Blood Supply: Risks, Perceptions and Prospects for the Future

Blood Supply: Risks, Perceptions and Prospects for the Future

Editor

Sandra Taddie Nance, MS, MT(ASCP)SBB
Director, Technical Services
American Red Cross Blood Services
Musser Blood Center
Penn-Jersey Region
Philadelphia, Pennsylvania

American Association of Blood Banks
Bethesda, Maryland
1994

American Association of Blood Banks
8101 Glenbrook Road
Bethesda, Maryland 20814-2749

ISBN NO. 1-56395-033-2
Printed in the United States

Text paper meets EPA guidelines for minimum recovered material content (50% recycled fiber, including 10% postconsumer waste).

Scientific Program Committee

Sandra Taddie Nance, MS, MT(ASCP)SBB
Chairman

Richard H. Aster, MD
Michael P. Busch, MD, PhD
Roger Y. Dodd, PhD
Joseph Fratantoni, MD
Dennis Goldfinger, MD
Gregory R. Halverson, MT(ASCP)SBB, DLM
Peter D. Issitt, PhD, FIMLS, FIBiol, FRCPath
Steven H. Kleinman, MD
Joann Moulds, PhD
Leslie E. Silberstein, MD
Marilyn Telen, MD
Patricia Tippett, PhD

Contents

Foreword

This year's Annual Seminar book entitled "Blood Supply: Risks, Perceptions and Prospects for the Future" is especially timely. It collates many of the issues that have required great concentrated efforts on the part of transfusion medicine scientists for the past 10 years. These chapters are written by scientists on the leading edge of their subject areas and are world-renowned for their expertise.

The first chapter is written by Roger Y. Dodd, PhD (Rockville, MD) on the topic of "Adverse Consequences of Blood Transfusion: Quantitative Risk Estimates." The major infectious adverse effects of blood transfusion are caused by viruses, bacteria and parasites. Dr. Dodd eloquently details the quantitative risks for each. The usual viruses are detailed (HIV, HCV, HBV, HTLV-I/II, CMV) as well as HAV and the B19 parvovirus. Parasitic infections, including malaria, Chagas' disease and babesiosis, are covered. Dr. Dodd discusses noninfectious risks such as acute hemolytic transfusion reactions, acute lung injury and graft-vs-host disease. He compares the relative risks of transfusion to other risks associated with medical care.

The second chapter, "The Use of Computers in the Blood Bank to Reduce Transfusion Risk," is written by William C. Sherwood, MD, Edward Bauman and Tasha Glenn (Philadelphia, PA). These authors review the data challenge in blood banking, and how the systems of the future will move into process control. Part of the chapter focuses on the challenge of "people" data bases and new technologies. The new symbology standards are discussed with regard to Codabar and Code 128. Biorecognition devices are explored. Massive parallel processing, human interfaces, interface standards and redefinition of documentation are some of the topics that are discussed in terms of what is necessary for the future.

The third chapter, written by Jay E. Menitove, MD (Cincinnati, OH), is on the "Perception of Risk." The first section introduces approaches to risk evaluation, risk analysis, damage assessment and risk perception. The second section discusses reasons for conflicts between the experts and the public. The third section collates the information as it pertains to transfusion medicine and contains suggestions for future action. Throughout the discussions, Dr. Menitove has relayed information from many areas to evaluate perceptions of risk.

The fourth chapter is the Emily Cooley Memorial Awardee's chapter, written by Paul V. Holland, MD (Sacramento, CA). Entitled

"Safety in the Blood Bank," it reviews the data on risks for patients and fully discusses the risk of infection for health-care workers. Part of this chapter is devoted to OSHA and includes the enforcement procedures proposed by OSHA. Facility exposure control plans are discussed. The prevention of viral infection in blood bank staff is a major section of this chapter. Finally, Dr. Holland gives a perspective on the comparative safety of health-care workers vs those working in other occupations.

The next chapter, "Normal Hemopoiesis," is written by Peter J. Quesenberry, MD, and colleagues (Worcester, MA). This chapter starts from the beginning of hematopoiesis in the primitive multipotent stem cell to nondividing end cells. Stem cells are discussed, but major emphasis is placed on clinical utilization of lymphohematopoietic growth factors. The role of G-CSF, GM-CSF and other cytokines in clinical practice is discussed.

The sixth chapter is on "Ex-Vivo-Generated Hematopoietic Progenitor Cells: Potential New Transfusion Product" and is written by Robert J. Tushinski, PhD; Mark P. Backer, PhD; and Ronald Hoffman, MD (Palo Alto, CA). This chapter can easily stand alone with its broad coverage of the topic. After a brief introduction, the major focus is ex-vivo expansion systems, reviewing stromal-cell-based systems and stroma-free liquid culture systems. An important consideration is the hematopoietic cell population to be used for expansion. Other major topics include: the clinical use of enriched hematopoietic stem cell populations, stem cell culture process development, establishment and operation of centers for stem cell expansion and the relationship of this to good manufacturing practice. This comprehensive chapter gives the reader an in-depth discussion of all the major considerations for ex-vivo expansion of progenitor cells.

The seventh chapter, written by Leonard I. Friedman, ScD; Robert R. Stromberg, PhD; and Stephen J. Wagner, PhD (Rockville, MD), is titled, "Reducing the Infectivity of Blood Components—What We Have Learned." This chapter gives an overview of virus removal and inactivation processes. Specific cell lines are discussed, including plasma processing, red cell processing and platelet processing. This comprehensive chapter is the ultimate for a review chapter, giving the reader discussion points as well as the necessary references for further investigation.

The last chapter is a fitting finale for a multidisciplinary text. It is written by Kathleen Sazama, MD, JD (Philadelphia, PA) and is titled, "Impact of Legal and Regulatory Changes During the Past Decade." Her unique perspective allows the reader to obtain an understanding of the complexity of the legal changes that have affected transfusion medicine. Dr. Sazama details the concerns of US governmental agencies whose authority embraces blood banking activities. Recent changes—both legal and regulatory—have had a sweeping impact on transfusion medicine, causing reorganization of services, implementation of new tests and computerization. Dr. Sazama gives us a view of the future based on the experiences of the past 10 years. One of the most useful tools this chapter provides, along with an insider's viewpoint, is the chronology of FDA oversight of blood banks.

This book, with its chapters written by pioneers in their fields, is an excellent book for transfusion medicine neophytes as well as experienced scientists and administrators because of its thorough review of diverse topics. These chapters allow readers to formulate their own views for the future based on the very latest data available today.

Sandra Taddie Nance, MS, MT(ASCP)SBB
Editor

The Emily Cooley Lecture

Today's lecture is the 30th in a series of annual lectures in honor of Emily Cooley, an outstanding medical technologist.

Emily Cooley was an attractive young woman raised in a distinguished family—her grandfather had been a Justice of the Supreme Court of Michigan and her father was a professor of pediatrics at Wayne State University. She had been brought up to be an artist, or a writer, or simply to preside over a household like her mother. She had attended a private school for girls and graduated from Vassar College with a degree in landscaping. Her mother, a kindly, gracious woman, was often incapacitated with attacks of melancholia and her father, then about to retire, was ailing much of the time. Emily ran the household and was her father's companion, chauffeur, travel aide, nurse, secretary and illustrator. It was she who drew the beautiful illustrations of blood films that appeared in Dr. Cooley's publications.

After the death of both her parents, Emily had to find a career in which to earn a living. Having been so intimately connected with medicine, and hematology in particular, she chose medical technology. She took her training at Henry Ford Hospital and received a master's degree before she started work. Returning to Children's Hospital, where her father had worked in the laboratory, she became the chief hematology technologist. An excellent morphologist, Emily became the mainstay of her department and was looked up to and beloved by her colleagues.

Emily Cooley was not only a fine technologist and a dedicated worker in the laboratory but also a warm, sensitive, intelligent and gracious human being. It is to her memory that this series of lectures is dedicated.

Emily Cooley Lecturers

1963 .... E. Eric Muirhead, MD
1964 .... Scott N. Swisher, MD
1965 .... Wolf W. Zuelzer, MD
1966 .... Alexander S. Wiener, MD
1967 .... Max M. Strumia, MD
1968 .... Hugh Chaplin, Jr., MD
1969 .... Emanuel Hackel, PhD
1970 .... Flemming Kissmeyer-Nielsen, MD, PhD
1971 .... Neva Martin Abelson, MD
1972 .... Bernard Pirofsky, MD
1973 .... Serafeim P. Masouredis, MD, PhD
1974 .... Paul J. Schmidt, MD
1975 .... Eloise R. Giblett, MD
1976 .... Richard E. Rosenfield, MD
1977 .... Herbert F. Polesky, MD
1978 .... Mary N. Crawford, MD
1979 .... Sir John Dacie, MD, FRCP, FRCPath, FRS
1980 .... Kathryn M. Beattie, MT(ASCP)SBB
1981 .... C. Paul Engelfriet, MD
1982 .... Edwin A. Steane, PhD
1983 .... Marjory Stroup, MT(ASCP)SBB
1984 .... Patrick L. Mollison, CBE, MD, FRCP, FRCPath, FRCOG, FRS
1985 .... Jeffrey McCullough, MD
1986 .... Peter D. Issitt, PhD, FIMLS, FIBiol, FRCPath
1987 .... Harvey J. Alter, MD
1988 .... W. Laurence Marsh, PhD, FRCPath, FIBiol, FIMLS
1989 .... George Garratty, PhD, FIMLS, MRCPath
1990 .... Sherrill J. Slichter, MD
1991 .... Lawrence D. Petz, MD
1992 .... Herbert A. Perkins, MD
1993 .... Richard H. Aster, MD

1994 Emily Cooley Memorial Lecturer:

Paul V. Holland, MD

Paul V. Holland, MD, is the 1994 Emily Cooley Memorial Awardee. Dr. Holland graduated from the University of California, Los Angeles, Medical School in 1962 and subsequently served a straight medical internship at the UCLA Medical Center. From there, he entered the US Public Health Service (USPHS) and spent the next 3 years in the Blood Bank and Clinical Pathology Departments at the Clinical Center of the National Institutes of Health in Bethesda, Maryland. While still in the USPHS, Dr. Holland completed a medical residency at the University of California, San Francisco from 1966-68 and then returned to the NIH Blood Bank Department, where he remained until September 1983. For his last 9 years at NIH, he was Chief of the Blood Bank Department. After retiring from the USPHS, Dr. Holland returned to California as Medical Director and Chief Executive Officer of the Sacramento Medical Foundation Blood Center, positions he still holds. Dr. Holland is also Clinical Professor of Medicine in the Division of Hematology/Oncology at the University of California at Davis Medical Center and is actively involved in many teaching programs at the Medical School.

Dr. Holland has served the AABB in various capacities, including the Editorial Board of *TRANSFUSION*, Scientific Section Coordinating Committee, Technical Manual Committee and Standards Committee; currently, he is the Chairman of the Transfusion-Transmitted Diseases Committee. Dr. Holland is actively involved in other disciplines; for example, he is a member of the American Society of Hematology, the American Society of Histocompatibility and Immunogenetics, and the International Society for Hematotherapy and Graft Engineering.

Dr. Holland is the author or coauthor of over 175 published works based upon his research, especially transfusion-associated viral hepatitis and its prevention. Last year, Dr. Holland spoke at international meetings in Lyon, France; Tokyo, Japan (two conferences); and Barcelona, Spain. In addition, he was a guest lecturer for a week-long course on blood banking issues in Melbourne, Australia. Dr. Holland has given lectures or presentations at many area hospitals as well as at local and national meetings. In recognition of his leadership and vision at the Sacramento Medical Foundation Blood Center, Dr. Holland received AABB's 1993 Bernice Hemphill Award, an award given to recognize an individual for administrative insight, outstanding accomplishments and excellence in blood center operations.

On a personal note, Dr. Holland is married and has four children. Paul and his wife, Pat, also have two grandsons. Pat graciously accepts Paul's absence to attend meetings and conferences, many of which are held on weekends.

In: Nance ST, ed.
Blood Supply: Risks, Perceptions and Prospects for the Future
Bethesda, MD: American Association of Blood Banks, 1994

1

Adverse Consequences of Blood Transfusion: Quantitative Risk Estimates

Roger Y. Dodd, PhD

He is a man born to be useful to society. And so is a mosquito, a horse-leech, a ferret, a polecat, a weasel: for these all are bleeders, and understand their business full as well as Doctor Rush does it.

—William Cobbett (1762-1835), writing of Benjamin Rush.

ALTHOUGH BENJAMIN RUSH HAS been characterized as the Hippocrates of medicine in the United States, he was notorious for his reliance upon bleeding as a therapeutic measure, and it is clear from the quotation that there is nothing new about a negative public perception of blood in the context of medicine. Yet, in quantitative terms, blood transfusion is one of the safest invasive medical procedures—indeed, it is considerably safer than hospitalization itself.[1] Those who are professionally responsible for the provision and oversight of the blood supply continue to add to and improve measures to ensure its safety and adequacy; yet these efforts do not appear to satisfy the public or their representatives. Unfortunately, public perception of risk is poorly correlated with the

Roger Y. Dodd, PhD, Head, Transmissible Diseases Department, American Red Cross Holland Laboratory, Rockville, Maryland actual magnitude of the risk—indeed, it is well established that individuals are unable to adequately comprehend very low estimates of risk.[2] Rather, response appears to be a complex function of the degree to which the individual feels in control of the risk, the severity of the outcome and "outrage," based upon the concept that the risk may appear to be preventable by appropriate action. Finally, in the context of transfusion medicine, an additional concern may be that the risk is not diffuse, in the sense that an adverse drug reaction is; rather, it is focused to a single blood component unit. The purpose of this chapter is not to deal with the management of public perception, but rather to develop realistic estimates of the risks of adverse outcomes of transfusion. Such estimates can, perhaps, support efforts to educate the public and professionals and serve as one component of the public discourse.

The major adverse effects of blood transfusion are the result of infection or immunologic incompatibility. Simplistically, in each of these major categories, the adverse outcomes would appear to be either preventable—for example, use of the wrong unit or failure to test—or nonpreventable, as in the case of window period infections or rare incompatibilities. However, the degree to which an outcome may be preventable really covers a wide spectrum, and there are numerous examples of risks that might be reduced if additional procedures were introduced. Testing for HIV antigens or genome sequences or screening to prevent transfusion-associated acute lung injury (TRALI) are cases in point.

Infectious risks include viruses [notably hepatitis B virus (HBV), hepatitis C virus (HCV), human immunodeficiency virus (HIV), human T-cell lymphotropic virus (HTLV) and cytomegalovirus (CMV)], bacteria, and parasites, including malaria, babesia and *Trypanosoma cruzi*. The vast majority of transfusion-transmissible agents establish long-term, asymptomatic infections, or carrier states, although a few nonpersistent viruses, such as hepatitis A virus (HAV), may be transmitted during a period of viremia just prior to acute disease. The situation is somewhat different for bacteria. In some cases, bacterial carrier states may be established, but persistent bacteremia is rare. Low levels of bacteria may enter, and be maintained in, the bloodstream during some enteric infections, and transient bacteremia may exist after other events, such as dental treatment. In addition, bacteria are normally present in or on the skin and thus may contaminate a blood donation; there are also remote possibilities of entry of environmental bacteria into the unit.

Quantitative Estimates of Infection Risk

Viral Infections

Human Immunodeficiency Virus

There is little doubt that the risk generating greatest concern is HIV infection. History suggests justification for this concern, with a total of 6311 transfusion-transmitted AIDS cases reported by September, 1993. The vast majority of these cases occurred before the implementation of routine testing for HIV antibodies in early 1985. In fact, only 29 cases have been attributed to transfusions that took place since that time.[3] Other studies on the validity of transfusion-associated AIDS reporting have also suggested that no more than five cases per year have occurred since the initiation of testing.[4] It must be remembered that AIDS represents end-stage disease, and the most important issue is the frequency with which blood components are capable of transmitting HIV. It is now accepted that essentially all transfusion-transmitted infections occur as a result of collection of blood from donors who present during the window period before development of detectable levels of anti-HIV. Each case of HIV infection will result in the development of AIDS, unless the infected individual dies before developing the disease. In fact, several studies indicate that any given component has a 50% likelihood of being administered to an individual who will die within one year of the transfusion.

How can the current risk of such transmission be measured or estimated? Several different approaches have been taken. Direct measurement of risk has been undertaken with two approaches. In the first, a population of blood recipients was serologically evaluated in order to define the number of infections that occurred. Recipients with preexisting infections or other risk factors were eliminated from the analysis. The number of infections was then related to the number of blood products transfused. Using this approach, Nelson and colleagues[5] found two HIV infections in a population of 11,532 recipients who had been transfused with a total of 120,312 blood components between 1985 and 1991. They concluded that the risk of infection was 1 per 60,000 units. It should be noted that one of these infections was associated with a transfusion that took place in 1986, relatively soon after the initiation of testing. This study was also undertaken in two cities with relatively high incidence rates for HIV infection.[5]

Another direct measure of risk was provided by Busch and colleagues,[6] who isolated HIV from pools of blood units that had been fully tested and were issued for transfusion. This group eventually found one viral isolate in a total of 1436 pools representing 71,800 blood donations cultured. They determined (after some adjustment) an infection risk of 1 per 61,171 units, assuming that the isolation system was sensitive enough to detect all infectious units. Again, it should be noted that this study was performed in a single city with a high incidence of AIDS cases.[6]

An alternate approach has been to estimate risk by considering the frequency of seroconversion among blood donors and combining this figure with an estimate of the length of the infectious window period in order to define the chance that blood would be collected during the window period. Ward was first to use this approach, developing an estimate of 1 in 40,000.[7] Subsequently, Cumming and colleagues used the same approach to arrive at a somewhat lower estimate of 1 in 153,000.[8] A significant improvement on this approach was developed by Kleinman and Secord,[9] and extended and improved by Petersen and others.[10] This approach involved the use of data from look-back investigations to provide an actual measure of HIV transmission incidence from preseroconversion blood donations. Kleinman arrived at a risk estimate of 1 in 68,000 for Los Angeles.[9] Petersen and colleagues looked at the outcome in recipients of 136 preseroconversion units, finding an overall frequency of infection of 20% from such units.[10] As might be expected, the risk of such a unit being infectious correlated inversely with the time period between that donation and the subsequent seropositive one. Careful mathematical modeling of this relationship showed that the infectious window period was 45 days, with relatively little variation. By using the mean value of 45 days for the window period, and combining this figure with the measured rate of seroconversion in a large blood donor population, plus estimates for the likely frequency of seroconversion among first-time donors, these investigators arrived at an estimate that the risk of HIV infection was 1 in 225,000. This estimate was based on studies reflecting a large portion of the United States and data reflecting conditions in 1990.[10]

However, it is critical to recognize that change continues to occur. Perhaps the most important change after 1990 was the widespread adoption of anti-HIV screening tests with greater sensitivity and the ability to detect seroconversion at an earlier time. Busch has estimated that, since 1990, the use of tests of increased sensitivity reduced the length of the infectious window period by about 13 days.[11] Because the risk of infection is directly proportional to the length of the window period, this clearly implies that the current risk of HIV infection could be less than 1 in 300,000 per component unit, even if the continuing decline in donor seroprevalence rates is ignored.

A subject of continuing concern and inquiry is the extent to which this risk may change in the future. It is possible that the risk may be somewhat reduced by more intensive screening efforts, although this may be offset by increases in the rate of infection among individuals who do not perceive themselves to be at risk. Second, improved procedures for testing for HIV antibodies may result in somewhat earlier detection of antibodies among seroconverting donors. Finally, consideration has been given to the addition of other test modalities, such as those for circulating HIV antigens or genomic materials. Each of these procedures might result in some diminution in the length of the infectious window period, but such measures are unlikely to fully eliminate the risk. Data reviewed by Busch, in fact, suggest that the best that may be expected would be an overall reduction in risk to about 1 in 500,000, were it to prove possible to perform DNA polymerase chain reaction (PCR) tests for HIV genomic sequences on all donor samples, thus reducing the window period to about 20 days.[11]

There may also be some concern about the possibility that HIV risk may increase. At the time of writing, the epidemic is considered to have reached a stage of maturity in the United States, with the annual incidence of new infections approximately matching the annual mortality from AIDS. It is possible that this situation could change, with a reemergence of an epidemic growth phase. However, what seems more likely is that the demography of the disease will change. Indeed, at this time, heterosexually transmitted cases are growing more rapidly than those in which infection occurs by other routes. If a significant proportion of these cases occur among individuals who fail to recognize that they are at risk, and if they present to give blood, then there would clearly be potential for increased infectivity.

Hepatitis C Virus

Although HIV infection is probably the most feared complication of transfusion, infection with the hepatitis C virus is still the most likely adverse outcome. Transfusion medicine professionals continue to express concern about HCV infection, although it does not appear to generate nearly as much public concern. Remarkably, there are few contemporary measures of the risk of HCV infection among blood recipients in the United States. Much information was derived from extensive posttransfusion hepatitis studies that were performed in the late 1970s and early 1980s. These studies defined the incidence of posttransfusion hepatitis by looking for posttransfusion elevations of serum alanine aminotransferase (ALT), along with available serologic markers. At least 95% of the occurrences were defined as non-A,non-B hepatitis; it is now clear that at least 85% were a result of HCV infection. These studies led directly to the introduction of surrogate marker screening of donors to reduce the incidence of posttransfusion non-A,non-B hepatitis. Starting in late 1986, donors were tested for the presence of antibodies to hepatitis B core antigen (anti-HBc) and elevated levels of ALT (although some locations had initiated ALT screening in 1982).

Donahue and colleagues evaluated the frequency of HCV seroconversion among a large population of blood recipients.[12] When first published, the study used the first generation, single-antigen (c-100-3) test for anti-HCV to define the frequency of infection among recipients. As a result, they showed that the per-unit risk of transmission was 0.45% immediately before initiation of surrogate testing. After surrogate testing was implemented, the risk declined to 0.19% per unit. After first-generation HCV testing was implemented, the per-unit risk dropped to 0.03%. No data were available representing rates after the implementation of second- or third-generation tests. This group did subsequently reevaluate infection rates using the second-generation tests and found a total of 11 HCV seroconversions among 1122 patients who had received a total of 18,392 units of blood, for a rate of 1 infection per 1672 units.[13]

Kleinman and others reviewed the increased detection rates achieved by second-generation tests for anti-HCV among donors, and came to the conclusion that the residual risk of HCV infection among current, fully tested units was between 1 in 2000 and 1 in 6000 per component unit.[14] A number of posttransfusion studies performed outside the United States have found no infections among recipients of anti-HCV tested products; these studies were all relatively small, and the results are compatible with Kleinman's estimate. Not incidentally, these studies also invariably show that surrogate testing does not appear to have any significant additional contribution to the prevention of HCV infection, once anti-HCV testing has been implemented. Unfortunately, at this time, there are no means of estimating the infectious window period for HCV, and information on seroconversion rates among donors is very limited. Consequently, other approaches to estimation of risk are not available. Alter has suggested that there may now be about 150,000 HCV infections per year in the United States; if 2-3% of these are transfusion-associated, then there would be 3000-4500 infections annually—a figure that is entirely compatible with the risk figures presented above.[15]

The difficulty of providing estimates of the risk of HCV infection from blood is doubly complicated when attempts are made to define the incidence of disease that may result from such infection. It has been estimated that 25% of patients may be acutely symptomatic, although it appears that such symptoms are mild and rarely lead to hospitalization.[16] Almost all infections become chronic. It is also well established that transfusion-transmitted HCV infection results in chronic liver dysfunction in about 60-70% of patients, as indicated by ALT elevations lasting more than one year. Further, on biopsy, some 60% of these individuals are found to have microscopic evidence of chronic persistent or chronic active hepatitis or cirrhosis. Despite this evidence of disease, many such patients appear to be asymptomatic. Seeff and colleagues showed no increased mortality among about 500 transfused individuals with posttransfusion hepatitis relative to those who did not have hepatitis, even after about 20 years' follow-up, but there was some evidence of increased liver disease in this group.[17] Similar studies by Koretz and others suggested evidence of overt liver failure in about 20% of those with chronic posttransfusion hepatitis C, with an overall death rate of about 5-6%.[18] In addition, prolonged observation of individuals with posttransfusion hepatitis C in Japan has shown occasional progression to cirrhosis and liver cancer over a period of 23 years or more.[19]

Thus, in summary, HCV infection probably does continue to occur among blood recipients. In most cases, little or no acute disease occurs. Some proportion of those infected, perhaps 10% to 20%, may develop chronic, clinically apparent liver disease 15 to 20 years after transfusion. A proportion of these, perhaps 25%, may eventually die of liver-related disease. Clearly, the impact of this disease will not be apparent unless the patient survives for such a period after transfusion.

The incidence of hepatitis C in the United States appears to be declining, although there has also been a shift in risk factors, with more cases associated with injecting drug use.[15] At the same time, further "generations" of test reagents that include additional antigens expressed from the HCV genome are under development or, indeed, available in some parts of the world. Consequently, it is reasonable to anticipate that the incidence of transfusion-associated HCV infection will continue to decline.

Hepatitis B Virus

Evidence that transfusion-associated HBV continues to occur originates mainly from anecdotal reports of patient hepatitis linked to donors who have subsequently seroconverted. The frequency is very low, and no direct measures of transfusion-transmitted HBV infection exist. This low risk is a result of donor screening and the use of sensitive tests for hepatitis B surface antigen (HBsAg). In addition, anti-HBc testing was anticipated to have some impact upon prevention of posttransfusion HBV infection. This concept has not been definitively validated, but reporting rates for posttransfusion hepatitis (B and C) did decline after the implementation of surrogate testing in some studies; at least a portion of this decline was probably attributable to the testing.[20] Current reporting rates for clinical posttransfusion hepatitis B are about 100 cases per year for the American Red Cross system. Because this probably represents around two million transfused patients, this would translate to about five cases per 100,000 individuals per year, substantially less than the overall population incidence of nine cases per 100,000 per year. At a minimum, this would imply that several cases reported as transfusion-associated are not caused by transfusion, but are merely coincident in time. Admittedly, reporting rates are known to be underestimated, but presumably, this applies to both transfusion- and community-acquired cases. Surveillance studies indicated that, in 1989, prior receipt of transfusion is reported from about 1.1 percent of the 23,000 cases of hepatitis B reported each year, or about 250 cases. Finally, and more recently, Alter and others[21] estimated that the per-unit risk of HBV transmission was about 1:200,000. This estimate was based upon the number of donors found positive for HBsAg and for anti-HBc, along with estimates of the potential failure rates of each test. This would suggest only about 100 transfusion-transmitted infections per year.

The clinical outcomes of posttransfusion HBV infection are not well defined. About 35% may lead to acute disease of varying severity.[22] Studies involving a large population of iatrogenically infected individuals suggest that only a small proportion of adult-acquired infections become chronic, with very little long-term disease and no evidence of development of liver cancer.[23] It is reasonable to anticipate little change in the overall risk of transfusion-associated

HBV infection, at least until the impact of large-scale use of the hepatitis B vaccine becomes apparent.

Human T-Cell Lymphotropic Retroviruses

Currently, all blood collected for transfusion in the United States is tested for antibodies to HTLV-I. Because of the close genetic homology between HTLV-I and HTLV-II, this procedure also detects an unknown, but probably high, proportion of infections with HTLV-II. Even so, more than 50% of all donations that are confirmed to be positive for HTLV-I/II are found to reflect infection with HTLV-II on further testing.[24] Only one published study has provided a measure of the residual risk of infection with HTLV-I/II since testing was initiated. One infection was found in a population transfused with 69,272 blood component units, translating to a risk of 1:70,000, with an upper 95% confidence limit of 1 in 15,000. The single infection detected was with HTLV-II.[5] Although it is clear that no rational conclusions can be drawn from a single event, it is of interest that current tests for antibodies to HTLV-I are known to be less than 100% sensitive for HTLV-II infection.[25] An alternate approach to assessing the risk of infection is to make some assumptions about the sensitivity of existing tests and to apply such assumptions to current seroprevalence rates. Dodd suggested, on this basis, that the residual risk of infection was on the order of 1 in 50,000, but there is very little factual basis for this approach.[1]

Other factors may affect the risk of posttransfusion HTLV-I/II infection. First, these viruses do not appear to be transmitted by acellular components; it is not clear whether or not leukocyte-reduced components are infectious. The efficiency of infection appears to be profoundly affected by storage. Both in Japan and in the United States, it has been shown that stored red cell concentrates are much less likely to transmit the viruses than are fresh ones.[24,26] Finally, few studies seem to address the incidence of new infections in the donor population, or the length of any infectious but seronegative window period.

The extent to which transfusion-transmitted HTLV-I/II infection leads to clinical disease is also poorly characterized. At least for HTLV-I, it is generally accepted that an infected individual has a 2-4% chance of developing the neurologic disease HTLV-I-associated myelopathy/tropical spastic paraparesis (HAM/TSP) or adult T-cell leukemia/lymphoma (ATL). There are no recorded cases of ATL associated with transfusion, perhaps because of the lengthy incubation period, or perhaps because, like HBV, early or perinatal infection is a prerequisite. It is clear that TSP may result from transfusion-transmitted HTLV-I infection. To date, there do not appear to be any reports of disease resulting from transmission of HTLV-II. While this is regarded as comforting by many authorities, such complacence may be ill-advised. HTLV-II is so closely related to HTLV-I that it would appear unlikely that infection would not lead to disease. In fact, published studies have reported neurologic disease among HTLV-II-infected individuals.[27] Nevertheless, it is still reasonable to assume that disease will only be manifested among about 4-8% of individuals who are infected with HTLV-I/II as a result of transfusion.

It is reasonable to expect that the risk of posttransfusion HTLV-I/II infection will decline, as manufacturers modify enzyme immunoassay (EIA) tests to be more sensitive for HTLV-II infection. Also, increased leukocyte reduction may have some impact upon residual infectivity, either by frank removal of infected leukocytes or, perhaps, by damaging them so that they can no longer replicate and/or express virus. It appears unlikely that any significant upward trend in HTLV-I infection will become apparent in the United States, although the course of the HTLV-II epidemic among injecting drug users cannot be foreseen.

Cytomegalovirus

There is no simple way to estimate the risk of disease from transfusion-associated CMV infection, because many factors appear to influence both the risk of infectivity in the donor population and the nature of the outcomes in the recipient population. In addition, when the recipient is at particular risk of significant disease, interventions are undertaken to prevent transmission of the virus to susceptible patients.[28] The risk of transmission of CMV from cellular components appears to be approximately 1-2% per unit. However, for immunocompetent recipients, it is generally accepted that significant disease will not result from such transmission. The effects of transfusion-transmitted CMV infection on severely immunocompromised patients are profound, and are frequently fatal. Consequently, those recipients most at risk of such disease are usually treated with CMV-seronegative components, which do not appear to have significant risk of transmission. Consequently, no attempt will be made to develop a risk estimate for posttransfusion CMV disease.

Hepatitis A Virus and the B19 Parvovirus

Two other viruses have been discussed in the context of transmission risk. About 25 cases of transfusion-transmitted hepatitis A virus had been reported in the literature by 1989,[29] representing an overall risk of less than one per million units. HAV is transmitted only as a result of the collection of blood during a short viremic phase immediately before the appearance of symptoms. Attention has been focused on HAV solely because of some puzzling outbreaks of HAV infection among recipients of pooled plasma products in Europe.[30] These products had been inactivated by the solvent/detergent-treatment process, which has little effect on nonenveloped viruses. There seems to be little reason for concern relating to single donor products in the United States.

Another nonenveloped virus that has been cited as a cause for concern is the B19 human parvovirus. Again, it is difficult to assess the risk of transmission, which has been variously estimated as from 1 in 10,000 to 1 in 50,000, with a frequency of 1:24,000 measured by an assay for viral antigen.[31] In a subsequent study using PCR methods, a frequency of 1 positive result per 3300 donations was found.[32] One of the difficulties in making such an estimate is the fact that B19 infection is highly seasonal. Once again, infection is almost always acute and self-limited, and risk is essentially confined to collections made during the pre-acute phase. It appears that, as with CMV, the adverse outcomes of infection with this virus would be expressed in only a subset of the recipient population. B19 infection during pregnancy can have serious adverse effects on the fetus. Also, infection can cause aplastic crises for some individuals with hemolytic anemias, or persons with HIV infection.[33] At present, there are no preventive measures that can be taken. For the majority of transfused patients, B19 infection would appear to represent a very minor risk.

Parasitic Infections

Several parasitic infections may be transmitted from donor to recipient by transfusion. However, in the absence of wide-scale studies to define the prevalence of infections among donors, or of seroconversion among recipients, it is almost impossible to define the risk of infection. At best, the incidence of reported disease among blood recipients may serve as a guide. In most cases, these events are reported with a frequency of five or fewer cases per year and thus, even in aggregate, appear to offer negligible risk to blood recipients. Nevertheless, it is important to try to develop accurate assessment of true risk and to engage in surveillance to ensure that circumstances are not changing.

Malaria

Perhaps best known of these low-incidence diseases is malaria. An average of about three cases of transfusion-associated malaria are reported each year in the United States, with little variation except for an increase during the Vietnam conflict. It is likely that current screening procedures to identify those potential donors who have been exposed to malaria are effective. Whether the increase in drug-resistant strains of plasmodia will affect this situation is unknown.[34]

Chagas' Disease

The possibility of transmission of *T. cruzi*, the agent of Chagas' disease, is currently receiving some attention. In the United States and Canada, three cases of acute posttransfusion Chagas' disease have been reported in the literature since 1987. Each of these reports involved immunocompromised patients. At the same time, it has been estimated that there are at least 100,000 individuals with chronic *T. cruzi* infection in the United States and that, at least in South America, blood from such individuals appears to have a 14-49% risk of transmission in a transfusion.[35] Thus, even using conservative estimates of transmission frequency and assuming that no more than 1% of the infected individuals present to give blood, there could be more than 100 transfusion-associated *T. cruzi* infections each year in the United States. Other studies suggest that about one in every 1000 donors judged to have some evidence of risk of infection may have serologic evidence of *T. cruzi* infection.[36] It has not proved possible to estimate the frequency of this donor subset on a nationwide basis. Some of the discrepancy between reported cases and the potential incidence of infection may be a result of the difficulty of diagnosing Chagas' disease and the frequency of asymptomatic infection. Studies are clearly needed to better define the risk of *T. cruzi* infection among blood recipients.

Babesiosis

Babesiosis is another parasitic disease with a poorly defined risk for blood recipients. A total of nine clinically apparent, transfusion-associated cases has been reported in the literature since 1982, with anecdotal reports of several more.[37] Thus, the risk, as defined by clinical outcomes, is probably on the order of 1 in 5 or 6 million.

Bacterial Infections

Yersinia

A low risk, similar to that for parasitic infections, appears to exist for *Yersinia enterocolitica* sepsis, with about seven cases reported over a 2-year period in the United States.[38] A complicating factor is the age of the component at transfusion, because significant outgrowth of contaminating bacteria (usually taking more than 20 days at refrigerator temperatures) must occur for the component to have observable effects upon the recipient. One interesting aspect of *Y. enterocolitica* contamination of red cell components is that at least one case of sepsis has been reported in an autologous blood recipient.[39] This is one case in which an autologous donation may have a negative infectious outcome. Other bacteria, including enteric pathogens, psychrophilic pseudomonads and skin or environmental contaminants, have been shown to cause sepsis among recipients of red cell components, at a frequency comparable to that for *Yersinia*.[40]

Bacterial Contamination of Platelet Concentrates

In addition to blood-borne infectious agents transmitted from donor to recipient, blood products may also become contaminated with a variety of bacteria. In some cases, these contaminants could represent transient bacteremia in the donor, but contamination from extrinsic sources may also occur. In general, such contamination offers little risk for red cells or plasma, because these products are stored at temperatures that inhibit or prevent bacterial growth. As pointed out above, psychrophilic organisms, *Y. enterocolitica* in particular, can grow in red cells. A much more frequent problem is the growth of bacteria in platelet concentrates, which are stored for up to 5 days at room temperature. Two prospective studies on platelet recipients suggest that approximately one in every 4-12,000 platelet concentrates may result in detectable sepsis in recipients.[41,42] Because random-donor platelets are usually administered as pools of five to seven donations, the per-recipient risk of sepsis is higher for random-donor than for single-donor platelet transfusions. The risk is increased for concentrates that have been stored for longer periods, presumably because bacterial growth is more likely to have reached pathogenic levels after several days. What is not clear is the inherent frequency of bacterial contamination of platelet concentrates. A wide range of contamination rates has been reported from quality control studies in which products have been cultured; however, it is not possible to assess the false-positive rates in such studies.[40]

The outcomes of identified events of transfusion-associated sepsis are often serious and may be directly or indirectly fatal. Among reported cases, some 26% have been fatal.[40] As with a number of other transfusion-transmitted infections, it is by no means clear that all cases are recognized or reported. The frequency of bacterial sepsis observed in two hospitals would translate to many more cases than are actually reported, if they represent the normal frequency of such sepsis. Indeed, in a study of transfusion-associated deaths reported to the Food and Drug Administration (FDA), Sazama noted only 26 deaths occurring over a 10-year period.[43] Interestingly, an equal number of deaths were attributed to red cells and platelets; however, it must be remembered that fewer patients receive platelets.

Table 1-1 presents best-guess estimates for the risk of infections from transfusion of one million component units, representing about 250,000 patients. The potential number of infections and cases of clinically significant acute and chronic disease and the corresponding number of deaths have been estimated, without any correction for mortality from underlying disease.

Laboratory Errors

Laboratory errors are a possible source of risk to blood recipients, inasmuch as improper performance of a test could lead to a false-negative finding, but there is no clear measure of the frequency of such errors. Systematic errors that might result in the failure of a complete test run are unlikely to occur, because of the need to obtain satisfactory results with test calibrators and (where used) external controls, along with routine quality assurance measures.

Table 1-1. Best Estimates of the Risk of Infectious Complications of Blood Transfusion per Million Component Units Transfused

Agent	Frequency	Clinical Disease Episodes: Acute	Clinical Disease Episodes: Chronic	Deaths
Virus				
HAV	>1	1.0	0	0.00
HBV	5	1.8	0	0.00
HCV*	333	84.0	67	17.00
HIV	4	0.0	4	4.00
HTLV	14	0.0	1	0.00
Parvovirus†	100	5.0	0	0.00
Bacteria				
Yersinia, etc	2	2.0	0	0.25
Platelet contamination‡	83	83.0	0	21.00
Parasite				
Babesia	>1	1.0	0	0.25
Malaria	>4	4.0	0	0.00
T. cruzi§	80	1.0	0	0.00
TOTALS	627	183.0	72	42.50

*Infectivity rate calculated as mean of values from Kleinman et al.[14]
†Infectivity derived from upper value from Cohen et al,[31] disease rate assumed.
‡Based upon a frequency of 1:12,000 concentrates.
§Based upon the assumption that there are 100,000 infected individuals in the US, and that 1% donate.

Random errors, such as sample transposition or omission, may occur, although modern, automated systems should preclude such problems. In order to affect a recipient, such an error would have to coincide with the presence of an infectious sample. Consequently, even if errors were to occur at a frequency of 1%, for example, the actual risk to recipients for HIV infection would be 1% of 0.006% (the current frequency of Western blot-confirmed HIV positives), or a rate of 1 in 1.7 million. On the other hand, Young reported that 18, 27 and 55 HBsAg testing errors were reported to the FDA in 1985, 1986 and 1988 respectively.[44] If every one of these reflected failure to identify an EIA-positive product (which is by no means clear), then the error rate could have been as high as 18 to 55 per 18,000, assuming 18 million collections of whole blood and plasma per year, and an EIA reactive rate of 0.1%. This would translate to an overall error rate of 0.1% to 0.3%, leading to an HIV transmission risk of one in six to 17 million. It is reasonable to assume that increased attention to transfusion safety and quality assurance in testing over the past years will have resulted in very much lower rates of laboratory errors. Consequently, laboratory testing errors probably have no significant contribution to the risk of infection from transfusion. Other, widely publicized errors certainly do occur, but most often reflect failure to withhold a safe, test-negative product because of a prior false-positive test result.[45]

Noninfectious Risks

Several noninfectious adverse outcomes are associated with blood transfusion, but there seem to be few comprehensive and current assessments of the incidence of such outcomes. Such risks are not amenable to estimation in the same way that infectious risk can be defined on the basis of serologic information from the donor population. Consequently, the frequency of these noninfectious adverse outcomes is largely defined on the basis of studies from a limited number of transfusion services, from summation of the number of occurrences reported in the literature, or from regulatory reports of errors, accidents and deaths. Walker[46] estimated that there was an adverse outcome for almost 20% of all units transfused. Only a small proportion of these were regarded as serious. In fact, Walker's estimate for the frequency of serious, noninfectious adverse effects was about 0.025% per unit, or one in 4000. This figure includes rates of 1:10,000 for circulatory overload, 1:10,000 for acute lung injury, 1:25,000 for acute hemolytic transfusion reactions and 1:150,000 for anaphylactic reactions. Additionally, Walker suggests that there may be a risk of 1:2500 for delayed hemolytic reactions. Also, febrile nonhemolytic reactions may occur at a frequency of 1:200 units, allergic reactions (urticaria) at a rate of 1:1000 and nonspecific chill reactions at the same rate; none of these outcomes was defined as serious.

Fatality rates have been presented for some of these outcomes. In particular, the fatality rate for acute hemolytic transfusion reactions has been estimated at 1:100,000 per unit[46] or per patient,[47] although Mollison reviews widely differing rates from different series.[48] Deaths are also attributed to delayed hemolytic transfusion reactions, but the mortality figures are difficult to establish, perhaps because they are often contributing, rather than direct, causes of death.

Sazama analyzed transfusion-associated deaths that were reported to the FDA over the 10 years from 1976-85, representing the transfusion of about one hundred million donations.[43] Although reporting was required from all registered blood establishments, it is likely that there was significant underreporting. There were 158 deaths due to acute hemolytic reactions, 31 due to acute pulmonary edema and 26 due to delayed hemolytic reactions. Interestingly, 12 donor deaths occurred in this same period. Overall, it was estimated that there was a fatality rate of 0.5 to 1 per 100,000 patients transfused. This figure excluded hepatitis deaths and did not include any cases due to HIV infection. It is of interest to note that this mortality rate is comparable with that for HIV. In a study of errors reported to New York State, Linden[49] found 92 cases of erroneous transfusions, including 54 that were ABO incompatible, in a 22-month period during which 1.78 million red cell products were transfused, for a rate of 1:33,000. Three patients died, representing a fatality rate of 1 per 600,000 red cell units. The overall true rate of transfusion error was estimated at 1 per 12,000 units transfused.[49]

The major cause of acute hemolytic transfusion reactions is transfusion of ABO-incompatible blood. As pointed out by Linden[49] and Sazama,[43] this is almost always the result of an error, most of which seem to occur outside the transfusion service. Presumably, the frequency of this outcome could be reduced, or even eliminated, by the appropriate use of improved systems for management of the transfusion process.

Other serious, noninfectious outcomes of transfusion occur, but it is difficult to define their frequency. Transfusion-related acute lung injury is one such adverse effect; Popovsky[50] reported on some 75 cases that had occurred over approximately 6 years, presumably reflecting a minimum frequency of about 1-2 per million units. Popovsky considers that this condition is greatly underreported, because 36 cases were diagnosed in a single institution over a 2-year period. The mortality for TRALI is approximately 5%. At least some cases of TRALI are thought to result from transfusion of plasma containing antileukocyte antibodies directed against host white cells.[50] Preventative measures have been proposed, but have not been widely adopted.

Another serious immunologic outcome of transfusion is graft-vs-host disease (GVHD), which may have a mortality rate of 68%-90%.[51] Again, the incidence of this outcome is poorly characterized, but it may well be underreported because patients who are at risk are generally very ill with underlying disease.[52] Indeed, in the United States, the major risk is to patients who are severely immunocompromised. Product irradiation can prevent or ameliorate this outcome. One study in Japan reported 96 cases among 63,257 immunocompetent patients, for a rate of 1 in 659,[53] but this figure is undoubtedly misleading, because GVHD is much more likely to occur when donor and recipient have histocompatibility antigens in common.[52] Thus, GVHD is more likely to occur in countries or populations with an inherently high frequency of genetic homogeneity. In the United States, the greatest risk for immunocompetent recipients seems to be when blood is received from a first-degree relative. Consequently, it is now routine to irradiate such donations before transfusion.

Several indirect, immunomodulatory effects of transfusion may contribute to an adverse outcome. However, such effects are inherently impossible to quantitate—indeed, it is not entirely clear whether or not some of them exist. Examples are the potential relationship between transfusion and recurrence of malignancies and the impact of transfusion on postsurgical infection. These effects are not discussed in detail in this chapter.

Finally, other nonimmunologic problems may occur occasionally. In particular, rapid administration of blood can lead to citrate toxicity or, in the case of stored red cells, hyperkalemia. Table 1-2 outlines estimates of the risk of clinically significant, noninfectious adverse outcomes per million component units transfused, and presents the observed number of deaths from Sazama's study.[43]

Relationship of Transfusion Risk to Other Risks

Taken together, the data below suggest that a clinically significant adverse outcome may occur with a frequency of about 400 per

Table 1-2. Estimated Risk of Serious, Noninfectious Adverse Effects of Blood Transfusion, per Million Component Units

		Deaths	
Outcome	Frequency*	Estimated†	Observed‡
Acute hemolytic reaction	40	2-10	0.2-1.6
Delayed hemolytic reaction	400§	?	0.25
Acute lung disease	100	?	0.30
Anaphylaxis	7	?	0.08
Other	?	?	0.08
TOTALS	≥550	(Est)≤15	2.30

*Figures from Walker.[46]
†Figures from Walker[46] and Consensus conference[47]: total estimated on the basis of observed frequencies of deaths.
‡From Linden[49] and Sazama.[43]
§See text: not regarded as "serious."[46]

million products transfused. Of these 400, 255 (64%) are due to transfusion-transmitted infections. Of these 255 transfusion-transmitted infections, 72 (28%) will not be manifested until many years after the transfusion. However, this 28% includes essentially all of the serious outcomes, with the exception of those attributable to bacterial contamination. As noted before, this number represents a potential, because approximately 50% of those at risk may actually die of their underlying disease before they suffer chronic hepatitis or AIDS. Of the serious infectious outcomes, about 43 may result in death, although the figure would be closer to 20 if the estimate of deaths due to bacterial sepsis were eliminated. Adding the potential for deaths from noninfectious causes, it appears that there could be a potential for up to 50-60 deaths per million component units transfused. Assuming about four units administered per transfusion episode, this would translate to about 0.2 deaths per 1000 patients. This figure is more than 10 times greater than that reported by Sazama,[43] presumably as a result of the combination of underreporting in that report and, perhaps, overestimation in this presentation.

It is of interest to compare these rates with other risks (both preventable and nonpreventable) associated with medical care. In particular, one large study in New York State revealed that adverse events occurred in 3.7% of all hospitalizations and that 6.5% of these led to permanent disability and 13.6% to death. That is, five patients in every 1000 actually died as an adverse outcome of their medical management. Approximately 51% of these deaths were considered to be a result of failure to follow the generally accepted standard of care; that is, they could have been defined as due to negligence.[54,55] In another study, the incidence of iatrogenic infections in the intensive care unit was 70-80 cases per 1000 patients.[56] McCullough has summarized other risks, quoting, for example, an annual risk of death of 1 in 50,000 among those who take contraceptive pills, and annual risks of death from leukemia and influenza as 1 in 12,500 and 5000, respectively.[57]

Three major points emerge from these data. First, the risk of adverse outcomes from transfusion is very low when compared to the overall risk of invasive medical procedures. Second, the public, and to a lesser extent the professional, response to transfusion risk is not necessarily commensurate with the quantitative risk of adverse outcomes or even deaths. For example, acute deaths from platelet contamination appear to be the single greatest risk of transfusion, and preventable deaths from mismatched transfusions may occur at least as frequently as deaths from transfusion-transmitted HIV infection. Yet neither of these outcomes has attracted a great deal of organized attention or calls for intervention. Thus, and finally, concern about the risk of HIV infection is on a different plane from that of other transfusion risks. The public policy response regarding transfusion-associated HIV risk would appear to be more like that relating to other areas involving public dread and outrage, such as the siting of nuclear power plants and high-voltage transmission lines or the safety of air travel or drinking water. It is of little consolation that the congressional and regulatory response to such issues may not be commensurate with general standards of cost-effectiveness; in fact, one EPA regulation relating to the monitoring of drinking water has been estimated to cost $93 billion for one life prolonged.[58] Thus, reasonable efforts to further reduce the low risk of transfusion-transmitted HIV will continue to be undertaken in a climate of public concern and pressure. This should not prevent responsible transfusionists from continuing to focus on problems of greater magnitude, but lesser public concern.

References

1. Dodd RY. The risk of transfusion-transmitted infection. N Engl J Med 1992;327:419-21.
2. Zeckhauser RJ, Viscusi WK. Risk within reason. Science 1990; 248:559-64.
3. Centers for Disease Control. HIV/AIDS Surveillance Report 1993;5(No. 3):1-19.
4. Selik RM, Ward JW, Buehler JW. Trends in transfusion-associated acquired immune deficiency syndrome in the United States, 1982 through 1991. Transfusion 1993;33:890-3.
5. Nelson KE, Donahue JG, Muñoz A, et al. Transmission of retroviruses from seronegative donors by transfusion during cardiac surgery. A multicenter study of HIV-1 and HTLV-I/II infections. Ann Intern Med 1992;117:554-9.
6. Busch MP, Eble BE, Khayam-Bashi H, et al. Evaluation of screened blood donations for human immunodeficiency virus type 1 infection by culture and DNA amplification of pooled cells. N Engl J Med 1991;325:1-5.
7. Ward JW, Holmberg SD, Allen JR, et al. Transmission of human immunodeficiency virus (HIV) by blood transfusions screened as negative for HIV antibody. N Engl J Med 1988;318:473-8.
8. Cumming PD, Wallace EL, Schorr JB, Dodd RY. Exposure of patients to human immunodeficiency virus through the trans-

fusion of blood components that test antibody-negative. N Engl J Med 1989;321:941-6.

9. Kleinman S, Secord K. Risk of human immunodeficiency virus (HIV) transmission by anti-HIV negative blood. Estimates using the look-back methodology. Transfusion 1988;28:499-501.
10. Petersen LR, Satten G, Dodd RY, et al. Current estimates of the infectious window period and risk of HIV infection from sero-negative blood donations (abstract). In: Program and Abstracts: Fifth National Forum on AIDS, Hepatitis, and Other Blood-Borne Diseases. Princeton, NJ: Symedco, 1992;37.
11. Busch MP. Retroviruses and blood transfusions: The lessons learned and the challenge yet ahead. In: Nance ST, ed. Blood safety: Current challenges. Bethesda, MD: American Association of Blood Banks, 1992:1-44.
12. Donahue JG, Muñoz A, Ness PM, et al. The declining risk of post-transfusion hepatitis C virus infection. N Engl J Med 1992;327:369-73.
13. Nelson KE, Donahue JG, Stambolis V. Post-transfusion hepatitis C virus infection (letter). N Engl J Med 1992;327:1601-2.
14. Kleinman S, Alter H, Busch M, et al. Increased detection of hepatitis C virus (HCV)-infected blood donors by a multiple-antigen HCV enzyme immunoassay. Transfusion 1992;32:805-13.
15. Alter MJ. The detection, transmission, and outcome of hepatitis C virus infection. Infectious Agents and Disease 1993;2:155-66.
16. Aledort LM. Consequences of chronic hepatitis C: A review article for the hematologist. Am J Hematol 1993;44:29-37.
17. Seeff LB, Buskell-Bales Z, Wright EC, et al. Long-term mortality after transfusion-associated non-A, non-B hepatitis. N Engl J Med 1992;327:1906-11.
18. Koretz RL, Abbey H, Coleman E, Gitnick G. Non-A, non-B post-transfusion hepatitis: Looking back in the second decade. Ann Intern Med 1993;119:110-15.
19. Kiyosawa K, Sodeyama T, Tanaka E, et al. Interrelationship of blood transfusion, non-A, non-B hepatitis and hepatocellular carcinoma: Analysis by detection of antibody to hepatitis C virus. Hepatology 1990;12:671-5.
20. Chambers LA, Popovsky MA. Decrease in reported posttransfusion hepatitis: Contributions of donor screening for alanine aminotransferase and antibodies to hepatitis B core antigen and changes in the general population. Arch Intern Med 1991; 151:2445-8.

21. Centers for Disease Control. Public Health Service inter-agency guidelines for screening donors of blood, plasma, organs, tissues, and semen for evidence of hepatitis B and hepatitis C. MMWR 1991;40(RR-4):1-17.
22. Bloom BS, Hillman AL, Fendrick AM, Schwartz JS. A reappraisal of hepatitis B virus vaccination strategies using cost-effectiveness analysis. Ann Intern Med 1993;118:298-306.
23. Seeff LB, Beebe GW, Hoofnagle JH, et al. A serologic follow-up of the 1942 epidemic of post-vaccination hepatitis in the United States Army. N Engl J Med 1990;316:965-70.
24. Sullivan MT, Williams AE, Fang CT, et al. Transmission of human T-lymphotropic virus types I and II by blood transfusion: A retrospective study of recipients of blood components (1983 through 1988). Arch Intern Med 1991;151:2043-8.
25. Hjelle B, Wilson C, Cyrus S, et al. Human T-cell leukemia virus type II infection frequently goes undetected in contemporary US blood donors. Blood 1993;81:1641-4.
26. Okochi K, Sato H, Hinuma Y. A retrospective study on transmission of adult T-cell leukemia virus by blood transfusion: Seroconversion in recipients. Vox Sang 1984;46:245-53.
27. Murphy EL, Engstrom JW, Miller K, et al. HTLV-II associated myelopathy in 43-year-old woman. Lancet 1993;341:757-8.
28. Preiksaitis JK. Indications for the use of cytomegalovirus-seronegative blood products. Transfus Med Rev 1991;5:1-17.
29. Giacoia GP, Kasprisin DO. Transfusion-acquired hepatitis A. South Med J 1989;82:1357-60.
30. Mannucci PM, Gdovin S, Gringeri A, et al. Transmission of hepatitis A to patients with hemophilia by Factor VIII concentrates treated with organic solvent and detergent to inactivate viruses. Ann Intern Med 1994;120:1-7.
31. Cohen BJ, Field AM, Gudnadottir S, et al. Blood donor screening for parvovirus B19. J Virol Methods 1990;30:233-8.
32. McOmish F, Yap PL, Jordan A, et al. Detection of parvovirus B19 in donated blood: A model system for screening by polymerase chain reaction. J Clin Microbiol 1993;31:323-8.
33. Frickhofen N, Abkowitz JL, Safford M, et al. Persistent B19 parvovirus infection in patients infected with human immunodeficiency virus type 1 (HIV-1): A treatable cause of anemia in AIDS. Ann Intern Med 1990;113:926-33.
34. Nahlen BL, Lobel HO, Cannon SE, Campbell CC. Reassessment of blood donor selection criteria for United States travellers to malarious areas. Transfusion 1991;31:798-804.

35. Schmuñis GA. *Trypanosoma cruzi,* the etiologic agent of Chagas' disease: Status in the blood supply in endemic and nonendemic countries. Transfusion 1991;31:547-57.
36. Kerndt PR, Waskin HA, Kirchhoff LV, et al. Prevalence of antibody to *Trypanosoma cruzi* among blood donors in Los Angeles, California. Transfusion 1991;31:814-18.
37. Popovsky MA. Transfusion-transmitted babesiosis. Transfusion 1991;31:296-8.
38. Tipple MA, Bland LA, Murphy JJ, et al. Sepsis associated with transfusion of red cells contaminated with *Yersinia enterocolitica*. Transfusion 1990;30:207-13.
39. Richards C, Kolins J, Trindade CD. Autologous transfusion-transmitted *Yersinia enterocolitica*. JAMA 1992;268:1541-2.
40. Goldman M, Blajchman MA. Blood product-associated bacterial sepsis. Transfus Med Rev 1991;5:73-83.
41. Morrow JF, Braine HG, Kickler TS, et al. Septic reactions to platelet transfusions. A persistent problem. JAMA 1991;266:555-8.
42. Barrett BB, Andersen JW, Anderson KC. Strategies for the avoidance of bacterial contamination of blood components. Transfusion 1993;33:228-33.
43. Sazama K. Reports of 355 transfusion-associated deaths: 1976 through 1985. Transfusion 1990;30:583-90.
44. Young FE. Efficacy of new tests and the safety of the blood supply. Transfusion 1990;30:4-5.
45. Dodd RY, Houlihan K, Lamberson HV. The specificity of enzyme immunoassays for antibodies to human immunodeficiency virus: Impact on record and donor management (letter). Transfusion 1993;33:693.
46. Walker RH. Special report: Transfusion risks. Am J Clin Pathol 1987;88:374-8.
47. NIH consensus conference. Perioperative red blood cell transfusion. JAMA 1988;260:2700-3.
48. Mollison PL, Engelfriet CP, Contreras M. Haemolytic transfusion reactions. In: Blood transfusion in clinical medicine. Oxford: Blackwell, 1993:498-542.
49. Linden JV, Paul B, Dressler KP. A report of 104 transfusion errors in New York State. Transfusion 1992;32:601-6.
50. Popovsky MA, Chaplin HC Jr, Moore SB. Transfusion-related acute lung injury: A neglected, serious complication of hemotherapy. Transfusion 1992;32:589-92.
51. von Fliedner V, Higby DJ, Kim U. Graft-versus-host reaction following blood product transfusion. Am J Med 1982;72:951-61.

52. Anderson KC, Weinstein HJ. Current concepts: Transfusion-associated graft-versus-host disease. N Engl J Med 1990;323:315-21.
53. Juji T, Takahashi K, Shibata Y, et al. Post-transfusion graft-versus-host disease in immunocompetent patients after cardiac surgery in Japan. N Engl J Med 1989;321:56.
54. Brennan TA, Leape LL, Laird NM, et al. Incidence of adverse events and negligence in hospitalized patients. Results of the Harvard Medical Practice Study I. N Engl J Med 1991;324:370-6.
55. Leape LL, Brennan TA, Laird N, et al. The nature of adverse events in hospitalized patients. Results of the Harvard Medical Practice Study II. N Engl J Med 1991;324:377-84.
56. Doebbeling BN, Stanley GS, Sheetz CT, et al. Comparative efficacy of alternative hand-washing agents in reducing nosocomial infections in intensive care units. N Engl J Med 1992; 327:88-93.
57. McCullough J. The nation's changing blood supply system. JAMA 1993;269:2239-45.
58. Abelson PH. Unfunded federal environmental mandates. Science 1993;262:1191.

In: Nance ST, ed.
Blood Supply: Risks, Perceptions and Prospects for the Future
Bethesda, MD: American Association of Blood Banks, 1994

2

The Use of Computers in the Blood Bank To Reduce Transfusion Risk

William C. Sherwood, MD; Edward T. Bauman; and Tasha Glenn

IN THE BLOOD BANK, as in everyday life, computers have come to be associated with almost everything we do. We easily recognize those functions that are initiated from a keyboard or a wand. However, we often fail to appreciate the many fundamental blood bank processes in which computers play a role. We tend to overlook the fact that the basic conditions of our operations, such as temperature, time or centrifuge speed, are under microprocessor control. Often such "computers" are invisible components of many of our blood bank instruments and devices.

Certainly, these simplistic computer systems that manage basic control functions have a role in blood transfusion safety. For most of the functions they control, the standards[1] and regulations[2] are quite precise. Frequently, the range of acceptable function is narrow. Many critical tasks that we consider routine would not be possible without this infrastructure of computing, constantly occurring in our background.

Typically, such computing systems are not recognized until they fail. Many experienced blood bank personnel have witnessed the discard of valuable blood products resulting from the failure of a device assigned to manage or monitor temperature of a blood stor-

William C. Sherwood, MD, Director, National Biomedical Computer System, American Red Cross; Edward T. Bauman, Senior Director, Blood Banking Systems, National Biomedical Computer System, American Red Cross; and Tasha Glenn, Consultant in Information Technology, National Biomedical Computer System, American Red Cross, Philadelphia, Pennsylvania

age apparatus. Table 2-1 lists many of the uses of computers in blood centers and transfusion services.

There are several basic reasons for the rapid and extensive use of computers in blood banking. The first of these is the extraordinary progress in information technology that has enabled the expansion of computers in the blood banking environment. The critical elements of this progress have included:

- An enormous increase in computer processing capacity at affordable prices.
- Reduction in size of data processing devices.
- Improved data communications.
- Improved systems reliability.
- Introduction of methods to capture data in an automated manner, such as optical symbology techniques.

Future directions in computer technology are discussed later in this chapter.

The second reason for computer use is the veritable explosion of data in the blood banking industry. This has occurred to the degree that data management in most blood centers and large transfusion services would not be possible without computers. Before 1985, only two tests were utilized in screening donated blood for transmissible disease. Beginning 1985 and in the years that have followed, six new screening tests have been added for these purposes.

The enormous increase in data requirements has involved much more than analyzing and managing the testing data. This challenge has included the appropriate management of the donors who produce abnormal results. These data management issues for donors have emerged as our most complex problems, and have included donor notification and counseling, donor "look-backs," donor deferral registries and donor reentry.

Contributing to the massive increase in data requirements in blood banking has been the increase in type and variation of blood products produced, including apheresis products. The introduction of autologous and directed donations has required specialized handling of many blood products, necessitating advanced product management systems.

A third basic motivator in the use of computer systems in blood banking has been the primary regulatory agency: the Food and Drug Administration (FDA). Inspection observations have repeatedly identified issues that were not satisfactorily controlled by manual management processes or required improved computer systems. These have included:

Table 2-1. The Use of Computers in Blood Banking

Monitor/Control Devices Refrigerators Freezers Platelet storage devices Timers Waterbaths Incubators Automated pipettes Centrifuges Automated blood typers ELISA reading devices Printers ALT testing devices Scales Apheresis machines	Laboratory Testing Sample management Data analysis Data storage Control devices Reagent qualification Proficiency results Compatibility results
Donor Recruitment Database marketing Telerecruitment Predictive dialing Donor scheduling Donor recognition Sponsor management	Manufacturing Production planning Product recording Product management Labeling Waste management
Blood Collection Donor registration Donor identification Donor deferral registry Donor history Donor CUE Donor education	Product Management Inventory control Distribution recording Quarantine management Routing
Patient Management Biographic data Product usage Transfusion history Serologic record Billing information	Quality Control Equipment management Materials management Personnel certification Product release Data certification Process control
	Document Management Document production Version control Document and record archiving
	Workload Recording

- Discrepancies in donor databases, including donor deferral registries.
- Laboratory testing irregularities.
- Inadequate standard operating procedure (SOP) management and version control.
- Failures to calibrate and maintain blood banking equipment.

These issues have prompted the development of more comprehensive computer systems and, more important, the development of systems with integrated quality control and process control. These control processes are similar to those used in manufacturing systems in other industries.

The pace of change in technology is likely to accelerate in the future, as will the complexity of the blood banking issues that need to be solved. The future of computer systems in blood banking will depend on the ability of innovators in this field to use the new and enabling technology to reengineer the process of this industry. Such changes can be far-reaching and, for some, may be difficult to accept.

The Data Challenge in Blood Banking

As noted, the rapid and massive increase in data production in blood banking caught the industry by surprise, and only now are systems catching up to the need. There is a realization that there are some fundamental differences in the data requirements for the blood banking industry, as compared with other manufacturing environments, such as pharmaceutical manufacturers. A basis for one of these differences is the extensive data record associated with each product. For most industries, data for each manufacturing "lot" apply to each component of the lot. Usually, there are many products per "lot." However, in blood banking each product is a separate "lot." Each product has an associated data record unique to the product.

An additional major difference between the data needs for blood banking compared with other manufacturing industries is the need for "people data." Compared with the precision of data produced in other manufacturing environments, the biographic information obtained from donors is less exact, is prone to errors and is subject to change over time. Most of the erroneous and constantly changing data obtained are not provided by donors with a subversive intent. Rather, donors innocently misspell their name or provide erroneous social security numbers, birth dates, telephone numbers and addresses. Over time, names, addresses and phone numbers may change as well.

The management of a "people data" database is a unique challenge for systems operators. It is a fair assumption that "people" databases with a large number of entries will never be 100% accurate. Usually, this is not a failure of the system or the system operators; it is a feature of human nature to be less than perfect when rendering biographic information.

For blood centers, the size of the combined "product" and "people" databases is considerable. Current needs are approximately 35 kilobytes per blood donor annually—almost 400 gigabytes, nationwide! In contrast, transfusion service data requirements are more modest—approximately 5 kilobytes per patient managed.

The Current Status

Upon examination of many of the information systems in use by blood collection agencies and transfusion services in early 1994, it is apparent that the industry is built on old engineering. Many systems do not have a modern structure, nor were they developed with a clear and documented methodology. The functionality of these systems grew over time and was not planned comprehensively.

At the end of 1993, many of the computer systems in use in blood banking in the United States still depended on portions of their code that were at least 10 years old. In the late 1970s and early 1980s, system developers were rewarded for their creativity and their speed. During those years, blood bank computer software was developing from the ground up. There was much to do with few resources in very little time.

These early computer programs were simple and tended to be data-capture systems that merely imitated and automated the paper environment, supporting the industry's critical manual systems. In the 1980s as donor data management, laboratory testing and product release matters grew more complicated and required additional data processing support, the computer became more essential in blood banking. Many of the older systems have been enhanced to accommodate the increasing needs, but often in a manner that continued to automate the previous paper system, without the business process re-engineering that has been needed.

As noted, the FDA has been particularly attentive to computer systems used by blood collection centers and transfusion services. An analysis of FDA inspection observations and product recalls indicates consistent deficiencies for a number of facilities. These include:

1. Failures in blood collection, testing and manufacturing operations that could be obviated by adequate process control and quality control in automated systems.
2. Inadequate testing and validation of installed systems.
3. Failure to document system development steps, methodology and trace requirements.
4. Inadequate backup and recovery methods.

Strict conformance to development standards is incorporated into many systems that are being developed currently. Traceability from the sources or cause of a change or new program through user requirements, design, coding, testing, validation and user support documentation is now a requirement and not a luxury. The proposed FDA Draft *Guideline for the Validation of Blood Establishment Computer Systems*[3] has established baseline standards for these functions.

Tomorrow's Systems Move Into Process Control

As current computer systems are replaced, we are beginning to see a new discipline arriving for both development and functionality. Again, an analysis of FDA citations shows that there is a failure to use computer systems to enable a much higher degree of process control and quality control than currently exists in this industry.

Process controls are automated "go/no go" controls that permit continuation to the next step in a process only if all the conditions are acceptable. For example, equipment maintenance systems that keep track of the calibration and maintenance of laboratory instruments can be integrated into the operations systems, preventing the use of uncertified instruments in the controlled environment.

An additional example of process control is the integration of personnel training certification with the operations to ensure that specific personnel who log on to a function are trained and currently certified to carry out the function.

"People" Databases: A Major Challenge

As long as our need for large files continues and inexact methods for donor identification exist, there will be a continuing emphasis on eliminating duplicate/discrepant records in blood bank databases. With the implementation of more aggressive file-matching tools and techniques, this situation should improve. The problem is now well understood and blood collection agencies are applying more rigorous checks to evaluate potentially duplicate data elements. Software tools and packages used by other industries exist to match names and other "look-alike" identifying information, such as social security numbers. However, the best solution is to identify the donor more accurately, each time, at the blood collection site before biographic data are entered into or matched against the record.

Phase-in of New Technologies

Computers provide the "glue" to enable many automated technologies that can improve the efficiencies in this industry and maintain the safety of blood products.

For example, thermal ABO label printers have been available for several years but are only recently being implemented in large numbers into blood labeling applications. Real-time machine-produced labels are a marked improvement over preprinted labels and virtually guarantee correct labeling in a well-designed and tested application.

The use of donor databases on site during donor registration, even at mobile collection sites, is an application that has been available for several years but is slow to be implemented. Donors with identification problems can be questioned face to face for accurate identification. On-site deferral using more extensive data-base information also provides the ability to screen donors more carefully and accurately and to reject those who may donate unsafe units.

Old Symbology Standards Undergoing Change

After more than 4 years of planning, the blood banking community is ready to see a new set of commonality standards introduced into the industry.[4] These evolving standards are being driven by the International Society of Blood Transfusion (ISBT) and the AABB Information Systems Committee, which has liaisons from other blood banking and manufacturing organizations. They are intended to replace those standards developed almost 20 years ago by the American Committee for Commonality in Blood Banking Automation (CCBBA).[5]

The CCBBA Codabar symbology has served blood banks well since its inception in 1975. This symbology has had only one minor modification. It remains identical to the original scheme and is performing as it was intended when the original guideline was published. However, the limited ability to expand Codabar symbology is, in part, the reason why the need to change is so acute. It has grown less useful over time and cannot satisfy the many changes that have occurred in the blood banking environment.

Unlike other symbology specifications that were developed after the CCBBA Codabar version was introduced,[6] such as in the food, health and automobile industries, the Codabar symbology has had no long-term maintenance process to help evolve and manage the standard. In the interim, other industries have adopted new and more robust optical symbols.

Too frequently, individual blood centers have needed to customize the CCBBA symbology to satisfy evolving needs and, in the process, caused a growing number of barcode compatibility problems. This became clear during the Persian Gulf War, when the US military received large numbers of products from multiple blood centers with product codes that were nonstandard and/or incorrectly printed and blood unit identification numbers that were printed contrary to published Guidelines for Uniform Labeling of Blood and Blood Components.[7]

The existing guidelines do not address the ability to uniquely identify divided or aliquoted products, nor is there adequate ability within this structure to bar-code product attributes, unit phenotypes, testing information or patient identifiers.

CCBBA Codabar raises some additional concerns. The symbol requires considerable space on the main label of blood products. There is a large amount of data competing for limited space on the face of these labels. The space on the label is inadequate for continued use of Codabar as well as the optimal amount of other information needed.

"Substitutions" a Recognized Problem

Erroneous barcode "substitutions" were known to exist when the CCBBA symbology was first introduced.[8] A substitution occurs when a reading device is passed over a barcode and a reading result other than that intended is interpreted by the reader output device. Without additional controls, such as multiple wanding or other automated verification techniques, other more serious substitutions can occur in either product testing or labeling.

When the original code was selected in the early 1970s, Codabar had the lowest known substitution rate among all of the existing technologies. The CCBBA published testing data that detailed nine substitutions for every 1,000,000 characters read. In 1987 the Automatic Identification Manufacturers (AIM) association commissioned a study that showed a higher rate. In this controlled study conducted at the State University of New York at Stony Brook, a substitution rate of 1 in 235,250 characters read was found.[9]

A recent study of over 50,000,000 characters read in a large blood center showed an actual substitution rate of 1 in 1,400,000.[10] This was lower than expected because the system also included other validity checking schemes that rejected invalid entries and filtered out many of the original substitution problems. All of these studies confirmed what was known when Codabar was first installed. Codabar has a substitution rate; originally considered low, by current standards it is too high when compared to other technologies that have become available.

Emerging New Standard

The US blood banking organizations and the ISBT have selected a modified version of Code 128 (ISBT 128) as the new barcode labeling symbology for all blood product (Fig 2-1).[4] Code 128 is now finding wide acceptability in a number of health, automotive and military environments.

Substitution rates for Code 128 are well documented. The SUNY study in 1987 showed 0 substitutions in 3,634,500 characters read.[9] Another study showed a substitution rate of 1 in 13,112,754.[11] A zero error read rate is probably impossible, but improvements in technology are moving us into an environment that is far more error-free than any environment experienced to date.

Code 128 offers other advantages. Twice the amount of data can be compacted into the same amount of space that CCBBA Codabar provides. With Code 128, two numeric digits will be combined into one barcode symbol character. This will enable the blood banking industry to add additional barcodes to the container, increasing the amount of data input directly from the product in a machine-readable form.

The product code design in the new ISBT structure uses coding schemes that assign product numbers serially. This allows almost

Figure 2-1. Proposed label for primary bag of multiple set.

unlimited ability to implement new product codes. It will also permit each code to identify a specific product no matter where it is assigned in the world. Other characteristics about the donor of the product may also be coded directly into the product code. This product code may also be used to help both blood centers and hospitals divide and aliquot products. Under the proposed scheme, blood collection agencies and transfusion facilities may make more than 25 divisions of any single product collected.

One of the greatest advantages of the new symbology is the ability to identify as unique any product anywhere in the world, produced in a 99-year time frame, using a single barcode number. This would overcome many of the problems we see today associated with manufacturing and testing divided among facilities and products transferred between and among regions.

New flag characters are available in the unit number for optional local use. New barcodes will be identified for the blood container lot number. Lot number information will no longer need to be entered manually but can be scanned accurately and quickly, providing for more accurate product tracking and current good manufacturing practice compliance. The type of donation—allogeneic, autologous, directed or apheresis—can be encoded on the unit label.

This new coding scheme should be finalized before the end of 1994, and plans are for a 4-year phase-in cycle after final approval. Equipment purchased over the last few years should be usable for both the old and new barcode standards. Coding structures are being designed so that even after final conversion, long-term products that remain in (frozen) inventory will be able to coexist without any significant need for relabeling.

What Is the Future?

The future of computer systems in blood banking will depend on the ability of developers to ride the crest of change in information technology and effectively introduce these enabling changes to our business processes.

For the last 30 years, the computing model was host-based, with dumb terminals connected to central processors in a self-contained, homogeneous and proprietary environment. This model is rapidly being replaced by network-oriented computing with multiple, heterogeneous, distributed processors connected to intelligent, graphic clients. Architecture has migrated from hardware-centered to software-centered, and is characterized by portability, extendibility, flexibility and interoperability.

Biorecognition Devices

A major challenge for those developing and utilizing databases of biographic information is the accuracy and continuing integrity of data[12,13] As noted earlier, "people data" tend to be inaccurate compared with other data in the manufacturing or pharmaceutical world. Often, there is no assured means to determine if the "people data" are correct. There are no physical properties that can be tested. For example, how can it be verified whether a person actually lives at the location provided in an address field without visiting him or her at the address? Although programming logic can provide a set of edits, constraints and consistency checks, the "correctness" of the data value itself cannot be inherently measured.

In the information processing field, great emphasis is placed on preventing erroneous data from entering a system by editing data at the time of entry, capturing data with automated rather than human techniques and continually improving and measuring the processes used to obtain the data.

Nowhere is the problem more acute than in the need for positive identification of blood donors. A range of techniques that may address this problem in the future is the use of biorecognition systems. These systems are used to verify a person's identity through the analysis of a physical characteristic or even a learned behavioral trait. Biorecognition systems may be used as verification systems for systems users (a tamper-proof password), or as an identification method for blood donors.

Currently, products based on the following biorecognition characteristics are reaching the marketplace: fingerprint pattern, hand geometry, retinal scanner, voice verification and signature dynamics. A new technology based upon the veins on the back of the hand is being tested.

Each biorecognition system is based on the following principles.[14] The user is enrolled into the system (fingerprint, hand or eye scanned; signature written; or words spoken). The results are digitized and stored in the system as reference data values for that user. In a verification mode, the person enters a "user ID" and undergoes the biorecognition process. The results are compared with the stored values to verify identity. A personal identification implies the ability to recognize the person at random from the entire database in the system.

Potential errors with biorecognition systems include rejection of a person whose identity claim is valid, and acceptance of an impostor. Specific error rates vary with each technique. Error rates for all techniques have been decreasing over the last decade.

Fingerprint Systems

Fingerprint systems use a reader to take a high-resolution photograph of one or more fingers, then digitize and store this in a database. Typically, the matching algorithms involve comparison of the minutiae of a fingerprint, including ridge endings and splits. The scan to enroll a user typically requires about a minute. The scan for verification requires about 2 seconds.

Hand Geometry

Hand geometry systems measure finger length, skin translucency, hand width, thickness and placement using ordinary light. Typically, 20 seconds are required to enroll, and 2 seconds to verify.

Signature Dynamics

Signature-based systems measure characteristics relating to how a signature is written with a light pen on a pressure pad, capturing data such as pen pressure and pen-in-air movement. Typically, 30 seconds are required to enroll, and 2 seconds to verify.

Retinal Scan

Retinal scanning systems use very low-powered light to scan the blood vessels in the rear wall of the eye. Typically, 1 minute is required to enroll, and 2 seconds to verify. Only one commercial manufacturer exists, and claims this technique can also be used as an identification system. Identification times would vary with the size of the database.

Voice Recognition

Voice recognition systems store data from the acoustic characteristics of a voice pattern. Typically, 30 seconds are required to enroll, and 2 seconds to verify.

DNA Patterns

Clearly, DNA "fingerprints," using multilocus probes, are a fundamental and ultimate "biorecognizer." The use of such methods in a routine, screening manner for blood donors seems to be in the remote future. The current costs and time required to obtain results for this purpose appear to be prohibitive for even the most innovative developer.

Any installation of a biorecognition system must address the issue of user acceptance. Fingerprints appear to be the biorecognition system ahead of the others in development and deployment. Commercial systems are in use by several state welfare boards to reduce welfare fraud. However, there is concern that many volunteer blood donors will not agree to be fingerprinted as part of a biorecognition system.

On-Line Access and Universal Connectivity

The need to improve productivity will force virtually all organizations to use fully on-line technology to become faster and better at what they do. To reduce costs and to improve quality and service, every user will be able to immediately input and access information in a database at any time, from any location.[15]

Geographically distributed operations, customers, suppliers, etc, will all have immediate access to current information. In the future, all computers will be linked together. The worldwide "any-to-any" communications expected and accepted for telephones will be true tomorrow for computers. By the late 1990s, the wideband networking infrastructure ("information highway") will be in place in the United States so that any type of information (voice, data, image, video) can be transmitted at anytime to anyone in the world.

Those managing blood banking operations require access to unexpected or surprising information immediately, not tomorrow. Computer reliability, availability and performance and networking capacity will all support fast, continuous, on-line applications.

Human Interface Approaches

The human interface is the gateway for the effective use of computer resources.[16] To the user, the computer system is synonymous with the interface. The graphic human interfaces characterized by windows, icons and mice that were popularized in the 1980s provided a degree of flexibility not found with the rigid and predictable keystroke-based terminals of the past. Today's graphic systems, however, are still operational in nature, and require specialized knowledge and training. Errors still occur during data entry and from misunderstanding the directions regarding how to operate the computer.

The future computer interface will have humans communicate with a computer in the way we do with other humans, so that no special training is required. Today, the burden of communication with the computer falls upon the human. In the future, the burden for interpreting human communication and compensating for human error will fall upon the human interface system of the computer. In the future, the human interface system will prevent errors by recognizing the user, and by using expert system technology to interpret and guide the user's interaction with the system.

The evolution of the human interface will be possible through the progression of the following enabling technologies:

- Voice recognition and response, and eventually continuous speech recognition and response.
- Three-dimensional graphic displays.
- Handwriting-based input.
- Gesture recognition.
- Vision-tracking devices.
- Enhanced input and output multimedia displays to mix text, voice, image, graphics, video and animation.

To implement future human interfaces, the following will occur:

- Increasing processing power to handle data compression and decompression.
- High communications bandwidth for video/animation/imaging.
- Enhanced storage technology to handle exponential storage growth requirements.
- Artificial intelligence and neural nets to improve pattern recognition.
- Faster signal processing chips.
- Artificial intelligence to determine characteristics of the user.

Information Manipulation and Management Techniques

In the future, computers will be thought of less as information processors and more as information sources. As more computers are networked together with access to local and remote data, with worldwide access to information databases and electronic documents, an overwhelming amount of information will be available.

Data will be available as text, image, animation, audio and simulations. In the future, the information explosion will be dealt with by applying knowledge to the information. Information will be subjected to automatic analysis, decision-making, simulation and visualization. Knowledge systems will provide a primary enabling technology.

Knowledge systems consist of structured information and a program that can interpret the information without human intervention.[18] Knowledge systems allow a user to apply the knowledge without first understanding the knowledge, allow the delegation of decisions and tasks to computers without human intervention, and allow the application of knowledge when humans are not available.

The potential impacts of knowledge systems are protean. The use of knowledge systems allows the actual decision-making process to be scrutinized and improved. Also, the specific data used in making the decision, such as the results of a test or a donor's health history, will be available. This will improve the decision-making process. In addition, decision-making can be published and standardized geographically, allowing more consistency across a widely dispersed range of practitioners.

Using the power of computers, knowledge systems will detect correlations that cannot be detected manually. These correlations, in essence, become new knowledge. Thus, knowledge systems will create more understanding.

Knowledge systems will proliferate in the area of mundane decision-making, providing consistency and sparing humans the drudgery of everyday routine decisions. The endless series of routine questions that constitute a manufacturing process can be answered by computer, leaving insightful thought for humans. Knowledge systems will allow the delegation of more trivial tasks to machines. Many mundane, repetitive, regulated and standardized functions in blood processing will be implemented in knowledge-based software systems.

Knowledge will be shared across an industry. The knowledge will be published in knowledge-based form, rather than in textbook or periodical form, just as today accounting data are published in spreadsheet form. Since this knowledge can be applied without understanding the underlying theory, it can be adapted universally.

Today, computers are described in terms of speed and processing power. Tomorrow, computers will be described in terms of storing, processing and disseminating knowledge. For example, in manufacturing in the future, a knowledge-based system can form a "command, control and communications" center in which all process control, process modeling, instrumentation, sensor input, maintenance and diagnostic expert system, scheduling and inventory management are integrated. Symbolic, numeric and image processing data will be integrated and interpreted in light of expectations and constraints, and respond in real-time with the appropriate actions.

Massive Parallel Processing

Massive parallel processing refers to the building of very high performance computers based on microprocessor technology and parallel processor computer architecture.[16] In a conventional computer, programming instructions are executed serially, with one instruction using one data item at a time. In a massive parallel computer, with thousands of microprocessors, each processor will act simultaneously and independently upon different data items.

There are two major potential impacts. First, because thousands of processors will be able to work effectively on one problem, researchers will be able to model complex phenomena with increasing realism. The models will be able to incorporate far greater complexity from multiple scientific disciplines, and interrelationships between subsystems and variables to produce results with far greater accuracy. This can be used in areas such as understanding how blood products affect the body, and in designing and analyzing the atomic structure of blood product substitutes.

Second, as the amount of information collected and stored keeps increasing over time (into terabytes), new techniques are required to access and manipulate the data. Databases that are designed to divide the total workload over the processors in a parallel processing computer will be able to support far greater workloads.

Massive parallel processing machines will be able to support both extremely fast transaction processing applications (very large numbers of users modifying small numbers of data elements) and decision support applications (complex queries that span most of the data in a database). Investigations into decades of data could occur routinely. Massive parallel processing computers will be able to provide data integrity; transaction integrity; controlled access; and control to load, store, retrieve and recover data—with predictable response times, while supporting huge databases.

Interface Standards

As noted for Code 128 and the efforts of the ISBT and related US organizations, standards will be required for all connections between computers. In order to have direct computer-to-computer interfacing, to allow computers to control other computer functions, to allow transactions to occur between computers and to exchange information without human intervention, computers must be able to exchange data. With a set of standards universally accepted by all vendors, effort will be put into defining function, and not into integration and interoperability. In the future, the transmission of all data types will be based on globally accepted standards.

Redefinition of Documentation

Today, paper documentation prevails everywhere. Paper is portable, inexpensive, reliable and familiar. Paper is also passive and limited. In the future, a new medium of electronic documents will replace the paper document.

However, electronic documents that can only be displayed on the desktop will not displace paper documents. The replacement of paper with electronic documents will be driven by hardware changes. The availability of a small, thin, lightweight, portable, inexpensive input/output device that provides the flexibility and convenience of paper will initiate the takeover of the electronic document.

Electronic documents will allow the incorporation of graphic, audio and animated images. Unlike passive paper documents, electronic documents will be able to respond to information from the external world, and the response can be linked to other logically connected documents. Humans will be able to interact with electronic documents, with their responses and input altering the document itself. Today, hypertext allows users to browse through information in documents as opposed to following the hierarchical and linear links imposed by the printed medium. Tomorrow, hypertext linkages between information will be expanded to support multidimensional and multimedia connections, at the control of the user.

References

1. Klein HG, ed. Standards for blood banks and transfusion services. 16th ed. Bethesda, MD: American Association of Blood Banks, 1994.

2. Code of federal regulations. Title 21 CFR, Parts 606, 607, 610, 640. Washington, DC: US Government Printing Office, 1993 (revised annually).
3. Food and Drug Administration. Draft guideline for the validation of blood establishment computer systems. October 28, 1993. Rockville, MD: Congressional and Consumer Affairs Branch, 1993.
4. Hohberger C. ISBT 128 bar code symbology and application specification for blood and blood products labeling. Vernon Hills, IL: Zebra Technologies Corporation, 1994.
5. Committee for Commonality in Blood Banking Automation. Final Report. Volume VII. Vienna, VA: American Blood Commission, 1977. [out of print]
6. Longe K, Brenner L. Bar code technology in health care. Cleveland, OH: Advanstar Communications, 1993:31-42.
7. American Association of Blood Banks, American Red Cross, Council of Community Blood Centers. Guidelines for the uniform labeling of blood and blood components. Arlington, VA: American Association of Blood Banks, 1989.
8. Committee for Commonality in Blood Banking Automation. Final Report. Volume III. Vienna, VA: American Blood Commission, 1977. [out of print]
9. Bar code system performance test. Report #1. Pittsburgh, PA: Automatic ID Manufacturers, Inc, 1987:11.
10. Carty L, Bauman E. A blood center's two-year experience with bar code substitutions (abstract). Transfusion 1991; 31(suppl):73S.
11. Longsacre A. Data integrity test results and observations. Paper presented at Scan-Tech 1991, November 5, 1991.
12. Naus JI. Data quality control and editing. New York: Marcel Dekker, 1975.
13. Redman TC. Data quality. New York: Bantam Books, 1992.
14. Datapro Research Group. Biometric access control systems: Maulet overview. Delran, NJ: McGraw-Hill, 1991.
15. Boar BH. The art of strategic planning for information technology. New York: John Wiley & Sons, Inc, 1993.
16. Wang RY, ed. Information technology in action. Englewood Cliffs, NJ: PTR Prentice Hall, 1993.
17. Winston PH. Artificial intelligence. Reading, MA: Addison-Wesley, 1984.

In: Nance ST, ed.
Blood Supply: Risks, Perceptions and Prospects for the Future
Bethesda, MD: American Association of Blood Banks, 1994

3

Perception of Risk

Jay E. Menitove, MD

MEDICAL INTERVENTIONS ARE ASSOCIATED with risk. The decision to proceed with a diagnostic or therapeutic procedure requires an analysis of the benefits and the hazards posed in conjunction with the underlying medical condition, the prognosis, the alternatives and the patient's consent. For a specific patient, this decision involves an assessment of risk following consultation with a physician, medical professionals and possibly family and friends.

Society approaches risk acceptance differently. In general, the public perceives risk as detached from an immediate, pressing and personal decision. For the public, riskiness relates to a general impression.

Several academic and intellectual disciplines study methods for evaluating risk (Table 3-1). Each of these has its own technical

Table 3-1. Approaches to Risk Evaluation

Discipline	Expertise
Risk analysis	Decision analysis
	Operations research
	Engineering and applied science
Damage assessment	Economics
Risk perception	Psychology
	Sociology

Jay E. Menitove, MD, Deputy Director, Medical Services, Hoxworth Blood Center and Professor of Internal Medicine, University of Cincinnati College of Medicine, Cincinnati, Ohio language and analytical methods for reaching conclusions and recommendations. In broad terms, these approaches fall into three categories: risk analysis, damage assessment and risk perception.[1]

This chapter is separated into three sections. The first introduces the three broad pursuits to understanding risk evaluation. The second discusses reasons for conflicts between experts and the public. The third section links the comments about risk perception to blood banking and provides suggestions for future action.

Professional Approaches To Risk Evaluation

Risk Analysis

Decision analysis and operations research experts engage in risk analysis. These individuals assess physical outcomes of rare, but serious events to determine what is "safe." They rely on observations, experiments and epidemiologic research. Their conclusions are formulated in probabilistic and objective terms, eg, the number of deaths per person per year such as 1 in 125,000 from leukemia or 1 in 588,000 from an earthquake in California; or deaths per million hours spent participating in an activity, such as 1 in 7150 from rock climbing.[2-4] A decision to undertake a "risk" becomes a personal decision based on quantifiable data.

Damage Assessment

Economists view risk acceptance in terms of damage assessment. These experts provide calculations of the value of lives lost or expected dollar damages. Unfortunately, a cost-benefit analysis may underestimate the public's reaction to an event, eg, the risk of a gas tank rupture and explosion following an accident involving a Ford Pinto.[5]

One approach to determining the value of a life involves an analysis of the dollar amount consumers, in aggregate, are willing to pay for certain safety devices divided by an estimate of the lifesaving potential of the item. For example, using 1987 dollars, if consumers were willing to pay \$100 for a smoke detector that had one chance in 1000 for saving a life, the public's view of the value of a person's life would be $\$100 \div 0.001 = \$100,000$. With additional mathematical modeling considerations, the value of a life calculated by smoke detector purchases was \$373,000.[6] Other such calculations valued lives at $541,000 for seat belt usage, $3,600,000 for premium tire usage, and $11,800,000 for a desire for safer airline travel.

Apparently, government agencies set values on lives from $400,000 to $7 million (based on 1987 considerations). One study of environmental carcinogens found that the public seeks regulation when lives can be saved for less than $2 million each.[6]

Risk Perception

Psychologists and sociologists study the ways that risk is perceived. These professionals ask why the public is concerned about certain technologies and not others, and why experts and the public view the same risk differently.[7,8] Because these questions are appropriately germane to transfusion medicine specialists, they are discussed in depth below.

Characterization of Risk

In an attempt to better define public judgment about risk, Paul Slovic, PhD (a student of human judgment, decision-making and risk analysis) used psychometric scaling methods and multivariant analysis techniques to produce "cognitive maps" of risk attitudes and perceptions (Fig 3-1).[7] These maps were formulated by considering quantitative judgments about the risk of certain activities, substances and technologies; the level of regulation desired for dealing with these risks; the associated benefits; the number of deaths ensuing each year; and other qualitative characteristics. The latter category included catastrophic potential, controllability, familiarity, voluntariness and severity.

In creating this conceptual framework, Slovic created a four-quadrant "map." In the vertical axis, risk characteristics varied from those that are observable, known and immediate to those that are not observable, unknown and delayed. On the horizontal axis, risks varied from controllable, not dread, equitable and voluntary to those considered uncontrollable, dread, not equitable and involuntary. Two factors emerged as most important, "dread risk" and "unknown risk." "Dread risk" associates with a perception of lack of control, catastrophic potential, fatal consequences and inequitable distribution of risks and benefits. If a hazard is seen as "dread," the perception of risk is higher, the public wants risks reduced and society

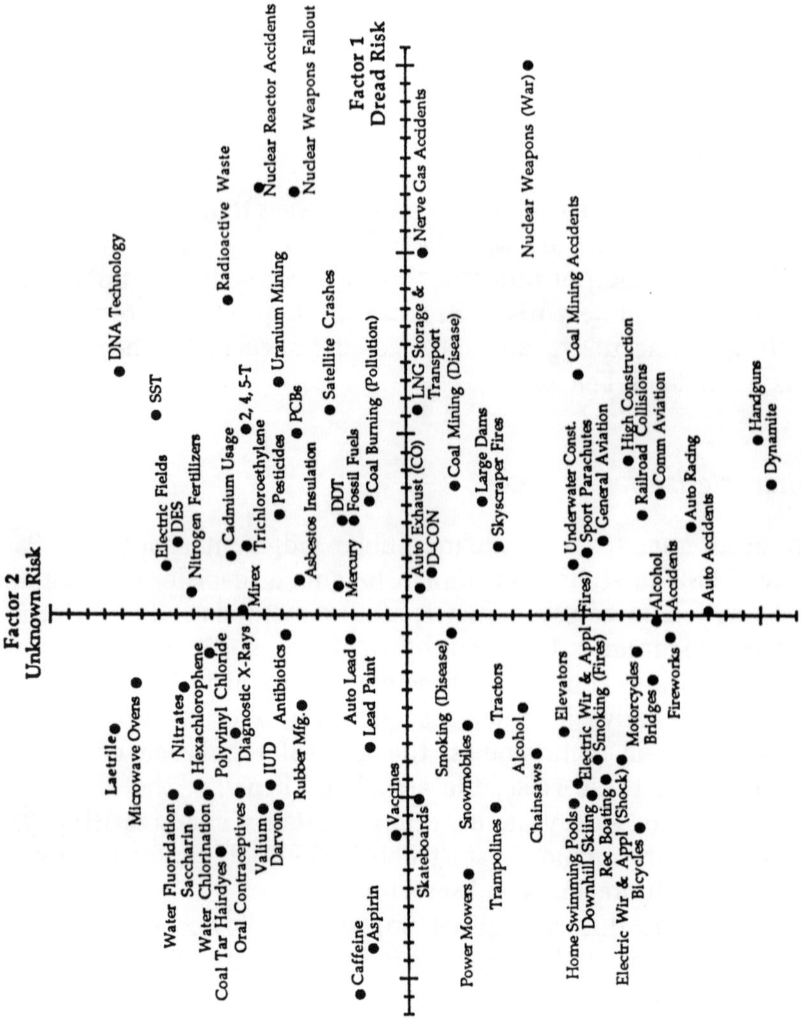
Factor 2
Unknown Risk
Factor 1
Dread Risk
DNA Technology
SST
Radioactive Waste
Nuclear Reactor Accidents
Nuclear Weapons Fallout
Uranium Mining
Satellite Crashes
Electric Fields
DES
Nitrogen Fertilizers
Cadmium Usage
2, 4, 5-T
Mirex
Trichloroethylene
Pesticides
PCBs
Asbestos Insulation
Mercury
DDT
Fossil Fuels
Coal Burning (Pollution)
Auto Exhaust (CO)
D-CON
LNG Storage &
Transport
Nerve Gas Accidents
Coal Mining (Disease)
Large Dams
Skyscraper Fires
Nuclear Weapons (War)
Coal Mining Accidents
Underwater Const.
Sport Parachutes
General Aviation
High Construction
Railroad Collisions
Comm Aviation
Auto Racing
Auto Accidents
Alcohol
Accidents
Handguns
Dynamite
Laetrile
Microwave Ovens
Nitrates
Hexachlorophene
Polyvinyl Chloride
Diagnostic X-Rays
Antibiotics
Rubber Mfg.
IUD
Water Fluoridation
Saccharin
Water Chlorination
Coal Tar Hairdyes
Oral Contraceptives
Valium
Darvon
Auto Lead
Lead Paint
Caffeine
Aspirin
Vaccines
Skateboards
Smoking (Disease)
Snowmobiles
Power Mowers
Trampolines
Tractors
Alcohol
Chainsaws
Elevators
Home Swimming Pools
Downhill Skiing
Electric Wir & Appl (Fires)
Smoking (Fires)
Rec Boating
Electric Wir & Appl (Shock)
Motorcycles
Bicycles
Bridges
Fireworks

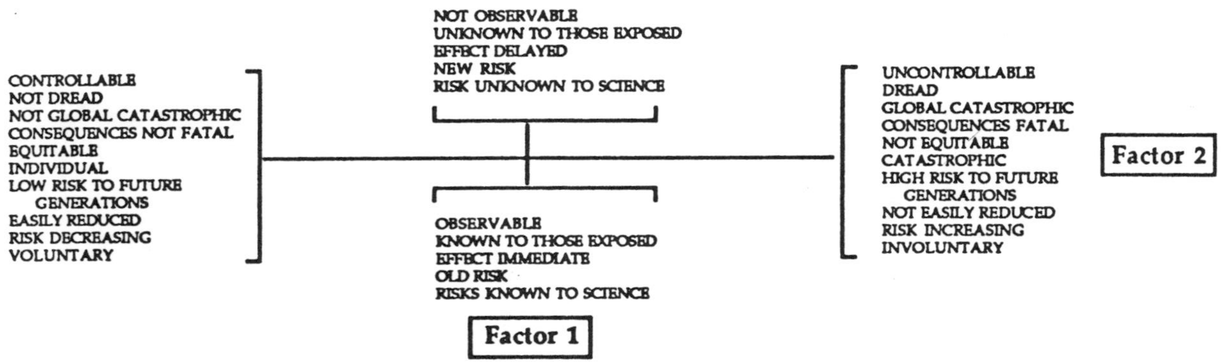

Figure 3-1. The relationship of two factors, dread risk and unknown risk, plays an important role in risk perception. The vertical axis varies from unknown risk to known risk. The horizontal axis depicts dread risk at one extreme and controllable, voluntary, low risk issues on the other end. (Used with permission from Slovic.[7])

requests more regulation. "Unknown risk" is unobservable, unclear, new and delayed in manifesting harm.

Notably, the perception of risk within broad categories is diffuse. For example, not all automobile accidents are perceived similarly. In the case of the Ford Pinto, the public identified fuel tank rupture with the possibility of fire and burn injuries as a "dread risk." However, cost-benefit experts interpreted the risk differently. In retrospect, this is not surprising. Experts perceive risk in technical, quantitative terms, such as expected annual mortality, or in damage assessment terms. On the other hand, the public views risks qualitatively and assigns attributes such as "dread," uncontrollable, catastrophic, inequitable and being a threat to future generations.

In addition, studies find large differences in perceived benefits from various products. People tolerate higher risks if the risks are balanced by significant benefits.[9] Benefit or pleasure from using a product decreases "dread" and perceived risk. That is, risk perception becomes the net of risk minus benefit. Apparently, people undervalue the benefit of items they do not use directly and voice concern about items controlled by others, such as corporations. Research results indicate personal benefits influence issues dealing with technological changes while catastrophe highlights perceptions about a technology. For example, nuclear power plant accidents are less acceptable to the public than adverse events at coal-fired plants or hydroelectric dams.

Amplification of Risk

On occasion, relatively minor risks or events result in strong reactions. This is explained by a theoretical model, "the social amplification of risks." According to this theory, the consequences of the event as well as psychological, cultural, social and institutional influences determine the social and economic consequences of an adverse event. In a study involving bleach, ammonia, oven cleaners and other household chemicals, there was consensus that injury could be reduced by following proper precautions and that the risks associated with these products were known. Nonetheless, if a serious accident or injury occurred, the adverse event might serve as a "warning signal," indicating that use of the chemicals was potentially more dangerous than initially considered.[5,7] Not surprisingly, the media would then communicate these risks because of the potentially large number of persons exposed to the products, even though the absolute level of risk may be small.

The way an event is managed and the likelihood of ongoing or future hazards also influence public impressions. Perceptions of managerial incompetence and threats of future risk create the potential for "dread" concern. Media coverage, along with public response, plays a significant role in determining societal reactions. Interestingly, the number of casualties or extent of property damage often has a lesser role in influencing public response than the possibility of future risk or perception of managerial incompetence. As an example, the public's reaction to the nuclear plant accident at Three Mile Island reflected "dread" adverse events, perceived management incompetence and the potential for future danger to others. There were few casualties, but if one concentrated on this factor, the event's impact was severely underestimated. Instead, the media focused on perceived managerial incompetence. Media coverage and public response redirected the impact of the event and transformed it into a "signal."

Signal Events

"Signal" incidents refer to events that indicate there may be reasons for concern.[7,8] The context is important. An accident resulting in the loss of many lives in a well-understood situation (eg, a train wreck) has less "signal" potential than a small accident involving unfamiliar circumstances (eg, an accidental spill in a recombinant DNA laboratory). While the proximate cause of the space shuttle Challenger explosion was failure of an O-ring, the investigation of the accident found extensive management and organizational problems at the National Aeronautics and Space Administration (NASA).[7,8] The overall impact of the initial event extended beyond the shuttle explosion and affected the entire space industry. Eventually, NASA's management reorganized and, incidentally, changed the O-ring. The accident at Three Mile Island also sent a "signal" that nuclear reactors were not as safe as the public believed. The entire nuclear power industry suffered disastrous consequences.

Obviously, risk perception, with its emphasis on the psychological and sociological aspects of public reaction, plays a more significant role than risk analysis and damage assessment. The public response is more dramatic when events have a high degree of unfamiliarity, unknown risks, uncontrollability and "dread." An appreciation for the way the public responds to riskiness and how this approach differs from that taken by experts are of paramount importance to those involved in risk management.

Conflicting Aspects of Managing Risk

As shown in Table 3-2, several factors can influence risk management, including public perception, media coverage, regret, errors, opinions and policymakers.

The reasons the public views some events with "dread" and others without this perception are not always understood. In practice, the media and the public interact in defining the impact of an event, eg, widespread exposure to a toxin or a contaminant. Surveys indicating high levels of radon gas in thousands of homes capture more news coverage than an accident involving a tractor-trailer carrying nuclear waste without release of radioactive material. The number of casualties magnified by future risk, perceived managerial incompetence, and large economic and property damage affects media coverage.[10]

Problems also arise when scientists lack precise estimates of risk. For example, the extent of risk following discovery of two cyanide-laced Chilean grapes in Philadelphia was unknown. The specific risk exposure was identified and blamed. The public avoided grapes. If no action had been taken and others became sick or died, there would have been significant regret. Regret looms as a significant factor and is magnified when expected behavior is not followed. For example, a babysitter will be condemned if a sleeping baby, left alone for 10 minutes while the babysitter does an errand, suffers an injury, even if the risk associated with running the errand were higher.[11]

Of interest, society has a "lopsided" opinion of errors of omission and commission. The perception that a person or agency made a decision involving significant risk may create more damage than the risk itself. Also, adverse outcomes of making a decision are more visible than positive effects resulting from not making a decision.[9]

In addition, attitudes about risk may reflect other and perhaps earlier formed opinions, such as those involving the role of government or military policymakers. Public risk managers are compromised when they are unaware of these preconceived attitudes. Out-

Table 3-2. Factors That Influence Risk Management

- Public perception
- Media coverage
- Regret
- Errors of omission/commission
- Previously formed opinions
- Policymaker competence

side influences, such as monetary and political pressures, influence decisions about risks and should be considered when the rationale for making a choice is not obvious. For example, North Sea oil exploration workers take risks to avoid consequences, rather than to make additional income. They opt to work in off-shore drilling in fear of being fired if they refuse the assignment rather than focusing on bonuses for taking a risk.[8]

If those involved in determining risk are concerned with minute details, difficulties may arise. In general, policymakers are charged with looking at the larger picture, not the smaller parts. Policymakers should question the validity of technical or specialist advice when 1) the specialists have direct interest in outcomes, 2) past recommendations were wrong, 3) global constraints are not recognized or 4) the advice of various experts is in conflict. Situations marked for concern include those that have: 1) large unknown elements, 2) consequences that are potentially severe and 3) errors that are likely to be irreversible.[8]

Problems also arise when those seeking risk reduction proposals have differing goals. There is unavoidable conflict in attempting to simultaneously minimize risk, avoid catastrophe and distribute risk equally. Saving lives takes precedence, but the data are not always clear. Tension arises when one attempts to avoid catastrophe and distribute risk equally. Hence, public and expert viewpoints are discernibly and sometimes unavoidably different.[1]

Blood Banking Aspects of Risk Perception

Between 1985 and 1993, the American Association of Blood Banks sponsored six public opinion surveys.[12] Respondents mentioned AIDS repetitively as the most serious health problem facing the United States. In response to questions about United States blood suppliers and the AIDS epidemic, 78% considered the nation's blood supply safer in 1993 than it was 5 years previously, when only 44% had this perception. Among those questioned, 79% knew about blood supply safeguards such as donor questioning and screening tests for infectious diseases. Approximately 88% said they had "some" to "a lot" of confidence in the blood banks' ability to recruit healthy donors, test blood and handle it properly. Nonetheless, 50% believed that there is some likelihood of contracting AIDS from a blood transfusion.

Despite these somewhat heartening results for those involved in transfusion medicine, a lingering impression remains that the public demands perfection in preventing AIDS transmission.[13] Monetary compensation awarded by juries deciding transfusion-associated AIDS cases indicates a lack of acceptance of any risk associated with transmission of HIV through transfusion.

For these reasons, blood bankers need new approaches to risk perception management that reflect the current perceptions about the safety of the blood supply, the level of transfusion-associated HIV infection, and the trend in AIDS-related and other health-care-related litigation decisions. Blood bankers need to consider several aspects of risk perception, such as risk analysis, rebuilding trust, benefits derived from transfusion, the frame of reference for evaluating improvements and compensation programs (Table 3-3).

Risk Analysis

During early 1983, transfusion experts used a risk analysis approach to describe the association between AIDS and transfusion. The public received information indicating that the risk of transfusion-transmitted AIDS was 1 in a million (perhaps), that 5%-7% of transfusion recipients developed transfusion-associated hepatitis and that approximately 1 per million transfusion recipients developed transfusion-associated malaria. For comparison purposes, 1 per 5000 died during appendectomy, 1 per 10,000 died following tonsillectomy, 1 per 626 died during a cholecystectomy, 1 per 5000 died during hernia repair and approximately 1 per 500,000 transfusion recipients died because they received the wrong unit of blood.

Table 3-3. Risk Perception and Blood Banking

Risk analysis	Acceptance of one risk does not imply acceptance of another, lesser risk
Trust	Easier to lose trust than regain it
Advisory/monitoring agencies	Help to reestablish trust
Frame of reference for evaluating improvements	Restoring a condition has a greater value than improving it from its present condition
Benefits of transfusion	Transfusion provides important benefits!
Compensation programs	Enhance communication and promote equity

The risk of transfusion-transmitted AIDS was compared favorably with other more general risks. On an annual basis, 1 per 10,000 persons died in automobile racing accidents, 1 per 50 died motorcycling, 1 per 16,600 died from being struck by an automobile and 1 per 455,000 died because of floods.[2,14] Initially, these comparisons were helpful, but they lost effectiveness and credibility over time. In part, this occurred because acceptance of one risk does not imply acceptance of a hazard with a lower risk.[15] Eventually, the public compared the risk of acquiring AIDS from a transfusion with less risky alternatives and also inferred that the stated comparisons involve voluntary activities, while blood transfusion is involuntary. Since the acceptability of involuntary risk is lower than voluntary activities, it is not surprising that the public grew weary of these comparisons. In addition, a risk analysis approach fails to consider that the public weighs many factors in determining risk such as "dread," involuntariness, uncontrollability, catastrophe and inequitable distribution of risks and benefits.

Trust

Loss of trust in the answers to questions about the blood supply reinforced the public's fear of transfusions in the early 1980s. In general, the public does not assess risk through technical analysis, but relies on experts to provide stewardship and maintain quality. In recent years, there has been a "crisis in confidence" in governmental and industrial management decisions.[16,17] If the recipient of the information has trust in an industrial or governmental spokesperson, information transfer is relatively straightforward. Communication effectiveness diminishes without that trust.

Risk perception experts are quick to point out the asymmetry between creating trust and destroying it.[17] The "asymmetry principle" includes the admonition that trust-destroying events are more noticeable than trust-building events, and that negative events receive more attention than positive ones. In addition, bad news appears to have more credibility than good news. Unfortunately, lack of trust becomes reinforced because of the natural tendency to avoid persons or institutions that are distrusted.

It is difficult to regain trust once it is lost. The process of reestablishing trust requires considerable time, effort and bidirectional communication. Clearly, these measures are necessary for those in blood banking.

Advisory/Monitoring Agencies

Establishing advisory groups to monitor decisions and suggest corrective actions provides a first step in regaining trust. In the early 1980s, blood banks looked to the Food and Drug Administration (FDA) for oversight. However, accusations of collegial relations between the two entities tarnished the FDA's image as a tough regulator. Currently, efforts are under way for the prestigious Institute of Medicine (IOM) to address pertinent transfusion medicine issues ranging from hepatitis C look-back to an investigation of HIV transmission through blood products and components during the early 1980s.

Frame of Reference for Evaluating Improvements

The Prospect Theory presents an interesting model for managing risk. This theory considers change from a reference position, rather than movement to a new, final outcome. Accordingly, benefits of an intervention have a more favorable perception if they are viewed as a restoration to a previous, better state than if viewed as an improvement of the current condition.[18] As an example, in contemplating proposed improvements to a polluted river, the present condition or a previous condition may serve as the reference point. The options, then, are to improve the river or to restore it to a previous condition. By focusing on the previous quality as the reference point, the proposed change restores it to the way it "ought to be." To many, restoration to a previous state offers greater value than an equal improvement over the current state.

In its current form, absolute safety of the blood supply is not an achievable option. Nonetheless, significant changes enhanced the safety record during the past decade. An appreciation of these benefits appears more significant if couched in terms of restoring the safety record to the pre-AIDS era, rather than stressing gains achieved since 1985.

Benefits of Transfusion

As a corollary, it is important to remember that benefits derived from a risky venture influence psychometric risk ratings, ie, perceived benefits ameliorate perceived risks.[9] The public is bombarded with constant reminders of transfusion risks. Yet, almost everyone knows blood transfusions provide substantial benefits. Blood collection agencies use benefactors of transfusions in emotional appeals to enhance blood donation rather than highlight the life-promoting potential of transfusion.

Compensation Programs

Communication, mitigation and compensation programs present another option for altering the public perception of risk.[1] Communication with concerned citizens provides an opportunity for bidirectional information exchange. Even if the public's perception of risk does not change, each group has an opportunity to learn the basis for an opinion. This may lead to risk mitigation or promote equity by determining compensation packages for those affected. These techniques falter if initiated in the context of an expanding epidemic or in the face of growing distrust about leadership competency. Nonetheless, this three-part program provides a plausible approach for future risk management initiatives.[1,10]

Conclusion

Economists, engineers and other scientists involved in decision analysis use technical models for risk assessment. In contrast, the public views riskiness in terms of perception. Accordingly, perceived risk, "dread," expected mortality, effects on future generations, immediacy, catastrophic potential and voluntariness affect public acceptance or rejection of risks. As such, it is not surprising that public perception and expert assessment differ. It is equally obvious that several risk management approaches, such as risk-decision comparisons, are not sufficient at all times. Regaining trust should be a priority for blood bankers. Espousing benefits associated with transfusion may diffuse negative perceptions. Additionally, blood bankers need to decide whether to stress improvements to the status quo or to tout a return to the way it "ought to be." Overall, transfusion medicine specialists have a daunting responsibility to understand how the public perceives and makes decisions about risk.

References

1. Gregory R. Implications of public perceptions of hazardous materials on risk management. In: Levine DG, Upton AC, eds. Management of hazardous agents. Vol. 2: Social, political and policy aspects. Westport, CT: Praeger, 1992:69-79.
2. Dinman BD. The reality and acceptance of risk. JAMA 1980;244: 1226-8.
3. McCullough J. The nation's changing blood supply system. JAMA 1993;269:2239-45.
4. Apostolakis G. The concept of probability in safety assessments of technological systems. Science 1990;250:1359-64.
5. Neil N, Slovic P, Hakkinen PJ. Mapping consumer perceptions of risk. Washington, DC: Chemical Manufacturers Association, 1993.
6. Barrett PM. Price of pleasure: New legal theorists attach a dollar value to the joy of living. Wall Street Journal 1988; December 12:A1, A7.
7. Slovic P. Perception of risk. Science 1987;236:280-5.
8. Freudenburg WR. Perceived risk, real risk: Social science and the art of probabilistic risk assessment. Science 1988;242:44-9.
9. Gregory R, Mendelsohn R. Perceived risk, dread, and benefits. Risk Analysis 1993;13:259-64.
10. Burns WJ, Slovic P, Kasperson RE, et al. Incorporating structural models into research on the social amplification of risk: Implications for theory construction and decision making. Risk Analysis 1993;13:611-23.
11. Zeckhauser RJ, Viscusi WK. Risk within reason. Science 1990; 248:559-64.
12. AABB Sixth National Survey conducted by the Gallup Organization. Attitudes of US adults toward AIDS and the safety of America's blood supply. Bethesda, MD: American Association of Blood Banks, 1993.
13. Cates WJ, Hinman AR. AIDS and absolutism—the demand for perfection in prevention (Sounding Board). N Engl J Med 1992; 327:492-4.
14. Bove JR. Statement on AIDS and blood transfusion. Hearings before the Subcommittee on Intergovernmental Relations and Human Resources of the House Committee on Government Operations, August 1, 1983. Washington, DC: Government Printing Office, 1983.
15. Slovic P, Kraus N, Covello VT. What should we know about making risk comparisons? Risk Analysis 1990;10:389-92.

16. Slovic P, Flynn JH, Layman M. Perceived risk, trust, and the politics of nuclear waste. Science 1991;254:1603-7.
17. Slovic P. Perceived risk, trust, and democracy. Risk Analysis 1993;13:675-82.
18. Gregory R, Lichtenstein S, MacGregor D. The role of past states in determining reference points for policy decisions. Organ Behav Hum Decis Process 1993;55:195-206.

In: Nance ST, ed.
Blood Supply: Risks, Perceptions and Prospects for the Future
Bethesda, MD: American Association of Blood Banks, 1994

THE EMILY COOLEY MEMORIAL LECTURE

4

Safety in the Blood Bank

Paul V. Holland, MD

USUALLY, WHEN THE ISSUE of safety is discussed in the context of blood banking, it is with the transfusion recipient in mind. Certainly, this has been the foremost concern over the past 12 years when one talks about transfusions. However, the safety of staff working in blood banking and transfusion medicine is also important. For health-care workers (HCWs) in blood banks and transfusion services, the risks of acquiring infectious diseases are small. Our efforts have made the environments for HCWs in a blood center or a transfusion service quite safe; at the same time, the risks of transmissible agents for transfusion recipients have also been reduced considerably.

The risks of transfusion-transmitted diseases were well summarized by Dodd in 1992.[1] These risks should be even lower now, but they are dramatically less than they were just 12-15 years ago. Viral hepatitis has always been the major risk of developing an infectious disease following a transfusion. Today, with careful recruitment of volunteer (unpaid) donors, along with careful screening of these individuals utilizing informative predonation material and extensive questions, coupled with several viral marker tests, the risk of hepatitis has never been lower. At this time, it is estimated that the risk per unit transfused for hepatitis B infection, or what used to be called "serum hepatitis," is no more than 1 in 200,000. The risk of

Paul V. Holland, MD, Medical Director/Chief Executive Officer, Sacramento Medical Foundation Blood Center, Sacramento, California hepatitis C, or what was formerly called "non-A,non-B hepatitis," was always much higher; today, it is probably no more than 1 in 5000.[2]

For the general public, the major fear of a transfusion-transmitted disease is the transmission of the human immunodeficiency virus (HIV), the virus that causes AIDS. Again, with the multiple means in place to recruit low-risk individuals, screen donors and test donations, the risk is less than 1 in 225,000 units in the US as a whole.[1] This is a remarkable change from a high of more than 1 in 100 in certain cities, not so many years ago.[3] Additional retroviruses may also be transmitted by blood transfusions, especially the human T-lymphotropic viruses, type I and type II (HTLV-I/II). These viruses may be transmitted by 1 in 50,000 transfusions, but recent changes in the screening tests probably make this risk even less at this time. However, for these two viruses, the vast majority of patients, even if they are infected, do not progress to any clinical disease.

When we consider all the other risks of a transmissible agent being transmitted by a transfusion in the US today, the risk is no more than 1 in a million. Based on reported cases, this includes not only viruses, but parasites and bacteria as well.[1]

If one adds all of the risks of a transfusion and compares the sum to other risks, eg, hospitalization itself, the comparison is quite striking. On balance, about 3 units of blood or blood components per 10,000 may transmit some infectious, microbiologic agent in the US; these may result in serious morbidity and mortality.[1] On the other hand, patients who are hospitalized in the US have a risk of about 6 per 1000 admissions of having a serious or fatal consequence unrelated to the disease or condition for which they were admitted.[4,5] Thus, there is a 20 times greater chance that patients will have a fatal complication in the hospital, unrelated to the initial reason for admission, compared to their developing a potentially fatal, transfusion-transmitted disease with each unit of blood or single donor component they receive.

In assessing the safety of HCWs who are in the field of blood banking and transfusion medicine, one usually focuses on their risk of developing AIDS; however, one should really assess their chances of being infected with HIV.[6] While this risk is certainly important, there are other risks for these individuals, too.[7] Again, as for transfusion recipients, the most important risks are infection with hepatitis B virus (HBV) and hepatitis C virus (HCV). However, in the blood bank setting, whether it be in phlebotomizing donors or patients, or testing donor or patient samples, the chance of acquiring any of these infections is remarkably low, especially if safe work practices are used.[8,9] One question, however, which relates to this, is whether the risk of HIV, HBV and HCV in the HCW in the field of blood banking/transfusion medicine is over- or under-estimated. It is certainly possible that such HCWs may fail to report their injuries or infections for fear of job loss, rejection by their co-workers or other reasons. On the other hand, it is equally possible that HCWs may be reporting these three infections as occupationally acquired to cover nonoccupational risks and infections. On balance, it is likely that work-related injuries that might result in infection, especially needlestick injuries, tend to be reported as HCWs wait anxiously for up to 6 months to see if they will develop laboratory evidence (seroconversion) or clinical illnesses from any of these three viruses.

Risk of HIV Infection

One way to assess the risk of HIV infection in HCWs is to look at those who have a clinical diagnosis of AIDS in the United States.[10,11] Since the virus of AIDS first entered this country in the late 1970's, well over a million Americans have become infected with HIV, and more than 300,000 have progressed to clinical disease (AIDS).[11] During this time, the major risk factors for HIV infection (and progression to AIDS) have remained remarkably consistent. The major risk factor for men is having sex with other men. Individuals who share needles while using intravenous drugs have the second highest risk. Some individuals have had both risk factors. Next are those individuals who have acquired HIV through heterosexual contact, primarily women who have had sexual contact with HIV-infected bisexual men or intravenous drug users. Two percent of individuals with AIDS have a history of being transfused; another one percent are patients with hemophilia who have received clotting factor concentrates. Finally, some children have been infected perinatally with HIV from their mothers. In any given series, 4-5% of patients diagnosed with AIDS do not admit to any of the above risk factors, and are classified as "no identified risk" (NIR). When such NIR individuals are further evaluated carefully, the majority appear to have the same distribution of risk factors as those with identified modes of acquiring HIV infection. Some patients are never fully investigated; some may die before in-depth investigation can be completed and others may refuse to reveal risk factors. Eventually, however, relatively few end up having no identified risk.

About 5.5% of AIDS cases have occurred in HCWs.[10] However, 5.7% of the labor force is employed in health services. So, on this basis, the number of AIDS cases occurring in HCWs is not disproportionate. Of the AIDS cases that have been identified among HCWs, 95% have had the usual, recognized, nonoccupational risk factors. However, about 5% have been reported as NIR. When further, in-depth evaluation was conducted of these HCWs with AIDS who were initially classified as NIR, 44% of them had the aforementioned, nonoccupational AIDS risks, and were reclassified. Fourteen percent still appeared to have no identified risk and 41% were still under investigation (and may, or may not, be reclassified eventually). In any case, HCWs in general, and blood bank workers in particular, do not appear, on the basis of the frequency of diagnosis of AIDS, to be disproportionately overrepresented.

It is clear, however, that between 1981 and 1993, a number of HCWs were or appeared to have been infected with HIV through their jobs. By July of 1993, at least 37 HIV infections had been documented as occupationally acquired by HCWs.[11] These 37 HCWs had careful follow-up with evidence of a nonreactive HIV antibody test at the time of occupational exposure with subsequent seroconversion. At least eight of these individuals have progressed to AIDS, and three have died of this disease. During this same period, an additional 78 *possible* occupationally acquired cases of HIV infection were identified in HCWs in the US. Of these, at least 54 have progressed to AIDS.

Of those HCWs who have been documented to have acquired HIV on the job, the individuals at most risk appeared to be laboratory technologists and nurses. Among the 37 HCWs with a documented occupational transmission of HIV, 15 (41%) were laboratory technologists and 13 (35%) were nurses. Of the 78 HCWs with possible acquisition of HIV on the job, 14 (18%) were laboratory technologists and 15 (19%) were nurses. Both professionals frequently deal with patient blood and excreta. Further, they are often exposed to sharps, such as needles, with sticks or cuts as the primary mode of acquisition of HIV infection.

The occurrence of HIV infection in HCWs, albeit rare, prompted the Occupational Safety and Health Administration (OSHA) to promulgate a number of actions utilizing its "general duty clause." At the time of the increased enforcement activity of OSHA, there were approximately 25 HIV-infected HCWs; of these, two had progressed to AIDS, but there were no deaths.[12] Then, OSHA itself estimated that many more infections with hepatitis B were occurring; of these, at least 2500-3000/year resulted in acute disease, and approximately

200 HCWs were dying each year. Nonetheless, it was the few cases of HIV infection in HCWs, including the two cases that progressed to AIDS, which prompted widespread action and response by OSHA, and not the thousands of cases of hepatitis B occurring among HCWs, with a resultant 1000 carriers and 200 deaths per year.

With pressure and potential enforcement from OSHA, a great deal of effort was begun to reduce the risk of HIV transmission to HCWs. As a secondary effect, efforts were directed toward reducing infections with hepatitis B and other hazards in the health care workplace. The general duty clause of OSHA[12] states that "each employer shall furnish to each of his employees, an employment and a place of employment, which are free from recognized hazards that are causing, or are likely to cause, death or serious physical harm to his employees." With this clause, OSHA was able to promulgate additional safety regulations and force far-reaching changes in the health-care environment.

With OSHA's 1989 proposed enforcement procedures, a number of elements were either strongly recommended or required.[12] These included universal precautions, which were intended to prevent HCWs from parenteral, mucous membrane and nonintact skin exposures to blood-borne pathogens. OSHA further defined potentially infectious body fluids, including those linked to the transmission of HIV and/or HBV. As infectious fluids, they included blood, semen and blood products; in addition, they included concentrated HIV or HBV viral or culture material. In defining those at risk, a phlebotomist was defined as any HCW who draws blood samples, irrespective of whether this had to do with patients or donors. All health-care employers were required to develop infection control programs. While these could be oral or written, there had to be a program in place. To ensure this, OSHA announced that it would inspect hospitals, laboratories, blood donor centers and any other facility where patients, blood or excreta might be present. Recognizing that a major means of preventing HBV infections would be the use of the hepatitis B vaccine, employers had to define circumstances that would warrant vaccination. While this regulation applied primarily to employees at substantial risk of blood exposure, it could, in fact, include individuals who were infrequently exposed to blood or excreta. All potentially exposed individuals were to be offered the hepatitis B vaccine, and it was to be paid for by the employer. Probably the most important aspects of the OSHA 1989 "rules" were the aspects of training and education that were to be established. Clearly, employees were to be educated about the risks and means of reducing them, were to be trained in their job duties to minimize risk, and had to be informed of means to reduce their risk through various precautions in handling blood and blood-containing materials.

With OSHA's expanded enforcement activities, much more was done to reduce the risk of infections with HIV and HBV in the workplace. While the risks had already been recognized,[12] and means of reducing risk were already present,[9,13] it was clear that OSHA was making a persuasive argument for employers to put these practices into place. Thus, they were able to demonstrate what Al Capone said a number of years ago, "You can get much further with a kind word and a gun, than you can get with a kind word alone."

Millions of Americans have apparently been infected with HIV,[14] so it is not unreasonable that HCWs would be exposed to such individuals when they seek medical care. While it was clear that HIV could be transmitted through occupational exposure,[15] and a number of such cases had been reported in the USA and abroad, the magnitude of the risk was not clear. If anything, the frequency of HIV transmission to HCWs was overestimated. In looking at 14 prospective studies of HCWs who were exposed to HIV material by a percutaneous route, only six out of 1948 personnel who had had 2042 exposures appeared to seroconvert. This is a rate of 0.29%. Based on seven studies in the literature from five countries, the rate was 1 in 214 (16 in 3430) for HIV seroconversions with percutaneous exposure.[6] Further, while three highly publicized cases of HIV infection appeared to occur among HCWs who had had mucous membrane or nonintact skin exposure to HIV-containing materials,[15] in the US prospective studies, none of 668 personnel, who had had 1051 such exposures, had evidence of HIV seroconversion. In the Italian Multicenter Study, there was one seroconversion among 1003 percutaneous exposures and one among 158 mucous membrane exposures.[16]

The most important approach to avoiding HIV infection for HCWs is the use of universal precautions.[9,12] By handling all materials as if they were potentially infectious for HIV, or other transmissible agents, the number of occupational exposures among HCWs can be reduced.[17] However, even the most elaborate and enforced universal precautions may not prevent or eliminate entirely the risk of HIV transmission on the job. Despite extensive training and use of universal precautions, some HCWs have, nonetheless, become infected with HIV. Further, in a preliminary study, evidence of HIV-specific T-helper activity was found in some HCWs who were exposed to HIV-positive blood but remained seronegative (and uninfected).[18]

For the rare instance of occupational exposure to HIV by a HCW, there should be in place a facility exposure control plan (Fig 4-1). Because of the urgency of the situation, the initial aspect to consider is the use of zidovudine (AZT) prophylaxis. While this has not prevented HIV infection in a number of situations,[19,20] it should be offered; if initiated, AZT should be started as quickly as possible, preferably within 1-2 hours of the HIV exposure. The next aspect to consider is baseline testing for HIV and hepatitis B viral markers. This provides a useful basis to determine if HCWs are at risk for these viruses. At this point, some counseling should be undertaken regarding the actual risk of infection. It should be made clear that, even with a deep needlestick exposure, the risk of HIV infection is still quite small, from 0.1% to 0.5% in various series. If the index patient is not only HIV-infected, but also HBV-infected, the latter situation poses a much greater risk for the HCW. From 6-30% of individuals who have been stuck with a needle from an individual who is HBsAg reactive will develop HBV infection.[7]

Individuals who have been exposed to the blood of a patient with HIV and/or HBV infection should have a medical evaluation and should be apprised of the signs and symptoms of an early HIV infection, as well as viral hepatitis. The former tends to occur from 6-12 weeks later, and to mimic an infectious mononucleosis-like

Facility Exposure Control Plan - HIV

1. **Counseling re AZT prophylaxis**
2. **Baseline testing for anti-HIV and HBV markers**
3. **Counseling re risk of HIV infection**
4. **Medical evaluation, including signs and symptoms of early HIV infection**
5. **Testing at 6 weeks, 12 weeks and 6 months**
6. **Counseling re prevention of transmission**

Figure 4-1. Elements of a facility exposure control plan for a health-care worker occupationally exposed to the human immunodeficiency virus.

illness; individuals exposed to HIV should be looking for such signs and symptoms. Symptoms of HBV infection may take up to 6 months to appear and begin with loss of appetite, nausea, low-grade fever and may progress to frank jaundice. To evaluate whether an individual has been infected with HIV and/or HBV, subsequent testing should be carried out at 6 weeks, 12 weeks and 6 months after the exposure. Virtually all individuals infected with hepatitis B virus or the human immunodeficiency viruses will seroconvert within this period of time. Very rarely, there may be seroconversions beyond this, but they are extremely unlikely. Finally, individuals exposed to either virus should be counseled regarding secondary transmission and means of prevention. Certainly, they should be cautioned about any type of parenteral exposure of their blood to others, eg, through needles, razors or other sharps, as well as the risk of sexual transmission. However, the risk of transmitting HIV to a patient by a HCW infected with HIV is extremely remote.[21]

Of the three most important viruses that can be potentially acquired in a health-care setting after a needlestick exposure or injury, HIV is the least likely to result in seroconversion; HBV infection is 12 to 300 times more likely. Of intermediate risk is that of HCV transmission. From 1-3% of individuals stuck with a needle from a patient with HCV may develop HCV infection (Fig 4-2).[22,23]

HCW Risk of Infection After Needlestick Injury

Patient HBsAg positive	**6% - 30%**
Patient anti-HCV positive	**1% - 3%**
Patient anti-HIV positive	**0.1% - 0.5%**

Figure 4-2. Risk of infection for a health-care worker following a needlestick injury from a patient with hepatitis B infection (HBsAg-positive), with hepatitis C infection (anti-HCV-positive) or with the human immunodeficiency virus (anti-HIV-positive).

Risk of HBV Infection

When one looks at the risk of HBV infections in the US, it is clear that this is a major risk for Americans in general, as well as for HCWs. It has been estimated that at least 300,000 Americans are infected annually, and approximately 5000 deaths occur each year from HBV infection, generally due to fulminant hepatitis, cirrhosis or subsequent hepatocellular carcinoma.[24] From various surveys, it appears that at least 5% of Americans have been infected with the HBV. Despite the licensure of the hepatitis B vaccine more than 10 years ago, there has been a 37% increase in hepatitis B infections in the US over that period.[24] While this increase is due to multiple factors, it might have been modified, in part, with more widespread use of the hepatitis B vaccine. Between 1982 and 1988, there was a 75% decrease in hepatitis B cases in HCWs due to HBV vaccination and universal blood precautions.[25]

Exposure in the health-care setting is not the major risk factor for acquiring HBV infection. Far and away, the major (known) risk factor is heterosexual contact with an individual infected with the hepatitis B virus.[23,26] This is closely followed by intravenous drug use and homosexual contact. HCWs account for about 2% of the cases of hepatitis B infection (and transfusions for no more than 1%). Unfortunately, a large proportion, approximately 38% of hepatitis B cases, have no known risk factors or, at least, no acknowledged ones. An important point to remember, however, is that 98% of HBV infections do not occur in HCWs exposed to HBV on the job. Nonetheless, there is a huge reservoir of HBV infection in hospitals.[27] Anywhere from 1-1.5% of hospital admissions are patients who are HBsAg-positive. Of these, 89% are never identified as such. Further, blood and all body fluids of these HBsAg-positive individuals are potentially infectious for HBV.

It has been known for some time, based upon HBV serologic markers, that certain HCWs are at increased risk of acquiring this infection.[27,28] Among those at highest risk are emergency ward nurses and blood bank personnel in hospitals. In addition, laboratory technologists, as well as pathology staff, have increased rates of HBV markers. When risk factors are weighed, it is clear that contact with patients' blood is more important than contact with patients themselves.[27] HCWs exposed to the blood of patients should receive the HBV vaccine, and thereby have immunity to HBV. However, certain host factors correlate with poor immunogenicity of the HBV vaccine; these include increased age, increased body mass and smoking. Thus, HCWs should be immunized early and the vaccine given intramuscularly with a longer needle if an individual is obese.[29,30]

When the 1991 OSHA regulations were published, there continued to be thousands of cases of hepatitis B among HCWs, with approximately 300 deaths each year.[31] By that time, approximately 100 HCWs appeared to be infected with HIV occupationally, but only 18 had documented seroconversion. However, three had progressed to AIDS and one had died (Fig 4-3). Thus, HBV infection remained a more important risk for HCWs. Among the strategies to decrease HBV transmission with the hepatitis B vaccine, the highest priority is HCWs who are potentially exposed to the blood of patients. Additional efforts should be directed at identification and vaccination of other at-risk individuals; these include prenatal testing of pregnant women, universal immunization of all infants and universal immunization of all 10-year-old children.[24,25]

A recent study looked for evidence of, and significant risk factors for, HBV exposure in HCWs.[28] This was carried out approximately 12 years after the HBV vaccine had been licensed, and 2 years after OSHA had seriously begun its enforcement activities. Among the HCWs involved in this study, the most significant risk factor for presence of antibody to the hepatitis B core antigen (anti-HBc)

Occupational Diseases in Health Care Workers

Agent/rate	# Infected	# Diseases	# Deaths
HBV/year	?	10,000	300
HIV/to date	100*	3	1

* only 18 with documented seroconversion

Figure 4-3. Frequency of occupational infections due to hepatitis B virus and human immunodeficiency virus among health-care workers in the United States (OSHA, Fed Register 1991;56:64004).

and/or HBsAg (and thus serologic evidence of HBV infection) was failure to receive the hepatitis B vaccine. The adjusted odds ratio was 16. A number of other factors for HBV infection were evaluated; age, race, total years involved in clinical practice, RN or MD, history of transfusion, and gender did not appear to have a significant odds ratio for those HCWs infected with HBV. Because the single most important risk factor was whether an individual had been vaccinated against HBV, a careful evaluation was performed of the individuals who had not received the hepatitis B vaccine, approximately 23% of those enrolled in the study. Among the reasons for not being vaccinated, the most common was, "I just haven't gotten around to it," for 91 (or 37%) of those unvaccinated. Other reasons given were that some individuals thought they had already been immunized from a previous hepatitis B infection; some didn't like to get stuck with a needle; certain individuals didn't feel their work involved any exposure; and, for some, the vaccine was felt to have too many side effects. Unfortunately, a few individuals feared getting AIDS, or other infections, from the hepatitis B vaccine. A small proportion of these HCWs claimed that no one told them about the vaccine's availability, while others stated that they did not know how to go about getting vaccinated. A few felt they couldn't afford it, and/or that they had a medical condition that would place them at some risk if they received the vaccine.

For HCWs exposed to HBV, a plan should be in place to determine whether they need hepatitis B immune globulin (HBIG) and/or the HBV vaccine after baseline evaluation and follow-up. Individuals with ≥ 10 mIU/mL of anti-HBs after the hepatitis B vaccine are protected against HBV infection; only one of 78 adults who had previously responded to this vaccine and "lost" anti-HBs had transient HBsAg while the rest had asymptomatic seroconversion (anti-HBc).[32] A reactive anti-HBs test by enzyme immunoassay (EIA) generally indicates a level of ≥ 10 mIU/mL.[33]

Risk of HCV Infection

In an evaluation of HCWs for evidence of HCV infection, there was little antibody to HCV (0.7%), especially compared to a control group composed of local blood donors (0.4%).[28] Considering that blood donors would have had to deny a history of hepatitis to donate, and many had been previously screened for hepatitis markers, the small difference is further minimized. Thus, being a HCW is not a major risk factor for acquiring HCV infections. In the Centers for

Disease Control (CDC) Sentinel Counties Study, only 1% of individuals with acute hepatitis C were HCWs.[25] Among the risk factors identified, intravenous drug use was the most important (38%), followed by possible heterosexual transmission (about 10%). Only 5% of individuals with HCV had been transfused. For 37% of the individuals with acute HCV infection, there was no identified (or at least acknowledged) risk factor. Overall, for HCWs the risk of HCV infection appears low; in the CDC Sentinel Counties Study, only 1% of cases occurred in those who identified themselves as HCWs. Nonetheless, a needlestick with a patient who has HCV infection, or apparent non-A,non-B hepatitis, can result in transmission of hepatitis C; the rate has been estimated as 1-3%.[22,23] Again, a facility's exposure plan should be in place for counseling, evaluation and follow-up. The only potential treatment modality, immune serum globulin, is no longer recommended as prophylaxis, however (M. Alter, CDC, personal communication).

Prevention of Infection

For the prevention of HIV, HBV and HCV, careful work practices, universal precautions, and the use of the hepatitis B vaccine should be quite effective. These efforts minimize the risk of these infections being transmitted in the workplace. While there are other occupational risks for HCWs in the workplace, these three viral infections can be largely prevented in health-care settings.

The major risk factor of a viral infection for HCWs is being stuck with a needle from a patient with HIV, HBV or HCV.[13] As part of a plan to address and reduce on-the-job risks, there should be an effort to reduce needlestick injuries among HCWs. The elements of such a plan are illustrated in Fig 4-4. The most important element of the plan is to obtain accurate reporting of needlestick injuries so that there can be a careful assessment of the circumstances under which needlestick injuries occur.[13] Using the epidemiology of needlestick injuries, efforts can be directed toward reducing their frequency, including procedure modifications such as not recapping used needles, one-handed recapping and proper disposal practices. While not recapping used needles should be safer than attempting to recap them, efforts should be directed toward safer technologies. These include such things as specially designed needles and needle guards for use after the needle has been used. Safer needles for taking samples from patients, as well as the phlebotomy of whole units or apheresis components from donors, have been developed.

Reducing Needlestick Injuries Among HCWs

1. **Epidemiology of needlesticks, including accurate reporting**
2. **Work practice modification, eg, not re-capping used needles, proper disposal practices**
3. **Safer technologies, eg, recessed needles, needle guard after use**

Figure 4-4. Means of reducing needlestick injuries to health-care workers.

A careful evaluation of the types and the frequency of needlestick injuries in a blood center has been carried out by Leparc.[34] Such findings can be used to make specific work practice modifications. The most important aspect is good technique, after careful training and proficiency, in the use of needles. Recessed needles, covered needles or a means to cover needles after a venipuncture have been developed.[35] Unfortunately, most are expensive and not in general use. However, these should be worth the cost and reduce risk, after careful training regarding proper use, for HCWs and their employers.

Exposure to viruses may be through nonintact skin or mucous membranes,[15] as well as by needlesticks or cuts.[31] Intact skin is a great barrier, but any breaks in it permit easy entry of viruses. Covering open wounds or nonintact skin is a very effective means of preventing infection with HIV, HBV and HCV. Some efforts to reduce HCW exposure to blood-borne pathogens may be simple and inexpensive, but may result in significant cost savings for both the employer and the HCW.[36]

Although the goal of zero risk of infections for HCWs is not possible, it should be sought. Even interventions to reduce risks have risks. The use of precautions such as gloves while drawing blood from patients may reduce the chance of HIV infection even after a needlestick injury,[37] but wearing gloves also has risks for the HCW[38,39] and for patients.[40] While extremely safe, the hepatitis B vaccine has side effects,[41] and is not always effective.[29] AZT given as prophylaxis for HIV exposure has significant side effects and a high failure rate.[20,42]

Comparative Risks

Working in the health-care field, especially in a blood bank or transfusion service, is, compared to other occupations, quite safe. An average of 15 Americans are slain on the job each week, but few are HCWs. If one looks at the most dangerous jobs in the US, health-care workers do not rank in the top 10. Some Americans are killed on the job by items that are not specific to health-care facilities, such as soft drink vending machines.[43]

Another way of looking at the relative safety of working in a health-care environment is to compare work-related fatality rates. In the US, about 7 employees per 100,000 each year die from work-related conditions.[44] For some areas and for some occupations, this figure can be considerably higher. For example, among individuals employed in private industry in Alaska, the rate is five times higher; the rate for those engaged in commercial fishing is 30 times higher. For individuals who attempt to make their living by catching shellfish, such as Alaskan king crabs, the fatality rate is 530 per 100,000 workers, or the equivalent of 1 in 187 employees, *each year*.

Several types of work have more serious occupational risks of death than HCWs. National Institute of Occupational Safety and Health (NIOSH) Alerts have been issued after investigating episodes of fatalities among farmers, storage bin workers, construction workers, refrigerator workers and painters.[45] For example, among farmers who have manure waste pits, there is a yearly average of 89 deaths.[46] Of these, 22% occur during rescue attempts to remove farm workers from the toxic gas and anoxic environment of the manure waste pits.

In assessing the risk of HIV infection for HCWs, especially on the job, it is clear that the risk is very small. The major risk factors for AIDS continue to be those that have always been present; they are not work-related. It should be noted that "unprotected sex from a one night stand on the way home from work" is a much more real risk for HIV infection in a HCW than is acquiring this virus on the job (Scott Sawyer, ACT Up, personal communication). Safe, or protected, sex is clearly the major means to protect all Americans from HIV infection. This is followed closely by avoiding the reuse of needles or other paraphernalia that have human blood on them; such material should be either sterilized or discarded and not reused, regardless of the environment.[47]

Conclusion

In summary, it should be noted that AIDS is difficult to contract if proper means are put into place to reduce one's risk. This is especially true at work, including health-care settings. Since HBV infection has always been a more significant risk than HIV, it is very important that individuals in the health-care field who are exposed to blood, especially that of patients, receive the hepatitis B vaccine. Further, they should use protective gear and assume that all patients are potentially infectious.[8] Universal precautions are warranted, and are effective[17] when there is the potential of being exposed to bloodborne pathogens.[9] Universal precautions should be so routine that they are like putting on a seat belt when getting into one's car. As Dr. Evatt pointed out, "the risk of acquiring HIV infection by health care workers...is incredibly low, *if* good precautions and procedures are routinely followed."[48]

References

1. Dodd RY. The risk of transfusion-transmitted infection. N Engl J Med 1992;327:419-21.
2. Kleinman S, Alter H, Busch M, et al. Increased detection of HCV-infected blood donors using a multiple antigen HCV enzyme immunoassay. Transfusion 1992;32:805-13.
3. Busch MP, Young MJ, Samson SM, et al. Risk of human immunodeficiency virus (HIV) transmission by blood transfusions before the implementation of HIV-1 antibody screening. Transfusion 1991;31:4-11.
4. Brennan TA, Leape LL, Laird NM, et al. Incidence of adverse events and negligence in hospitalized patients—results of the Harvard Medical Practice Study I. N Engl J Med 1991;324:370-6.
5. Leape LL, Brennan TA, Laird N, et al. The nature of adverse events in hospitalized patients—results of the Harvard Medical Practice Study II. N Engl J Med 1991;324:377-84.
6. Bignall J. Occupational HIV infection. Lancet 1993;342:980.

7. Alter HJ, Seeff LB, Kaplan DM, et al. Type B hepatitis: The infectivity of blood positive for e antigen and DNA polymerase after accidental needlestick exposure. N Engl J Med 1976;295: 909-13.
8. Bowden FJ, Pollett B, Birrell F, Dax EM. Occupational exposure to the human immunodeficiency virus and other blood-borne pathogens: A six-year prospective study. Med J Aust 1993;158: 810-2.
9. Centers for Disease Control. Recommendations for prevention of HIV transmission in health care settings. MMWR 1987; 36(suppl 25):1s-18s.
10. Lifson A, Castro KG, McCray E, Jaffe HW. National surveillance of AIDS in HCWs. JAMA 1986;256:3231-4.
11. Centers for Disease Control. HIV/AIDS Surveillance Report 1993;5(No.3):1-19.
12. Department of Labor, Occupational Safety and Health Administration. 29 CFR Part 1910. Occupational exposure to blood-borne pathogens: Proposed rule and notice of hearing. Fed Register 1989;54:23042-139.
13. Jagger J, Hunt EH, Brand-Einagger J, et al. Rates of needlestick injury caused by various devices in a university hospital. N Engl J Med 1988;319:284-8.
14. Centers for Disease Control. Current trends: Pilot study of a household survey to determine HIV seroprevalence. MMWR 1991;40:1-5.
15. Centers for Disease Control. Update: Human immunodeficiency virus infections in HCWs exposed to blood of infected patients. MMWR 1987;36: 285-9.
16. Ippolito G, Puro V, DeCarli G, et al. The risk of occupational human immunodeficiency virus infection in HCWs. Italian Multicenter Study. Arch Intern Med 1993;153:1452-8.
17. Wong ES, Stotka JL, Chinchilli VM, et al. Are universal precautions effective in reducing the number of occupational exposures among HCWs? A prospective study of physicians on a medical service. JAMA 1991;265:1123-8.
18. Clerici M, Levin JM, Kessler HA, et al. HIV-specific T-helper activity in seronegative HCWs exposed to contaminated blood. JAMA 1994;271:42-6.
19. Anonymous. HIV seroconversion after occupational exposure despite early prophylactic zidovudine therapy. Lancet 1993; 341:1077-8.
20. Tokars J, Marcus R, Culver D, et al. Zidovudine (AZT) use after occupational HIV exposure: Toxicity and failures reported to

CDC. Paper presented at the IX International Conference on AIDS, Berlin, Germany, June 8, 1993.
21. Centers for Disease Control. Update: Investigation of persons treated by HIV-infected HCWs—United States. MMWR 1993;42: 329-37.
22. Sodeyama T, Kiyosawa K, Urushihara A, et al. Detection of hepatitis C virus markers and hepatitis C virus genomic-RNA after needlestick accidents. Arch Intern Med 1994;153:1565-72.
23. Kiyosawa K, Sodeyama T, Tanaka E, et al. Hepatitis C in hospital employees with needlestick injuries. Ann Intern Med 1991;115: 367-9.
24. Bloom BS, Hillman AL, Fendick AM, Schwartz JS. A reappraisal of hepatitis B virus vaccination strategies using cost-effectiveness analysis. Ann Intern Med 1993;118:298-306.
25. Alter MJ, Hadler SC, Margolis HS, et al. The changing epidemiology of hepatitis B in the United States: Need for alternative vaccination strategies. JAMA 1990;263:1218-22.
26. Alter MJ, Coleman PJ, Alexander WJ, et al. Importance of heterosexual activity in the transmission of hepatitis B and non-A, non-B hepatitis. JAMA 1989;262:1201-5.
27. Dienstag JL, Ryan DM. Occupational exposure to hepatitis B virus in hospital personnel: Infection or immunization? Am J Epidemiol 1982;115:26-39.
28. Thomas DL, Factor SH, Kelen GD, et al. Viral hepatitis in health care personnel at the Johns Hopkins Hospital: The seroprevalence of and risk factors for hepatitis B virus and hepatitis C virus infection. Arch Intern Med 1993;153:1705-12.
29. Shaw FE Jr, Guess HA, Roets JM, et al. Effect of anatomic injection site, age, and smoking on the immune response to hepatitis B vaccination. Vaccine 1989;7:425-30.
30. Margolis HS, Presson AC. Host factors related to poor immunogenicity of hepatitis B vaccine in adults: Another reason to immunize early. JAMA 1993;270:2971-2.
31. Department of Labor, Occupational Safety and Health Administration. Occupational exposure to bloodborne pathogens: Rules and regulations. Fed Register 1991;56:64004-182.
32. International Working Group on Hepatitis B Immunization. Immunization against hepatitis B. Lancet 1988;1:875-6.
33. Centers for Disease Control. Sensitivity of the test for antibody to hepatitis B surface antigen—United States. MMWR 1993;42: 707-10.

34. Leparc GF. Precautions against human immunodeficiency virus infection for workers in blood donor centers. JAMA 1988; 260:2215.
35. Shinar E, Rotem S. Samplink: A new and safer method for collecting donor blood samples. Paper presented at AABB 46th Annual Meeting, Miami Beach, Florida, October, 1993.
36. Waldron HA. Needlestick injuries. Lancet 1992;340:975.
37. Mast ST, Woolwine JD, Gerberding JL. Efficacy of gloves in reducing blood volumes transferred during simulated needlestick injury. J Infect Dis 1993;168:1589-92.
38. Turjanmaa K. Incidence of immediate allergy to latex gloves in hospital personnel. Contact Dermatitis 1987;17:270-5.
39. Wolf BL. Anaphylactic reaction to latex gloves. N Engl J Med 1993;329:279-80.
40. Verkuyl DA. Glove powder introduced in the circulation by auto-transfusion and severe cardiac failure. Lancet 1992;340: 550.
41. Brezin AP, Lautier-Fran M, Hamedani M, et al. Visual loss and eosinophilia after recombinant hepatitis B vaccine. Lancet 1993;342:563-4.
42. Ciesielski R, Metier R, Hammett T, Ward J. Occupationally acquired HIV infection—United States. Paper presented at IX International Conference on AIDS, Berlin, Germany, June 8, 1993.
43. Cosio MO. Soda pop vending machine injuries. JAMA 1988;260: 2697-9.
44. CDC. Commercial fishing fatalities—Alaska, 1991-1992. MMWR 1993;42:350-9.
45. Centers for Disease Control. Lead poisoning in bridge demolition workers—Georgia, 1992. MMWR 1993;42:388-90.
46. Centers for Disease Control. Fatalities attributed to entering manure waste pits—Minnesota, 1992. MMWR 1993;42:325-9.
47. Centers for Disease Control. Improper infection-control practices during employee vaccination programs—District of Columbia and Pennsylvania, 1993. MMWR 1993;42:969-71.
48. Evatt B. HIV infection at home and in the workplace. J Clin Apheresis 1993;8:161-7.

In: Nance ST, ed.
Blood Supply: Risks, Perceptions and Prospects for the Future
Bethesda, MD: American Association of Blood Banks, 1994

5

Normal Hemopoiesis

Peter J. Quesenberry, MD; Hayley Ramshaw, PhD; Stefan Peters, MD; Sudhir Rao, MS; Cheryl Tiarks, MS; Phil Lowry, MD; F. Marc Stewart, MD; Pamela Becker, MD; Peter Newburger, MD; and Gary Stein, PhD

GRANULOCYTES, MONOCYTES, PLATELETS, red blood cells and a variety of lymphocyte types are produced primarily in marrow tissue in the adult mammal. This production proceeds from primitive multipotent stem or progenitor cells through progressively lineage-restricted progenitors to morphologically recognizable dividing and finally nondividing end cells. Production consists of a steady state baseline with rapid adjustments when demands are placed on the system such as tissue oxygen lack (erythroid production increases) or infection or inflammation (white cell and frequently platelet production increases). The target progenitor cells are regulated by a large number of circulating or membrane-based protein regulators. Both external and internal autocrine mechanisms may also be operative. Many cytokines or growth factors have a wide variety of effects on hematopoietic lineages and, in most cases, various nonhematopoietic tissues. These are outlined in Appendices 5-1[1] through 5-4.

Peter J. Quesenberry, MD, Professor of Medicine, Department of Medicine/Cancer Center; Hayley Ramshaw, PhD, Postdoctoral Fellow, Department of Medicine/Cancer Center; Stefan Peters, MD, Postdoctoral Fellow, Department of Medicine/Cancer Center; Sudhir Rao, MS, Research Associate, Department of Medicine; Cheryl Tiarks, MS, Research Associate, Cancer Center; Phil Lowry, MD, Assistant Professor of Medicine; F. Marc Stewart, MD, Associate Professor of Medicine; Pamela Becker, MD, Assistant Professor of Medicine; Peter Newburger, MD, Professor of Pediatrics and MGM, Department of Pediatrics; and Gary Stein, PhD, Professor of Cell Biology, Department of Cell Biology, University of Massachusetts Medical Center, Worcester, Massachusetts

Given the number of cytokines and the fact that different combinations of cytokines also invariably show additive or synergistic stimulatory or inhibitory effects, a wide range of potential outcomes exists when cytokines interact with target cells. Many, however, do have predominant effects, such as those of granulocyte colony-stimulating factor (G-CSF) on granulocytic/neutrophil production, erythropoietin on red cell production and CSF-1 or macrophage-CSF (M-CSF) on monocyte/macrophage production. Some general characteristics of these cytokines include the following:

1. Glycoproteins acting on cell surface receptors, sometimes at very low concentrations.
2. Most are lineage nonspecific. They stimulate or inhibit a number of cell types but some show predominant effects.
3. Synergistic interactions are the rule.
4. There are cell membrane or secreted forms.
5. Action may be to influence survival, proliferation, differentiation, renewal or function; action may be at stem cell level, on more differentiated progenitors or on functional end cells.
6. Usually produced by a variety of cell types.

The pleiotropic actions of some cytokines are illustrated by Interleukin-6 (IL-6), which acts on mature B cells, T cells, neutrophil-macrophage lineages, megakaryocytes and primitive marrow progenitor cells as well as on nonhematopoietic tissues. These cytokines act through cell surface receptors. A family of cytokine receptors, the hemopoietin family, are characterized by four conserved cysteine residues and a tryptophan-serine-X-tryptophan-serine motif. Several groups of cytokine receptors share chains, turning a low affinity receptor into a high affinity receptor. Human GM-CSF, IL-3 and IL-5 each have distinctive low affinity alpha chains, which in the presence[2-4] of a beta chain (common to all three) become specific high affinity receptors. There is a similar sharing of different chains for the leukemic inhibitory factor, IL-6, oncostatin and ciliary nerve growth factor receptors and by IL-2 gamma chain, IL-4 and IL-7 receptors. Other cytokine receptors are tyrosine kinases and are coded for by oncogenes; these include the c-Kit receptor, the CSF-1 receptor[5-7] (c-fms) and the platelet-derived growth factor (PDGF) receptor.[8]

Progenitor Cells

The cells of origin of the mature lymphohematopoietic end cells are termed progenitor or stem cells. These cells are characterized by their proliferative and differentiative potential; their cell cycle status; their physical, metabolic and antigenic properties; and, perhaps most important, by their cytokine responsiveness and cytokine receptor expression.[1] Early or primitive stem cells are generally characterized by their extensive proliferative potential and their ability to engraft and renew in-vivo lymphohematopoiesis including T cells, B cells, natural killer (NK) cells, neutrophils, eosinophils, basophils, mast cells, red cells, platelets and monocytes. They are generally felt to be quiescent (ie, not rapidly dividing), and they express a variety of cell surface proteins.

Human stem cells appear to be $CD34^+$ $CD38^-$, $Lineage^-$ and probably express the c-Kit receptor. Murine stem cells are Ly6 $(Sca)^+$, $Lineage^-$ and also probably express the c-Kit receptor.[9] Primitive murine or human lymphohematopoietic stem cells are quiescent (not in active cell cycle), have a relatively low DNA content (Hoechst low) and stain dully with the dye rhodamine, probably reflecting expression of the multiple drug resistance (MDR) gene. These primitive cells have been best characterized in myeloablated mice in which true marrow renewal and long-term persistence can be assessed. Data from gene marking studies indicate that a few cells can repopulate a mouse and that persistent oligoclonal hemopoiesis can occur after transplantation of marrow stem cells to irradiated hosts. The irradiated or myeloablated host represents an amplification system and may not be the best model in which to assess stem cell capacity. Transplantation into normal hosts, a competitive model, may monitor a different stem cell or at least a functionally different cell.[10]

The lymphohematopoietic system appears to be hierarchical in nature, with a progressive lineage restriction occurring until the stage of unilineage precursors is reached. Generally, these differentiated progenitors are in active cell cycle but have less total proliferative potential than their earlier precursors. They have a progressively diminishing capacity to repopulate the marrow of myeloablated hosts and eventually become restricted in their cytokine responsiveness. Other work has suggested that the system may in fact represent a cytokine cascade, although this needs to be confirmed. Certainly at some point, it appears that the system is hierarchical, but especially at more primitive stem cell levels there may be more complexity.

Elegant studies by Ogawa and colleagues[11-13] on the lineage fate of a percentage of separated sister cells under cytokine permissive conditions (ie, cells derived from the same parent) have indicated that in some cases totally different lineages may be produced. These results suggest that the different lineage decisions are possible during one cell cycle transit and that the position in the cell cycle of a stem cell may determine its response to cytokines or differentiation pathway, in turn suggesting a less ordered nonhierarchical system, at least for more primitive stem cells.

Recent work using purified murine Lin^- Sca^+ lymphohematopoietic stem/ progenitor cells and a serum-free clonal culture system has indicated that primitive high proliferative potential stem cells (HPP-CFC) respond to at least six to eight factors to provide their final in-vitro phenotype.[14-15] This work has further indicated that in the presence of optimal concentrations of certain cytokines, such as steel factor, other cytokines may act at very low subliminal levels. Thus, certain factors may be "anchor" factors in their ability to support the action of other factors at very low concentrations. These data also indicate that there may be a temporal hierarchy of action of such factors.

Clinical Utilization of Lymphohematopoietic Growth Factors

The cloning of lymphohematopoietic cytokines has made possible the availability of adequate amounts of cytokines for animal testing and, finally, clinical application. At present, three clinical hematopoietic cytokines are in general use, several other cytokines are utilized for therapy in different malignancies and a number of cytokines are in development. IL-2 and interferon have found small niches in the therapy of certain neoplasms, but this chapter concentrates on the major hematopoietic cytokines in clinical use.

Erythropoietin

Erythropoietin was the first hematopoietic cytokine established as effective in clinical therapy. Used in the treatment of anemia of renal failure (pre- and postdialysis), erythropoietin increases the red cell level, decreasing transfusion requirements and improving quality of life.[16-18] The in-vivo effects of erythropoietin on hematopoietic lineages are very selective, for although there are minor increases in the platelet count, for practical purposes only red cell production is influenced.

Studies of the effects of erythropoietin have thus established this cytokine as an important therapy for patients with the anemia of renal insufficiency. Studies have also established that the anemia of renal insufficiency is responsible for many of the adverse symptoms seen in patients with renal failure. The toxic-therapeutic ratio of erythropoietin was found to be very favorable in patients with renal failure, with some accelerated hypertension but otherwise little in the way of side effects. The complication of hypertension (or accelerated hypertension) is relatively easily treated and does not appear to be a problem in the anemia associated with other conditions. The administration of relatively small amounts of erythropoietin subcutaneously can be quite effective in correcting anemia and preventing the potential risks of a rapid increase in hematocrit. In general, therapy with erythropoietin should be in low doses and should gradually increase the level of the hematocrit. One of the complications associated with the use of erythropoietin is the creation of a relative iron deficiency state; thus, patients started on erythropoietin usually receive iron supplements.

Erythropoietin has also been approved by the Food and Drug Administration (FDA) for use in cancer and AIDS patients. Although its true role in this setting is not clear, it appears that the increase in hematocrit may have a favorable impact on the quality of life. Further information is needed to determine whether erythropoietin will be a major therapy in patients with cancer or AIDS.[19-20] A small percentage of patients with myelodysplastic syndrome may also benefit from erythropoietin treatment. Other areas of investigation for the use of erythropoietin have included preoperative administration and use in chronic inflammatory diseases such as rheumatoid arthritis[21] and neonatal anemia. The results in rheumatoid arthritis are instructive in that elevation of the hematocrit can be seen without any apparent clinical benefit (ie, quality of life unchanged). Erythropoietin may also be able to mobilize peripheral blood stem cells.

G-CSF and GM-CSF

Two cytokines—granulocyte colony-stimulating factor and granulocyte macrophage colony-stimulating factor—that elevate white blood cell counts have been approved by the FDA for specific indications and are presently being used in some cytopenic patients.[22-24] Both of these agents can elevate the granulocyte count, decrease the period of severe neutropenia after cytotoxic chemotherapy and, in most instances, decrease morbidity and infectious complications.

The effects of both G-CSF and GM-CSF are probably best illustrated by the first placebo-controlled, double-blind study published by Crawford and colleagues.[22] In this study, aggressive chemotherapy with cytoxan, VP16 and adriamycin was given with or without concomitant G-CSF to patients with small cell carcinoma. The number of days of severe neutropenia was reduced from 6 days to 1 day, with reduction in febrile neutropenia and an impression that mucositis and infectious morbidity were diminished. Any impact upon tumor growth could not be evaluated because most of the patients were crossed over in the double-blind, open-label, cross-over design of the study.

Many subsequent studies on both G-CSF and GM-CSF show essentially similar results. However, these studies have not shown any overall positive impact on disease outcome. In all of the studies published to date, there has been no study that indicates an increase in survival or an increase in cure rate of any cancer. In addition, a number of reports have indicated that up to 20-30% of solid tumor cell lines, including ovarian, small cell carcinoma, nonsmall cell carcinoma, renal cell, melanoma, breast and colon, have receptors and proliferate in response to G-CSF or GM-CSF. Thus, there is a real risk that tumor progression could be promoted by the administration of these agents. The nature of the studies carried out thus far would not detect a small but very significant increase in the growth rate of tumors. Thus it is not clear that G-CSF or GM-CSF administration benefits patients with cancer. One possible scenario is that the rate of tumor growth increases slightly, higher drug doses are administered and overall there is no net positive effect. Alternatively, the most likely scenario is that the therapy could be hurting some patients and helping others. The key question is whether identical results could be obtained in the solid tumor setting by either simply reducing the dose of the drug or giving G-CSF or GM-CSF.

GM-CSF has also been approved for graft failure after marrow transplantation. Both G-CSF or GM-CSF have been used to try to accelerate the recovery of patients who have not shown adequate engraftment after marrow transplantation or who have shown graft failure after initial engraftment. The results of the first cohorts of patients treated with GM-CSF did not show any survival advantage, and most of those patients have relapsed. Thus, the role of these factors in marrow transplant, regardless of FDA approval, is uncertain.

Whereas both G-CSF and GM-CSF appear effective in raising the granulocyte count, GM-CSF has a much broader range of effects in raising monocytes and eosinophils. The toxicity profile of the two agents is also different. G-CSF predominantly causes immediate bone pain and, with prolonged use, splenomegaly. GM-CSF has a much broader range of toxicities, including frequent skin reactions, malaise, fatigue and first-dose reactions, and can induce capillary leak syndrome, which at times can be fatal. Thus, with regard to toxicity profile and selectivity of action, G-CSF appears to be the superior agent. In addition, although claims have been made that both agents are cost-effective, there is no convincing evidence that support these claims. In fact, the way that these agents are now being used appears extraordinarily cost-ineffective.

A major clinical indication for the use of G-CSF appears to be one of the chronic neutropenic states—cyclical hematopoiesis, Kostman's syndrome or severe idiopathic neutropenia.[25] In these diseases, chronic administration of G-CSF reverses infectious morbidity in over 90% of patients, raising the neutrophil count to over 1500 μL and markedly improving the quality of life. Mucositis, oral infections and other infectious morbidity are eliminated or markedly decreased. The neutrophil count usually does not return to normal but returns to levels that prevent significant morbidity from the disease. Thus, at the present time it would appear that G-CSF is the treatment of choice for severe chronic neutropenic states. GM-CSF is relatively ineffective in this setting and, because of this and its toxicity, is not indicated.

Other clinical uses for G-CSF and GM-CSF include mobilization of peripheral blood stem cells for transplantation and possible use in various gene therapy protocols to cycle hematopoietic cells for retroviral DNA integration.

Other Cytokines

There has been a major search for agents that could increase platelet counts in thrombocytopenic patients. IL-3, Steel factor, IL-6 and IL-11 all have some effects on platelet levels and have been variably effective in thrombocytopenia. However, the ligand for the receptor encoded by the c-mpl protooncogene has recently been cloned and may represent the true thrombopoietin. Studies on this agent are awaited with interest.

Steel factor and IL-3 are intriguing agents that have major effects on multilineage and early stem cells. Both are also mast cell factors. However, because chronic administration of these agents appears to induce many allergic phenomena, they will probably not be important therapeutic agents, at least by themselves.

Conclusion

We have entered the age of cytokine therapy for many marrow disorders. This is an exciting time, and the potential of these potent biomolecules is tremendous. The challenge for clinicians is to adequately evaluate these biologics in appropriate controlled trials before their general widespread use. Each agent will undoubtedly find an important niche in therapy. Appropriate directions for the future will be in an aggressive definition of cytokine receptor expression and proliferative response of various neoplasms, guiding the use of these factors either to restore hemopoiesis or to stimulate tumor growth in a combined approach using cycle active chemotherapeutic agents and cytokines.

Acknowledgment

The authors would like to thank Glenna Cloutier for preparation of the manuscript.

References

1. Quesenberry PJ. Hemopoietic stem cells, progenitor cells and cytokines. In: Lichtman M, Kipps T, eds. Williams textbook of hematology. 5th ed. New York: McGraw-Hill, 1994:211-58.
2. Cosman D, Lyman SD, Idzerda RL, et al. A new cytokine receptor superfamily. Trends Biochem Sci 1990;15:265-70.
3. D'Andrea AD, Fasman GD, Lodish HF. A new hematopoietic growth factor receptors superfamily: Structural features and implications for signal transduction. Curr Opin Cell Biol 1990; 2:648-51.
4. Bazan JF. Structural design and molecular evolution of a cytokine receptor superfamily. Proc Natl Acad Sci USA 1990;87:6934-8.
5. Sherr CF, Rettenmier CW, Sacca R, et al. The c-fms proto-oncogene product is related to the receptor for the mononuclear phagocyte growth factor, CSF-1. Cell 1985;41:665-76.
6. Sacca R, Stanley ER, Sherr CJ, Rettenmier CW. Specific binding of the mononuclear phagocyte colony stimulating factor CSF-1 to the product of the c-fms oncogene. Proc Natl Acad Sci USA 1986;83: 3331-5.
7. Rettenmier CW, Sacca R, Furman WL, et al. Expression of the human c-fms proto-oncogene product (colony stimulating fac-

tor-1) receptor on peripheral blood mononuclear cells and choriocarcinoma cell lines. J Clin Invest 1986;77:1740-6.
8. Ross RE, Raines EW, Bowen-Pope DF. The biology of platelet-derived growth factor. Cell 1986;46:155-69.
9. Quesenberry PJ. The blueness of stem cells (editorial). Exp Hematol 1991;19:725-8.
10. Stewart FM, Crittenden R, Lowry PA, et al. Long-term engraftment of normal and post-5-fluorouracil murine marrow into normal myeloablated mice. Blood 1993;81(10):2566-71.
11. Ogawa M, Pharr PN, Suda T. Stochastic nature of stem cell functions in culture. In: Cronkite E, Dainiak N, McCaffrey R, et al. Hematopoietic stem cell physiology. New York: Alan R. Liss, Inc., 1985:11-19.
12. Suda J, Suda T, Ogawa M. Analysis of differentiation of mouse hemopoietic stem cells in cultures by sequential replating of paired progenitors. Blood 1984;64:393-9.
13. Suda T, Suda J, Ogawa M. Disparate differentiation in mouse hemopoietic colonies derived from paired progenitors. Proc Natl Acad Sci USA 1984;81:2520-4.
14. Lowry PA, Zsebo KM, Deacon DH, et al. Effects of rrSCF on multiple cytokine responsive HPP-CFC generated from SCA^+Lin^- murine hematopoietic progenitors. Exp Hematol 1991;19:994-6.
15. Lowry PA, Deacon DH, Witefield P, et al. SCF induction of in vitro murine hematopoietic colony formation by "subliminal" cytokine combinations: The role of "anchor factors." Blood 1992;80:663-9.
16. Eschbach JW, Egrie JC, Downing MR, et al. Correction of the anemia of end-stage renal disease with recombinant human erythropoietin: Results of a combined phase I and II clinical trial. N Engl J Med 1087;316:73-8.
17. Winearls CG, Oliver DO, Pippard MJ, et al. Effects of human erythropoietin derived from recombinant DNA on the anaemia of patients maintained by chronic haemodialysis. Lancet 1986; 2:1175-8.
18. Rudnick SA, Abels RI. Erythropoietin: Evolving clinical applications. Exp Hematol 1991;19:842-50.
19. Fischl M, Galpin J, Levine JD, et al. Recombinant human erythropoietin for patients with AIDS treated with zidovudine. N Engl J Med 1990;322:1488-93.
20. Oster W, Herrmann F, Gamm H, et al. Erythropoietin for the treatment of anemia of malignancy associated with neoplastic bone marrow infiltration. J Clin Oncol 1990;8:956-62.

21. Means RT, Olsen NJ, Kranz SB, et al. Treatment of the anemia of rheumatoid arthritis with recombinant human erythropoietin: Clinical and in-vitro studies. Arthritis Rheum 1989;32:638-42.
22. Crawford J, Ozer H, Stoller R, et al. Reduction by granulocyte colony-stimulating factor of fever and neutropenia induced by chemotherapy in patients with small-cell lung cancer. N Engl J Med 1991;325:164-70.
23. Williams ME, Quesenberry PJ. Hematopoietic growth factors. In: Stass SA, ed. Hematologic pathology. New York: Marcel Dekker, Inc., 1992;6:105-24.
24. Grosh WW, Quesenberry PJ. Recombinant human hematopoietic growth factors in the treatment of cytopenias. Clin Immunol Immunopathol, 1992;62:S25-S38.
25. Dale DC, Hammond WP, Gabrilove J, et al. Long-term treatment of severe chronic neutropenia with recombinant human granulocyte colony-stimulating factor (abstract). Blood 1990; 76:139a.

Appendix 5-1. Interleukins, Colony-Stimulating Factors and Erythropoietin

Growth Factor	Initially Described or Highlighted Bioactivity
Granulocyte-macrophage colony-stimulating factor (GM-CSF)	Granulocyte and macrophage colony formation
Granulocyte CSF (G-CSF) differentiation	Granulocyte colony formation and factor for murine leukemia cells, probably granulocyte releasing factor
Colony stimulating factor-1 (CSF-1)	Macrophage colony formation
Erythropoietin (EPO)	Red cell formation in vivo and in-vitro inducer of other factors
Interleukin-1 (IL-1)	B and T cell regulator, endogenous pyrogen
Interleukin-2 (IL-2)	T cell growth factor
Interleukin-3 (IL-3)	A multi-CSF stimulator, granulocyte, macrophage, eosinophils, mast cell, megakaryocyte colony formation and interaction with epo to stimulate erythroid colonies
Interleukin-4 (IL-4)	B-cell proliferation and immunoglobulin secretion
Interleukin-5 (IL-5)	B-cell differentiation and immunoglobulin secretion; eosinophil differentiation
Interleukin-6 (IL-6)	B-cell differentiation and immunoglobulin secretion
Interleukin-7 (IL-7)	Stimulation of pre-B-cell production
Interleukin-9 (IL-9)	Erythroid colony formation and stimulation of proliferation of a megakaryocyte cell line
Interleukin-10 (IL-10)	Inhibits cytokine synthesis by T cells. Increases cytotoxic T-cell number and function
Interleukin-11 (IL-11) stimulator	B-cell, megakaryocyte and stem cell

continued on page 90

Appendix 5-1. Continued

Growth Factor	Initially Described or Highlighted Bioactivity
Interleukin-12 (IL-12)	Natural killer cell stimulator. Helper T-cell proliferation and interferon gamma production by T and NK cells
Interleukin-13 (IL-13)	Similar to IL-4. B-cell immunoglobulin production and isotope switching. Stimulates T-cell proliferation and inhibits monocyte inflammatory cytokine production

(Used with permission from Quesenberry.[1])

Appendix 5-2. Cytokines with Stimulatory Activity of Lymphohematopoietic Lineages

Growth Factor	Initially Described or Highlighted Bioactivity
Steel factor or c-kit ligand	Acts synergistically with many other factors on early stem cells
Basic fibroblast growth factor (bFGF)	Acts in concert with Steel factor and others on early stem cells and megakaryocyte progenitors
Platelet-derived growth factor (PDGF)	Erythropoietic and granulopoietic progenitors
Hepatocyte growth factor or scatter factor	Synergistic activity on progenitors
Insulin-like growth factor II	Erythroid and granulopoietic progenitors
Activin	Stimulates erythroid progenitors
Leukemia inhibitory factors (LIF)	Megakaryocyte progenitor stimulator
Membrane bound burst-promoting activity	BFU-e and CFU-e

Appendix 5-3. Cytokines With Inhibitory Effects on Lymphohematopoiesis

Molecule	Effect on Progenitor/Stem Cell
Transforming growth factor-beta (TGF-β)	Interacts with serine threonine kinase receptor. Inhibits BFU-E, CFU-S and HPP-CFC and stimulates or has no effect on more differentiated progenitors, ie, GM-CFC. Has a direct effect, may take days to exert maximum effect and may downmodulate IL-3 and Steel receptor while upmodulating GM-CSF receptor.
H-subunit ferritin	A 21,000-dalton protein that inhibits BFU-E, CFU-GEMM and CFU-GM. Suppresses during S phase and this is linked to expression of HLA-DR (human) or 1a (mouse). Exerts a direct action; key may be ferroxidase action, which keeps iron in the ferric form. In vivo in mice inhibits CFU-GM, BFU-E and CFU-GEMM, decreasing cycle status and number in spleen and marrow. Also decreases peripheral blood neutrophils.
Interferon-α, β and γ (IFN) and tumor necrosis factor-α and β (TNF)	TNF and IFN induce many cytokines. IL-4 suppresses through these molecules. IFNα and γ (and to a lesser extent β) act synergistically to suppress BFU-E, CFU-GEMM and CFU-GM. IFNγ synergizes with TNFα and TNFβ to suppress. Action is direct.
Prostaglandin E_1 and E_2 (PGE_1 and PGE_2)	Has a direct action in suppressing CFU-M, CFU-GM and CFU-G but no inhibition of BFU-E. Can enhance BFU-E through an effect on CD8T lymphocytes. Myelopoiesis is suppressed in mice treated in vivo with PGE. CFU-GM of leukemic cells may be less sensitive to inhibition by PGE.
Inhibin	Suppresses CFU-E, CFU-GEMM and BFU-E by an indirect effect. Does not suppress CFU-GM. When administered to mice in vivo, it decreases CFU-GM, BFU-E and CFU-GEMM.

continued on page 93

Appendix 5-3. Continued

Molecule	Effect on Progenitor/Stem Cell
Lactoferrin	An iron-binding protein that inhibits indirectly by suppressing the release of CSFs or IL-1 from monocytes and macrophages. It is active in vivo, but action is abrogated by IL-6 or lipopolysaccharide.

Appendix 5-4. Inhibitors of Hemopoiesis, Chemokine Family and Small Peptides

Molecule	Effect on Progenitor/Stem Cell
Macrophage-inflammatory protein-1α (MIP-1α)	Part of chemokine family of small inducible proinflammatory intercrine molecules, 8 kD and is identical with the previously described CFU-S Dexter culture inhibitor. Has a G-associated receptor. Suppresses CFU-S, CFU-a, CFU-GEMM, BFU-E and CFU-GM (especially with Steel combination stimulus). Can enhance certain GM-CFC, M-CFC and mature BFU-E. Appears to enhance single factor responsive progenitors. Works in hours, action is direct and reversible and appears to both block entry of cells into S and move cells out of S. Action blocked by MIP-1β. Acts on mice to decrease the percent of CFU-GM in cycle in marrow and spleen.
Macrophage-inflammatory protein-2α (MIP-2α), Platelet factor-4 (PF4), Interleukin-8 (IL-8), Macrophage chemotactic and activating factor (M-CAF), Interferon inducible protein-10 (IP-10)	All members of chemokine family that act synergistically with each other and MIP-1α to suppress the same range of progenitor/stem cells as MIP-1α. Mode of action presumably similar to that of MIP-1α.
P Glu-Glu-Asp-Cys-Lys (pentapeptide)	Inhibits CFU-S, pre-CFU-S and CFU-GM by moving cells out of phase. Action is reversible and studies have been initiated in humans.
N-acetyl-Ser-Asp-Lys-Pro (seraspenide)	Represented in terminal part of thymosin B4 and included in TNFα. Stops the entry of CFU-S and HPP-CFC into the cell cycle. Has no effect on leukemic blasts. Effect is direct, reversible and dose-dependent. In mice and monkeys, neutrophils, monocytes and cell cycle status decreased for GM-CFU, BFU-E and CFU-GEMM. Human phase I trials have been initiated. Decreased progenitor levels have been seen with a 48-hour infusion in humans.

In: Nance ST, ed.
Blood Supply: Risks, Perceptions and Prospects for the Future
Bethesda, MD: American Association of Blood Banks, 1994.

6

Ex-Vivo-Generated Hematopoietic Progenitor Cells: Potential New Transfusion Product

Robert J. Tushinski, PhD; Mark P. Backer, PhD; and Ronald Hoffman, MD

OVER THE LAST TWO decades the molecular and cellular basis of human hematopoiesis has been clarified significantly. These achievements have been in large part due to the isolation, purification and molecular cloning of a number of hematopoietic growth factors that regulate human hematopoiesis and the identification and isolation of the various classes of hematopoietic progenitor cells from which the formed elements of blood originate.[1-11]

Circulating blood cells are highly specialized, and are composed of terminally differentiated cells that have a finite life span. A continued production of blood cells by marrow precursor cells is required to maintain normal blood cell counts. These marrow precursors originate from lineage-committed hematopoietic progenitor cells (HPCs), which are detected with the use of colony-forming unit (CFU) assays in which candidate cell populations are plated in semisolid media in the presence of growth factor mixtures. After a period of incubation the number of hematopoietic colonies is enumerated. Each colony is composed of mature blood cells and represents the progeny of a single CFU. HPCs divide extensively during their differentiation, which leads to expansion of cells belonging to a particular lineage. HPCs ultimately originate from a common

Robert J. Tushinski, PhD, Research Scientist; Mark P. Backer, PhD, Director of Clinical Product Development; and Ronald Hoffman, MD, Vice President of Research, Systemix Inc, Palo Alto, California pluripotent hematopoietic stem cell (PHSC). The entire lymphohematopoietic system is derived from this small pool of PHSCs. PHSCs are capable not only of producing numerous progenitor cells of multiple lineages but also of producing additional PHSCs. Stem cell self-renewal is required so that PHSC exhaustion and marrow failure are not a normal consequence of aging.

Hematopoietic Stem Cells

The existence of PHSCs was first demonstrated experimentally by Till and McCulloch, who injected lethally irradiated recipient mice with the bone marrow of healthy syngeneic donor mice.[1] The mice receiving the donor marrow were reconstituted, while the mice not receiving donor marrow died after one week. Donor cells formed macroscopic colonies in the spleens of the recipient mice. This led to the development of the CFU-S (spleen colony-forming unit) assay. More recent studies have indicated that the populations of cells that give rise to spleen colonies are heterogeneous and probably do not represent the true PHSC.[2-6] In fact, the CFU-S has been shown to represent a more differentiated cell than a true PHSC.[2,5,7] A definitive assay for a PHSC has been defined by the ability of a candidate cell population to initiate long-term hematopoietic reconstitution of lethally irradiated mice. Recently, a murine stem cell population (Thy-1.1^{lo}/Sca-l^{+}/Lin^{-}) has been isolated from murine bone marrow and shown to promote long-term engraftment. Injecting as few as 5-20 cells has resulted in the rapid and long-term radioprotection and engraftment of both myeloid and lymphoid cells.[6,8-11] Others have shown that both lymphoid and myeloid long-term engraftment can be obtained by the injection of a single genetically marked cell.[12-16] These studies have confirmed the existence of a PHSC in mice and suggest that stem cells can undergo self-renewal in vitro.[12,15]

Currently, the ability of candidate PHSC populations to initiate and sustain human hematopoiesis in the presence of a pre-established bone-marrow-derived stroma for up to 10 weeks is the best in-vitro qualitative assay of human PHSCs. This assay detects a long-term culture-initiating cell (LTC-IC).[17-18] Whether the LTC-IC assay actually measures a cell that confers long-term in-vivo repopulating ability in humans is not certain; however, for murine cells there appears to be some correlation between the LTC-IC assay and in-vivo repopulating ability.[5] Recently, there has been success in developing models for the engraftment of human PHSCs into immunodeficient mice[19-20] and sheep fetuses.[21-22] These models have proven to be invaluable as in-vivo assays for human PHSCs.

In addition to the creation of assays capable of demonstrating the presence of putative PHSC cell populations, the development of methods for isolating human PHSC has been described by a number of investigators.[23-28] Each of these procedures utilizes monoclonal antibodies to the CD34 antigen, which is present on the surface of approximately one percent of bone marrow cells. The CD34+ population includes the most primitive human hematopoietic cells as well as more committed progenitor cells. This discovery has had profound effects on the experimental approaches to determine the identity and biology of human PHSCs. Our capacity to identify and ultimately to purify PHSCs makes it ever more probable that we will eventually be able to expand ex vivo this rare cell population. Based on data gathered from a number of laboratories, the phenotype of the human PHSC appears to be CD34+, HLA-DR–, c-kit+, Thy-1+ (CDw90+), CD38–, CD71– and to express little or none of the phenotypic markers associated with a variety of lineages (Lin–).[3-11] These PHSC populations are characterized by poor retention of the mitrochondrial specific dye, rhodamine 123, and resistance to a variety of chemotherapeutic drugs, including 5-fluorouracil (5-FU), 4-hydroxyperoxycyclophosphamide (4-HC) and mafosfamide.[3-11]

The Hematopoietic Growth Factors

The hematopoietic growth factors (HGFs) are a family of glycosylated proteins, which are the products of stromal cells, endothelial cells and certain hematopoietic cells. HGFs regulate the production, maturation and function of hematopoietic cells.[29-31] The initial discovery of these growth factors, followed by their characterization, purification and subsequent cloning, has revolutionized the fields of experimental and clinical hematology. Along with the discovery of the need for growth factors for expansion of hematopoietic cells, the observations that multiple HGFs act in synergy during the regulation of primitive progenitor cells have been crucial to our understanding of the HGF regulation of stem cells.[32-35] The initially discovered HGFs (cytokines) were referred to as colony-stimulating factors (CSFs) and include granulocyte/macrophage-CSF (GM-CSF), granulocyte-CSF (G-CSF) and macrophage-CSF (M-CSF or CSF-1), eosinophil-CSF (Eo-CSF) and erythropoietin (EPO). In addition to the CSFs, another family of glycosylated proteins, the interleukins (ILs), are also involved in regulating hematopoietic cells. Except for IL-3, the CSFs and EPO appear to act primarily on committed progenitor cell production. The other interleukins (IL-1, -6, -8, -11 and -12) act only in synergy with the CSFs, including IL-3, to affect the proliferation and differentiation of primitive hematopoietic progenitor cells.[4,14,32,34,36-49] Another synergistic HGF has been cloned and identified as stem cell factor (SCF,[50] MGF,[51] c-kit ligand, SLF52). SCF has been shown to greatly enhance the biological effects of IL-3, IL-6, IL-11, IL-12, GM-CSF, G-CSF and EPO.[36-39,46-49,53-62] Currently, SCF appears to be a critical factor needed for the expansion of early multipotential hematopoietic cells.[36,53-54,61-66] Another synergistic type growth factor, flt3/flk-2, which has also been recently cloned, appears to affect the proliferation of PHSCs.[67] The potential use of this cytokine for ex-vivo expansion remains at present unknown.

The Concept of Ex-Vivo Expansion of PHSC, HPC and Marrow Precursors

The knowledge of PHSC and HPC biology as well as access to a variety of HGFs has led investigators to question whether ex-vivo production of PHSC, HPC and hematopoietic precursors might be possible and whether such cell sources might serve as potential transfusion products in the future. Traditional transfusion therapy involves the infusion of blood products that are composed of terminally differentiated blood cells that have a finite life span and are incapable of further cellular amplification once transfused. Such transfusions of terminally differentiated cells dictate the need for repeated transfusions, which ultimately leads to alloimmunization. Delivery to the recipient of cytokine-expanded cells including PHSC, progenitor cells and mitotic precursor cells that are capable of significant in-vivo cellular amplification once transfused might markedly diminish the number of transfusions required. Such an approach would diminish the risk of alloimmunization and reduce the potential infectious episodes associated with traditional transplant therapy.

Mobilized peripheral blood mononuclear cell (MPBMNC) grafts result in a far more rapid recovery of neutrophils and platelets than marrow grafts, thus leading to the reduction of the time to hematologic reconstitution following high-dose chemotherapy. It is possible that ex-vivo activation and production of PHSCs and progenitor cells could generate a graft with biological function similar to that of peripheral blood. An ideal ex-vivo product for infusion would contain sufficient numbers of PHSCs, progenitors and precursor cells, including megakaryocyte progenitors, which would lead to a shortening of the time to hematologic reconstitution after the administration of myelosupressive or myeloablative therapy.

Ex-Vivo Expansion Systems

Stromal Cell Based Systems

The ex-vivo long-term growth and maintenance of hematopoiesis derived from murine[68] and human[17-18,69-75] bone marrow can be sustained for several months. In these long-term bone marrow cultures (LTBMC), the establishment of a stromal cell layer derived from bone marrow cells maintained in the presence of hydrocortisone during the first 3 weeks of culture is critical for the long-term growth of the hematopoietic cells seeded into the culture. The stroma consists of endothelial cells, fibroblasts, adipocytes and macrophages. These stromal cells have been shown to produce CSF-1, G-CSF, GM-CSF, IL-1, flt3/flk-2 ligand, SCF and IL-6.[51-67,74-77] Hematopoiesis in these LTBMCs is localized in foci of cobblestone areas that contain primitive progenitor cells. These LTBMCs have been shown to support myelopoiesis but not lymphopoiesis; however, cells are maintained in such cultures that can reconstitute lymphopoiesis when transplanted into irradiated mice,[78] or seeded onto bone marrow stroma produced in the absence of hydrocortisone.[79] These studies suggested that hematopoietic cells require direct contact with the stroma for their growth, maturation and survival in vitro.[17-18,69-80] Stroma probably exerts its effects in part by the secretion and presentation of cytokines,[73-75,81-82] and production of extracellular matrix components. The matrix components within the marrow microenvironment include collagen, laminin, fibronectin,[74-83] hemonectin,[84] thrombospondin[85] and numerous glycosaminoglycans[86-89] (chondroitin, heparan, dermatan, keratin sulfate, hyaluronic acid). A more detailed review of the role of cytoadhesion molecules on hematopoietic cell interactions within their microenviroment has recently been published by Long.[90]

The inoculation of human mononuclear cells isolated from bone marrow, mobilized peripheral blood or cord blood in LTCs in the presence of stroma yields modest expansion of both total cells (10-20 fold), committed progenitor cells (CFU-GM), and a much smaller increase in the more primitive progenitor cells (LTC-IC).[42,91] Initiating cultures with a more highly purified progenitor population (CD34$^+$ cells) results in much greater expansion of total cells and progenitor cells (861- and 55-fold, respectively).[92] Considering the fairly large number of CD34$^+$ cells that one can purify from rather small (10-20 mL) volumes of bone marrow and mobilized peripheral blood, it remains possible that a hematopoietic graft that would be used for transplantation might be generated by ex-vivo expansion of such CD34$^+$ hematopoietic cells. In another study, it has been shown that incubation of a population resembling PHSC (CD34$^+$/Thy-1$^+$/Lin cells) in the presence of a murine-derived stromal cell line after the addition of IL-3, IL-6, GM-CSF and leukemia inhibitory factor (LIF) resulted in an expansion of total cells, CD34$^+$, CD34$^+$/Lin$^-$ and CD34$^+$/Thy-1$^+$/Lin$^-$ cells by 1770-, 110-, 45- and 4-fold, respectively.[93] Thus, there was a 4-fold expansion of the CD34$^+$/Thy-1$^+$/Lin$^-$ cell population that has been shown previously to contain PHSCs capable of reconstituting both myelopoiesis and lymphopoiesis (B-cell and T-cell) compartments.[20] This study indicates that ex-vivo expansion not only of progenitor cells but also of PHSC is possible.

These data suggest that it might be possible to achieve clinically significant expansion of progenitor cells in such stromal-based systems; however, due to a variety of regulatory considerations, it is not clear if such systems will be clinically relevant or usable. Could one use preformed stroma from allogeneic cell lines or fresh allogeneic donor marrow? Would it be possible to use stroma derived from mice or other nonhuman species? Even with the use of autologous stroma, one can encounter a graded spectrum in competency in supporting hematopoietic cells that would prevent the production of a cellular product with a known potency.

Stroma-Free Liquid Culture Systems

Direct contact between hematopoietic and stromal cells has now been shown to be unnecessary for the differentiation and maintenance of primitive progenitors in LTBMC systems. Physical separation of adult hematopoietic cells from the stromal cells by a microporous membrane does not prevent the generation of mature progenitors (CFU-GM) and at least conserves the numbers of primitive progenitors (LTC-IC) seeded into such cultures.[94] Furthermore, Brandt et al have shown that primitive progenitor cell populations from human marrow can sustain production of both primitive (HPP-CFC) and committed progenitor cells (CFU-GM, BFU-E, CFU-

GEMM, CFU-MK) in vitro in the presence of recombinant cytokines, but in the absence of stromal cells.[36,54,95] These results have been confirmed by a number of laboratories and indicate that ex-vivo expansion of hematopoietic progenitor cells occurs in the presence of exogenously added cytokines in the absence of a supporting stromal cell layer.[36,38-41,43,53-54,57-58,60-63,96-99]

The potential clinical use of stroma-free, ex-vivo expanded HPCs has been demonstrated in the murine system.[100-101] In these experiments, cytokine (IL-1+SCF; IL-3+SCF; IL-1+IL-3+SCF)-stimulated ex-vivo expanded bone marrow produced by adding such cytokine combinations to bone marrow obtained from 5-FU-treated mice was injected into irradiated mice. Mice receiving these cell suspensions experienced accelerated recovery of peripheral blood leukocytes, platelets, erythrocytes and a reduction in the number of infused cells needed for short-term and possibly long-term radioprotection when compared to the freshly harvested 5-FU-treated marrow or unperturbed bone marrow.[96,100-101] There was no evidence of damage to either the proliferative capacity or viability of the stem cell compartment in the ex-vivo expanded populations.

Hematopoietic Cell Populations To Be Used for Expansion

Unfractionated marrow or peripheral blood, CD34+ cell populations of these hematopoietic tissues or stem-cell-enriched populations (CD34+/Thy-1+/Lin–) of such tissues can be used as the starting cellular population with which to generate ex-vivo expanded blood products. Marrow contains large populations of mature cells and nonmitotic precursor cells that would provide no benefit to the recipient of an expanded cellular transfusion product (Fig 6-1). After 2-3 weeks in cytokine-driven culture, stem cells, progenitors and mitotic hematopoietic precursor cells would likely compose the cell population that would contribute to hematopoiesis when transfused into a recipient; more terminally differentiated hematopoietic cells would likely undergo cell death and lysis either in the culture system or during postculture processing (especially cryopreservation and thawing). Mature granulocytes that do reach the patient are expected to be cleared from the recipient within one day, playing a minimal role in restoration of hematopoietic function.

The availability of more primitive hematopoietic cells with which to initiate ex-vivo expansion allows the generation of a postculture cell mixture that contains a much higher proportion of progenitors

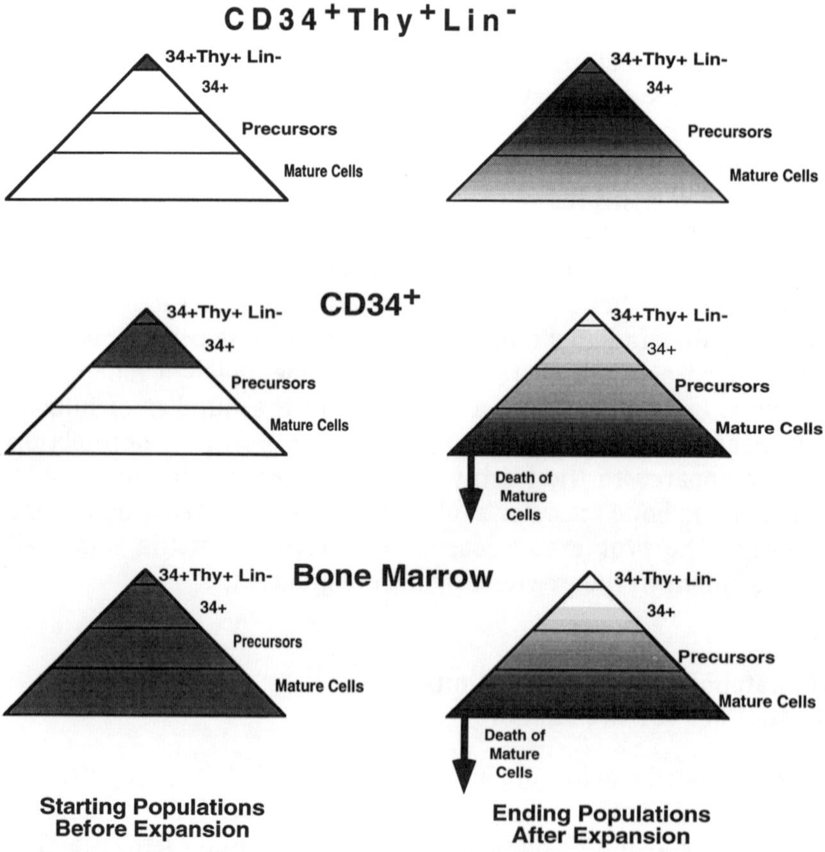

Figure 6-1. Illustration of various source tissues for stem cell expansion. Larger cell concentrations are represented by darker shading. The use of highly enriched stem cell compositions enables the highest degree of control over the proportion of various progenitor cells in the expanded cell product.

and stem cells (Fig 6-1). Whether it is optimal to initiate expansion cultures with CD34+ cells only or actual stem cells (CD34+/Thy-1+/Lin–) remains an area of controversy. As experience is gained in the use of cytokines to direct expansion and lineage commitment, it is hoped that cytokine administration and dosing schedules can be adjusted to maximize the degree of expansion and produce the numbers of target progenitors that correlate most closely with patient benefit, while reducing the proportion of unwanted cells (Fig 6-2). In a similar fashion, one can limit growth factor administration to those acting on either early progenitors or late progenitors, in order to adjust the number of cells that retain some degree

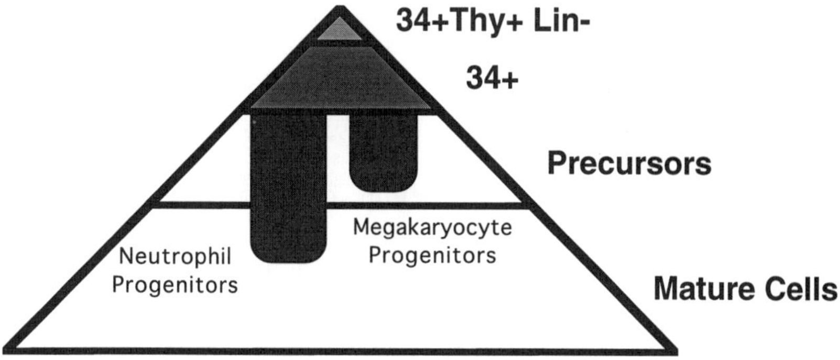

Figure 6-2. Illustration of the effect of growth factor additions to output composition. Growth factors and lineage specific inhibitors can be used to preferentially expand multipotent progenitors into the desired lineages.

of self-renewal. This may be important in generating sufficient cell numbers for transplantation.

Self-Renewal of Stem Cells

Control and regulation of the capacity for self-renewal of stem cells in vitro would enable much wider application of purified stem cell compositions. Using technology and cytokines available today, it appears that retention of PHSC self-renewal is possible albeit to a limited extent; in-vitro cultures do, however, tend to "run down" after 10-12 weeks as stem cells differentiate into cell types that lack self-renewal potential. It is difficult to determine whether these observations reflect inherent limits in the potential of adult stem cells or an inability to maintain culture conditions that support PHSC self-renewal. Muench et al, however, have demonstrated in the murine system that stem cells cultured ex vivo can be used to generate cell populations that provide both complete long-term engraftment and short-term recovery superior to uncultured stem cells.[100-101]

Kinetics of Stem Cell Expansion

Stem cells maintain very high levels of multipotential growth in vitro. Studies using single highly enriched stem cells have demonstrated some key aspects of stem cell expansion kinetics including: 1) stem cells cultured in vitro display various periods of quiescence before initiation of cell growth, even when provided with cytokines that enhance proliferation and 2) individual cells that match the expected behavior of stem cells in vitro (quiescence, lymphoid and myeloid progeny, production of hundreds of CD34+ cells) show a wide variation in the number of progeny produced in vitro (Young J, personal communication).[102]

This information and other studies demonstrate that maintenance of long-term hematopoiesis in vitro is accomplished by the sequential recruitment of stem cells from a quiescent pool.[98] In vivo this recruitment is presumably under active feedback control by mechanisms that are not fully understood; in-vitro stem cell recruitment can be increased using cytokines, but it is not clear what factors control recruitment either at initiation (using highly enriched populations) or in the presence of differentiated hematopoietic cells. Some stem cells enter active proliferation immediately on placement into culture and generate hundreds to thousands of progeny with extensive multilineage proliferative potential. Other stem cells remain quiescent during the entire culture process, retaining their full proliferative potential for support of engraftment after transplantation. Multipotential cells other than stem cells that are present in stem-enriched compositions are also important in producing substantial numbers of CFUs over a 2-3 week period; these proliferate immediately and lack the ability to return to quiescence or undergo self-renewal.

Ex-Vivo Expansion Using Unfractionated or Low-Density Fractions of Bone Marrow, Mobilized Peripheral Blood and Cord Blood

A summary of results of the ex-vivo expansion of unfractionated or low-density mononuclear (LDMNC) cells isolated from human bone marrow, peripheral blood and cord blood is shown in Table 6-1. These data clearly show that one can expand the number of total cells and committed progenitor cells (CFU-GMs) from a variety of hematopoietic tissues. It is important to note that several of the studies also indicate the ability to expand the numbers of LTC-ICs, suggesting that one can produce a graft containing PHSCs that would be capable of rescuing an individual receiving myeloablative therapy.[103,105-106] The range of the ex-vivo expansion of total cells, progenitors and LTC-ICs reported in Table 6-1 is 5- to 20-fold, 6- to 62-fold and 4- to 8-fold, respectively. It has been reported that transfusing CD34+ selected populations containing approximately 2.86×10^6 CFU-GM results in engraftment in patients who have received myeloablative chemotherapy.[107] Therefore, from the two reports in which the absolute number of progenitors in the expanded population was reported, one can conclude that sufficient numbers of CFU-GM to permit engraftment were produced.[100-103] To date, expanded cells alone have not been tested for efficacy in initiating hematopoiesis after myeloablative therapy. However, ex-vivo expanded cells ($1\text{-}3.6 \times 10^9$) have been infused into patients along with nonexpanded cells and were shown to be well tolerated by the recipients.[104,107]

Ex-Vivo Expansion of CD34 Selected Cells From Bone Marrow, Mobilized Peripheral Blood and Cord Blood

The CD34 selected population appears to be an excellent cell population with which to initiate ex-vivo expansion of hematopoietic cell transplants. This cell population contains both primitive and committed progenitor cells.[24-25] Large numbers of CD34+ cells (1-4% of marrow LDMNC) can be isolated from a variety of hematopoietic tissues. In addition, since most solid tumor cells do not express CD34 monoclonal antigen, it might be possible to purify a tumor-free CD34+ cell population from patients with a variety of malignancies with which to initiate ex-vivo expansion of hematopoietic cells.[108] Such tumor-free grafts would therefore avoid the reinfusion of contaminating tumor cells to patients receiving myelosuppressive chemotherapy. However, presently available means of obtaining isolated CD34+ cells are less than optimal because of the low purity of the selected population (64 ± 16%) that is often obtained.[109] This low purity suggests that such CD34+ populations may be contaminated with residual tumor cells that might contribute to relapse. It has been reported that breast cancer tumor numbers can be reduced by only 1-≥4 logs with use of such selection.[110] The data from various studies on the ex-vivo expansion of hematopoietic cells utilizing CD34+ populations as the starting cell population are shown in Table 6-2. These data clearly show that CD34+ cells have a greater capacity than unfractionated marrow for expansion of total cells. Because the original selected population contains a high percentage of committed progenitors, the cellular expansion reported here actually represents about a 10-fold greater increase in the absolute number of expanded cells per input cell than that obtained with unselected tissue (Table 6-1). The efficacy of transfusing such ex-vivo expanded CD34 selected cells into nonhuman primates and humans has yet to be demonstrated.

Table 6-1. Expansion of Whole or Low Density Mononuclear Cells

					Fold Expansion or (Absolute Cell Number)			
Tissue	Growth Factor Additions	Cell Input Fraction	Number of Input Cells	Incubation Time (Days)	Total Cell Output	CFU-GM	LTC-IC	Ref.
ABM	SCF, IL-3, GM-CSF, EPO	LDMNC	2.25E+08	14	9X (2.00E+09)	(1.20E+07)	(1.90E+04)	101
MPB	SCF, IL-1, IL-3, IL-6, GM-CSF, G-CSF	Whole	2.50E+08	14	20X	6X	NR	102
ABM n=10	IL-3, GM-CSF, EPO, SCF	LDMNC	3.00E+07	14	10X	21X	7.5X	103
ABM	IL-3, GM-CSF, EPO, SCF	Whole	3.09E+06	14	11X	28X	NR	89
BM	IL-3, GM-CSF, EPO, SCF	LDMNC	3.00E+06	14	11X	14X	NR	89

NPB	Pixy 321, SCF	LDMNC	1.00E+07	8	1X	16X	NR	39
ABM	IL-3, GM-CSF, EPO, SCF	Whole	3.00E+06	14	8X	10X (138,000)	4X	104
ABM	IL-3, GM-CSF, EPO, SCF	LDMNC	2.56-4.50E+08	14	(1.1-3.60E+09)	4.6-38X	NR	105
CB	Pixy 321, EPO, SCF	LDMNC	3.00E+06	14	7-8X	49-62X	NR	60
MPB		LDMNC	1.00E+07	14	≤5X	38X	NR	60

Abbreviations: adult bone marrow (ABM), cord blood (CB), mobilized peripheral blood (MPB), low density mononuclear cells (LDMNC), stem cell factor (SCF), interleukin-3 (IL-3), interleukin-1 (IL-1), granulocyte-macrophage colony-stimulating factor (GM-CSF), erythropoietin (EPO), IL-3/GM-CSF fusion (Pixy 321), colony-forming units–granulocyte/macrophage (CFU-GM), long-term culture-initiating cell (LTC-IC), X=fold expansion, NR=not reported.

Table 6-2. Ex-Vivo Expansion of Hematopoietic Cells From CD34+ Selected Populations

Tissue	Media Additions	Cell Input Fraction	Number Input	Incubation Time (Days)	Fold Expansion: Total Cell Output	Fold Expansion: CD34+	Fold Expansion: CFU-GM	Fold Expansion: Early Progenitors	Ref.
MPB	SCF, IL-1, IL-3, IL-6, EPO	CD34+	0.5-15.0E+03	~12	1260X	3X	190X	NR	58
MPB	SCF, IL-1, IL-3, IL-6, EPO	CD34+	1.50E+06	~12	170-240X	130X	~210X	NR	58
MPB	SCF, IL-1, IL-3, IL-6, GM-CSF, G-CSF	CD34+	2.50E+05	~21	1324X	11-22X	~66X	NR	35
MPB	SCF, IL-1, IL-3, IL-6, GM-CSF, G-CSF	CD34+	2.50E+06	21	1324X	11-22X	66X	NR	35
ABM	IL-3, GM-CSF, EPO, SCF	CD34+	4.76E+04	14	861X	NR	55X	NR	89
ABM	IL-3, GM-CSF, EPO, SCF	CD34−	2.90E+06	14	10X	NR	13X	NR	89

CB	CBPL, Pixy 321, SCF	CD34+	NR	21	1044X	7X peak day 7	NR	11.4X CFU-GEMM peak day 7	111
CB	CBPL, Pixy 321, SCF	CD34+	NR	21	1044X	7X peak day 7	NR	11.4X CFU-GEMM peak day 7	111
CB	CBPL, Pixy 321, SCF	CD34+	NR	21	1044X	7X peak day 7	NR	11.4X CFU-GEMM peak day 7	111
ABM	IL-3, GM-CSF, G-CSF	CD34+	0.5-1.00E+05	10-12	18X	NR	3	NR	41
ABM	IL-3, GM-CSF, G-CSF, SCF	CD34+	0.5-1.00E+05	10	24X	NR	8	NR	41

Abbreviations: adult bone marrow (ABM), cord blood (CB), mobilized peripheral blood (MPB), low density mononuclear cells (LDMNC), cord blood plasma (CBPL), colony-forming unit–granulocyte/macrophage (CFU-GM), colony-forming unit–granulocyte/erythrocyte/macrophage/megakaryocyte (CFU-GEMM), interleukin-1 (IL-1), interleukin-3 (IL-3), interleukin-6 (IL-6), stem cell factor (SCF), erythropoietin (EPO), IL-3/GM-CSF fusion (Pixy 321), X = fold expansion, NR = not reported.

Ex-Vivo Expansion of Subsets of the CD34 Selected Cells From Bone Marrow and Cord Blood

Other groups have proposed generating progenitor cell transfusion products from isolated stem cells. Because PHSCs have a greater proliferative and self-renewal capacity than any other cell in the hematopoietic hierarchy, the cellular output of such a cell population should be greater than that observed with the use of more differentiated cell populations. This approach may be hindered by the relatively rarity of this cell population and the inability to isolate sufficient numbers of these cells. The ex-vivo expansion of more highly purified progenitor cell populations should prove valuable in helping to produce a cellular graft essentially free of contaminating tumor cells and a population for more efficient transduction of genetic material during human somatic gene therapy. These populations of CD34+ subsets, which are enriched for PHSCs, should also represent the best target for ex-vivo expansion, because they contain a higher percentage of the earliest progenitor cells with the greatest proliferative potential. Table 6-3 shows the behavior of such stem cell populations, obtained by a variety of isolation methods, during ex-vivo expansion. Ex-vivo exposure of marrow cells to 4-HC has been utilized as a means of selecting for PHSCs. Calculations using the data shown in Tables 6-1 and 6-4 indicate that the expansion potential of the 4-HC-treated cells in terms of the absolute number of CFU-GMs generated after 21 days in culture is no better than that reported with unfractionated marrow (Table 6-1). Unfractionated and 4-HC-treated marrow both generated 1 CFU-GM for every 50 cells seeded into the original culture. However, the yield of cultures initiated with PHSCs isolated by monoclonal antibody staining and cell sorting is far greater. For example, a CD34+/DR–/CD15–/Rho^{dull} population from human marrow was shown to generate 15 CFU-GMs for each starting cell, which represents a 750-fold greater capacity to generate progenitor cells than either unfractionated or 4-HC-treated marrow. These data also demonstrate that reporting the absolute number of progenitor cells (CFU-GM and LTC-IC) generated in such cultures is a more informative way to compare the expansion potential of different populations of hematopoietic cells.

Recently, a human pluripotent progenitor cell population (CD34+/Thy-1+,Lin–) has been isolated from human fetal and adult bone marrow. This population represents approximately 25% of the CD34+ cells from marrow and was shown to form both myeloid and B lymphocytes when assayed in a LTBMC system containing bone-

Table 6-3. Ex-Vivo Expansion of Hematopoietic Cells From Purified Stem Cells

					Fold Expansion or (Absolute Number of Cells)				
Tissue	Media Additions	Cell Input Fraction	Number Input	Incubation Time (Days)	Total Cell Output	CD34+	CFU-GM (Absolute Number)	Early Progenitors	Ref
ABM	IL-3, SCF	CD34+/Lin– (2,10,19,20,33)	NR	21	NR	NR	50X	NR	48
ABM	Pixy 321, SCF	CD34+/DR– /15–	5.00E+03	21	5X	NR	66X	NR	92
CB (SF)	IL-6, Pixy 321, M-CSF, G-CSF, EPO	CD34+/45^{lo} /71^{lo}	1.00E+03	8	1429X	56X	41-71X	2-3.5X	52
ABM	IL-3, GM-CSF, EPO, SCF	4-HC treated	3.00E+06	14	1.63X	NR	60X (49,000)	1X LTC-IC	104
ABM	IL-3, GM-CSF, EPO, SCF	4-HC treated	3.00E+06	21	NR	NR	190X (156,000)	NR	104
ABM	Pixy 321, SCF	CD34+/DR– /15–/Rho^{dull}	1.00E+03	21	430X	56X	18.7X (15,336)	5.5X HPP-CFC	56

Abbreviations used: adult bone marrow (ABM), cord blood (CB), high proliferation potential-colony forming cells (HPP-CFC), long-term culture-initiating cell (LTC-IC), stem cell factor (SCF), interleukin-3 (IL-3), IL-3/GM-SCF fusion (Pixy 321), macrophage colony-stimulating factor (M-CSF), erythropoietin (EPO), granulocyte-macrophage colony-stimulating factor (GM-CSF), colony-forming unit-granulocyte/macrophage (CFU-GM), not reported (NR).

Table 6-4. Ex-Vivo Expansion of Hematopoietic Cells Initiated with $CD34^+/Thy\text{-}1^+/Lin^-$ Cells*

		Day 21 Culture Output				
Experiment	Number of Input Cells $\times 10^4$	Total Cells $\times 10^4$	% $CD34^+$	$CD34^+$ $\times 10^6$	CFU-GM $\times 10^3$	% $CD34^+/Thy\text{-}1^+/Lin^-$
1	1	1895	ND	ND	51	ND
2	1	1690	ND	ND	83	ND
3	4.5	1350	15	2.025	249	2.8
4	6	1500	13	1.95	305	2.4
5	3	4650	4	1.86	196	0.1
6	1	1740	ND	ND	63	ND
7	2	460	14.1	0.65	46	1.6
8	2	1050	9.45	0.993	116	1.8
9	2	1380	6.93	0.956	161	0.34
10	1	344	15	0.516	ND	4
11	2.5	440	8.77	0.386	49.2	2.3
12	1	588	7.8	0.59	ND	ND

*Each of the experiments shown above was carried out with marrow aspirates from 12 consenting healthy donors. The cells were sorted by FACS after staining with monoclonal antibodies for CD34, Thy-1 and a lineage panel (CD2, CD14, CD15, CD16, CD19, glycophorin). The cells were then incubated in IMDM supplemented with 10% FBS and human recombinant cytokines (IL-3, GM-CSF, IL-6 each at 10 ng/mL and SCF at 50 ng/mL). The cultures were refed every 48 hours with the same medium. After 21 days, the cells were harvested and analyzed for their cell surface phenotype, progenitor cell (CFU-GM) content. Abbreviations: colony-forming unit–granulocyte/macrophage (CFU-GM), not determined (ND).

marrow-derived stroma. This cell population is also able to reconstitute both myeloid and lymphoid compartments when assayed in SCID-hu mice.[20] This population has been further characterized as CD38^{lo}, CD45RO^{+}, CD45RA^{-}, CD71^{lo}, c-kit^{lo} and Rhodamine^{dull}.[112] The potential for the ex-vivo expansion of this population in stroma-free liquid culture is shown in Table 6-4. The high proliferative potential of this cell population is indicated by the large numbers of total nucleated cells and CFU-GM produced in suspension cultures initiated with this cell population to which cytokines are added. Each day, 0 input CD34+/Thy-1+/Lin^{-} cell generated six CFU-GMs. This represents approximately 300-fold better cellular output than that calculated for the ex-vivo expansion of unfractioned or 4-HC-treated bone marrow. In addition, there was expansion of the cells that expressed the starting phenotype which represented approximately 1.9% of the expanded cells. The CD34+/Thy-1+ cells in the expanded population have a similar frequency of LTC-ICs as compared to the starting population (about 1 of 20 cells are LTC-ICs). These data suggest that it may be possible to generate a graft for use as support after ablative chemotherapy from relatively small numbers of CD34+/THy-1+/Lin^{-} cells. Such grafts appear to contain large numbers of HPCs, PHSCs and significant numbers of marrow precursor cells capable of further mitosis.

Clinical Use of Enriched Hematopoietic Stem Cell Populations

The potential uses of ex-vivo expanded hematopoietic cells are enormous. Their uses are, however, in large part dependent on the composition and size of the cell product to be infused. With the use of currently available recombinant cytokines and cell populations enriched for primitive hematopoietic cells, it seems likely that tumor-free autografts can be generated ex vivo from marrow aspirates that are obtained under local anesthesia. Such ex-vivo-generated grafts might avoid both the use of general anesthesia for marrow harvesting as well as the costly, time-consuming process of peripheral blood mobilization and leukapheresis. The ability to generate such grafts ex vivo might require use of carefully defined cytokine combinations, purified matrix components, development of a medium optimized for HPC expansion and carefully controlled bioreactor systems in which to carry out these cell expansions. Such grafts will be required to contain sufficient numbers of PHSCs to ensure early, short-term and delayed, sustained engraftment. Because the number of PHSCs needed for engraftment remains unknown, careful Phase I trials will be required to determine a safe engraftment dose.

Attempts to increase the dose intensity of chemotherapeutic agents to treat malignancies have been limited by hematologic toxicity in spite of the use of HGFs. To address this problem, multiple cycles of dose-intensive chemotherapy have been administered successfully in the outpatient setting using HGFs and peripheral blood progenitor cell graft support.[113-117] Leukapheresis of peripheral blood progenitor cells for 3-6 days is required to provide hematologic support for sequential cycles of high-dose chemotherapy. In addition, approximately 10-15% of patients do not mobilize adequate peripheral blood grafts. Ex-vivo expansion of mobilized peripheral blood hematopoietic cells obtained after one apheresis procedure could be used to decrease the numbers of leukaphereses performed, to expand the grafts of patients who do not mobilize adequately, or to avoid mobilization totally and create an expanded hematopoietic cell graft from marrow aspirate specimens that could be obtained under local anesthesia. Another possibility would be to generate an expanded graft ex vivo from the mononuclear cells present in a unit of whole blood, thereby avoiding the inconvenience and cost of mobilization entirely. Although these approaches appear highly speculative, the technology to achieve many of these goals is presently available.

Transfer of genetically modified somatic cells will likely play an important role in the treatment of a growing number of diseases. Gene transfer into hematopoietic stem cells has remained problematic. Bienzle et al have recently shown that gene transfer into hematopoietic cells is facilitated by long-term ex-vivo culture.[118] By exposing canine hematopoietic cells to a replication-defective retrovirus bearing the reporter gene *neo* on multiple occasions during 21 days of LTBMC, these investigators have shown remarkable success in transferring genes into cells that can sustain hematopoiesis for several years.[118] These studies suggest that such ex-vivo expansion systems may serve as optimal targets for gene therapy involving adoptive transfer of transduced hematopoietic cells.

Regulation of Cell Products

The development of a useful process for ex-vivo expansion of hematopoietic cells involves novel and significant challenges. Stem cell purification and cell expansion involve the development and application of new technology. This new technology will require the development of new methodologies and standards. These efforts will likely be under increasing regulatory scrutiny. While blood transfusions and bone marrow transplantation are practiced routinely, transfusion of cultured cells is a relatively new activity that potentially introduces new patient risks as well as benefits. These risks are primarily associated with the opportunity for infection (due to the number of cell manipulations required) or transmission of etiologic agents (due to contact with biological materials). The use of cultured cells following the administration of myeloablative or myelosuppressive chemotherapy involves an additional set of issues more related to "reconstituting potency." The Food and Drug Administration (FDA) has signaled its intent to regulate this therapeutic area.[119-120] The FDA has published a notice asserting full regulatory authority over "cells manipulated in a way that changes the biological characteristics of the cell population,"[121] stating that these will be regulated by the Center for Biologics Evaluation and Research (CBER) through existing mechanisms for biologics products. The agency's viewpoint and rationale for regulation and control have been discussed in detail.[122]

The level of control defined by the above documents includes conformity to current good manufacturing practice (GMP), clinical trial and product licensure through the investigational new drug (IND) and product license application (PLA) process, facility licensure through an establishment license application (ELA) and general conformance with the Points to Consider documents that FDA has issued relating to ex-vivo cell manipulation. Antibodies or other biological materials placed in direct contact with the transfused cells are also expected to be manufactured in compliance with standards associated with biological products. For example, Points to Consider have been issued for characterization of cell lines used to manufacture biological products,[123] and for manufacturing and testing of such products.[124]

The degree of control described above is substantially beyond current requirements for centers handling blood products for transfusion; the associated issues will affect the development of cell therapies. This section addresses technical, regulatory and logistics issues related to the ex-vivo culture of human HPC, PHSC and hematopoietic precursor transfusion products.

Culture Systems for Stem Cell Expansion

A variety of basal media are suitable for stem cell expansion. Basal media consist of vitamins, amino acids, salts, buffers and other small molecule components, such as lipids and lipid carriers. Most media used for routine cell culture work (eg, DMEM, F12, IMDM, RPMI) were originally developed for balanced growth of transformed cell lines. These media have been applied successfully to the large-scale production of proteins from hybridomas and recombinant mammalian cell lines; more recently, they have also been applied to LTBMC and culture of hematopoietic cells. Because purified populations of stem cells have only been available recently, basal media that are optimal for the particular requirements of ex-vivo stem cell culture have not been described to date.

Animal sera, particularly fetal bovine serum (FBS), are commonly used in mammalian cell culture. Serum has a variety of effects on cultured cells, including supply of proteins and hormones supporting cell proliferation, specific inhibition of proteolysis and oxidation, and binding of ions and other small molecules for optimal delivery to the cultured cells. Most effects are beneficial; however, serum also contains components that are toxic or inhibitory to particular cell types or functions. Contaminated sera can also transmit viral pathogens or other adventitious agents to cultured cells. A class of agent called transmissible bovine spongiform encephalopathy (BSE) has raised concern due to the lack of a rapid screening test; however, recent data suggest that these agents represent a minimal human health risk.[125] Transmission risks can be addressed by purchasing serum from vendors who document acquisition from screened donor herds in a BSE-free country and process serum in a manner that removes or inactivates potential pathogens. Serum is also expensive and impossible to characterize fully; all animal sera vary considerably in the concentrations of hormones, steroids and other factors that can have significant effects on culture behavior (Table 6-5). For these reasons, a culture system that avoids the use of animal sera or serum extracts is strongly preferred for culture of human cells intended for infusion into patients. It is possible, however, to use serum or plasma obtained from the intended recipient of such a transfusion to support the culture.[126,127] This use of autologous serum or plasma introduces new issues related to consistency of performance, clearance of tumor cell contamination, infection risk, etc.

Purified protein components are often added to media to promote cell growth; ideally, these permit the construction of serum-free culture to generate HPC transfusion products. Insulin (for general cell growth promotion), transferrin (for iron delivery) and albumin (for binding or delivery of a variety of small molecules) are present in some form in most serum-free media. When culturing cells for

Table 6-5. Selected Components of Fetal Calf Serum

Proteins	Average*	Range
Albumin	2300 mg/L	2000-3600
Transferrin[†]	1790 mg/L	NR
Insulin	10 mU/L	6-14
Growth hormone	39 mg/L	19-52
Hemoglobin	113 mg/L	24-181
Thyroid stimulating hormone	1220 ng/L	<200-4500
Parathyroid hormone	1718 ng/L	85-6180
Follicle stimulating hormone	9.5 ng/L	<2-34
Leutinizing hormone	790 ng/L	120-1800
Platelet-derived growth factor[†]	770 ng/L	NR
Lipids and Fatty Acids		
Triglycerides[†]	210 mg/L	NR
Phospholipids[†]	630 mg/L	NR
Cholesterol	310 mg/L	12-63
Steroids		
Progesterone	80 ng/L	<3-360
Testosterone	400 ng/L	210-990
Corticosterone[†]	67 ng/L	NR
Cortisol	5 μg/L	<1-23

*Average values and ranges measured using several dozen lots of fetal bovine serum purchased from various suppliers.[126]

†Average values measured by a commercial serum supplier using multiple lots available for purchase.[127] NR = not reported.

infusion into humans, protein additives should ideally be produced using recombinant DNA technology to avoid any risk of contamination with adventitious agents from the source organism or serum. It may be possible to use conditioned medium prepared by culture of stroma lines or other cell types for hematopoietic culture support[94]; these may supply soluble factors that affect culture performance but are as yet unidentified. Conditioned medium, if used, should be prepared under GMP using a controlled cell bank, documented culture and purification procedures, and full quality control in order to ensure process consistency.

Culture of Hematopoietic Cells for Infusion

Most cell culture processes conducted in industry were developed for the manufacture of highly purified protein products using hybridomas or transformed recombinant cell lines. During these pro-

Table 6-6. Differences Between Regulated Processes for Manufacturing Biologic Protein Products and Expanded Stem Cell Products

	Protein Products	Expanded Stem Cells
Doses per lot	Up to hundreds of thousands	One (usually)
Source material	Controlled master and working cell banks	Autologous (generally) or allogeneic marrow or blood donor
Cell population characteristics	Continuous cell line	Expansion and lineage differentiation
Disposition of cells	Discard after protein manufacture	Recover with high yield and viability
Viral safety measures	Validate removal in purification	Avoid virus contact with cells
Definitive potency measurement	Biological assay	Long-term cell culture assay or engraftment in immunodeficient animal model

cesses, a controlled cell bank is expanded in culture through a series of seed vessels and finally cultured in a large production reactor. The producer cells are removed by physical methods; the resulting supernatant fluid is purified using chromatography, formulated and finally packaged under sterile conditions into vials for shipment to customers. Each production lot consists of hundreds to up to tens of thousands of doses. FDA guidelines for the production of biologic products generally relate to the production scenario. The culture of hematopoietic cells for autologous reconstitution differs from these procedures in a number of key respects (Table 6-6). Operations and regulatory considerations will need appropriate adjustments to accomplish licensure.

Stem Cell Culture Process Development

It is important in any culture process to maintain controlled conditions favoring production of the cell product. It is especially relevant in the culture of cells for clinical administration that all cells receive a consistent environment that ensures high viability and consistent cell division rates. Regardless of scale, it is necessary to consider mass transfer effects on the delivery of nutrients and factors, and the removal of toxic metabolites.

Passive Culture

Some expansion of progenitor cell number can be accomplished by the culture of enriched progenitors (eg, CD34+) in a passive culture system (eg, T-flasks or gas-permeable bags).[108] This process, while fairly simple, has some drawbacks. The culture environment will change through the course of the process as nutrients are converted to waste products; a pH change may occur as lactic acid levels increase. The level of oxygen supply throughout the culture vessel will vary due to limitations in oxygen transfer through multiple layers of cells; in severe cases, this can lead to cell necrosis in dense areas. Replacement of medium in a passive system, if performed, involves a risk of contamination with infectious agents with each sterile connection or operation.

Perfusion Culture

Some of the drawbacks of static culture can be overcome by medium perfusion. In a perfusion system, pumps are attached to sterile reservoirs of culture medium before bioreactor inoculation to supply medium. In a similar fashion, waste medium is pumped or allowed to overflow into a sterile waste container. This supply can be continuous or intermittent, and can be programmed to match a predetermined administration schedule. A controlled perfusion system allows operators to adjust the medium supply for optimal performance as the cells expand, without frequent sterile connection steps. Studies have shown that perfusion culture improves expansion performance, probably due to the creation of a more consistent cellular environment.[128-129]

Process Control and Data Acquisition

While some aspects of stem cell culture are fairly static for long periods, the large expansion of cell number requires some adjustment of environmental conditions through the culture period. For example, the concentration of oxygen in contact with hematopoietic progenitors strongly affects growth behavior. Optimal culture of stem cells requires a mechanism for maintaining a relatively constant level of oxygen delivery to cells; active computer control of oxygen concentration is helpful in achieving this goal. Culture processes for the manufacture of biologics are typically conducted using a full computer control system for maintenance of appropriate temperature, oxygen tension, pH, agitation rate, etc. The records of these variables are part of each batch production record file and must be kept in FDA-reviewable format for seven years. In addition, the computer control system must be validated according to industry standards. Because of scale effects for stem cell bioreactors, it is not always possible to incorporate sensors in the bioreactor compartment itself. Nevertheless, the variability inherent in the hematopoietic cell expansion process requires that process control and data acquisition be implemented to the greatest reasonable extent.

Scale Issues

The culture of highly enriched hematopoietic cells for readministration is unusual among biotechnology processes in that the number of cultured cells is very small. Optimal performance requires "scaledown" of reactor engineering principles to account for reactor wall effects and other flow irregularities, mass transfer issues in a very slow perfusion regimen, etc. Most commercially available bioreactors (eg, hollow fiber reactors) are not designed for even distribution of cell mass or full recovery of highly viable cells; these are prone to gravity settling and necrosis when inoculated with highly enriched stem cells. It is also critical to avoid transfer surfaces that promote cell adherence, or multiple handling steps with cell losses; these will directly affect the deliverable potency. The wide application of expansion technology must also address "scaleout" issues; the treatment of each culture process as an individual lot of manufactured product implies that the economic benefits of scale will be limited. Scaleout issues provide incentive to minimize the need for highly skilled operators through appropriate automation and rigorous process validation.

Establishment and Operation of Centers for Stem Cell Expansion

Licensure

Facilities that manufacture biological products for human use must be licensed with respect to the manufacturing process and the facility used to perform such processing. The licensing procedure emphasizes the viewpoint that "the process is the product" when dealing with complex biological materials. A PLA describes in detail the processes used for obtaining, processing, assaying, formulating and delivering the biological product, as well as a full review of clinical trial data from an approved IND. An ELA describes the facility to be used for this work. The ELA describes facility controls, including utility requirements (typically including dedicated water-for injection and clean steam systems for sterilization and product formulation), air handling systems (designed to minimize risk of contamination), and personnel and materials flows through the facility. Critical utility systems must be dedicated to the GMP processing functions to avoid cross-contamination risks. Typically, the cost of converting a portion of an existing multipurpose facility (such as a research-based medical center) to an ELA-licensable facility is similar to the cost of a completely new facility because of the high utility standards and stringent degree of segregation required for producing a licensed product. Each facility used for cell processing must be licensed; however, the FDA may reduce the regulatory requirements for licensure of new facilities after a record of operating success is established.

Ancillary Products

Ancillary products are defined as components of the process that exert their impact on the cell product rather than having an independent effect on the patient. Examples in this context include bioreactors and related systems, components of cell culture media, cytokines used in bioreactors, and purging or selection systems. Recent regulations[121] state that FDA has authority to regulate these ancillary components as medical devices through the Center for Devices and Radiological Health (CDRH). If the device is used only for the process of manufacturing the somatic cell product, device-related sections of the IND and PLA applications may be reviewed by CDRH, but a separate regulatory submission is generally not necessary and no independent device approval will be awarded. It should be noted that the regulation of bioreactors as medical devices represents a significant strengthening of control compared to regulatory requirements for bioreactors manufacturing protein products; any commercial systems used for cell products need to be reviewed against CDRH standards even if already in use for the manufacture of approved protein products.

Good Manufacturing Practice

The implementation of current good manufacturing practice is key to meeting regulatory requirements for product safety, potency and consistency. GMP standards are formal requirements for drug products, defined through the US Code of Federal Regulations (21 CFR Parts 200 and 600). While an in-depth review is beyond the scope of this chapter, it is important to realize that a GMP compliance program for a biological product involves substantial investments of time and capital as well as the permanent employment of trained technical staff in a formal quality control organization. These requirements will be beyond the capabilities of most academic centers and many commercial firms; the associated costs will have some impact on the ultimate scope of cell therapy practice. Very few centers have developed a track record describing the conduct of cell therapy under full GMP; an exception is the description of autolymphocyte therapy for renal cell cancer published by Cellcor, Inc.[130-131] GMP compliance is also required for operations under an IND; however, greater flexibility is allowed in some instances (eg, the rigor of stability studies to justify expiration dating for all materials used).

Documentation

Documentation is the cornerstone of regulatory compliance; a strong documentation system should be complete before IND submission. All documents must be approved by the functional department responsible for the activity described as well as the responsible quality assurance (QA) or quality control (QC) managers. The single most important document is the description of the documentation system itself and the conventions, lot numbering systems and terminology to be used. Another critical document will describe the "change control" strategy for documents, ie, the system that records the rationale for each document change and ensures that only current, approved and released documents are used to produce clinical material. Other key elements are listed in Table 6-7.

Validation

Validation is necessary to demonstrate the suitability of physical systems and procedures for performing the required manufacturing

Table 6-7. Elements of a Documentation System for Drug Manufacture

1. **Master Record and Batch Production Record System**
   These documents describe the "main path" of an individual manufactured lot of material. All steps and data recorded are to be initialed by the responsible operator; "key steps" of each procedure must be observed and countersigned by a witness. Completed batch production record (BPR) must be reviewed and approved before release of the final product for clinical use.

2. **Specifications**
   These documents describe the allowed ranges for each material used or produced by the process. Each specification should refer to a specific, validated and approved analytical procedure.

3. **Standard Operating Procedures**
   These documents describe procedures that are performed routinely, possibly at several points in the manufacturing process. Procedures may be referenced by SOP number instead of writing out each procedure in the BPR.

4. **Deviation Reports**
   Events or circumstances that are outside the approved or validated range for manufacture must be thoroughly documented using a preapproved deviation report system. A deviation must trigger a process of data review and approval by the functional group and quality groups before use or rework of the material.

5. **Training Records**
   All staff performing drug manufacture or support activities must have documented training both in the specific steps to be performed and in GMP compliance.

6. **Lot Number and Item Code Number Systems**
   Every item involved in manufacturing must have a title, description, specification, and lot number. These items are typically identified with code numbers to ease tracking and avoid confusion among similar materials.

7. **Labeling Systems**
   Manufacturing documents should specify exactly how each material is to be labeled. In general, labels should specify item name, manufacturer, code number, lot number, manufacture or process date, expiration date, volume or amount of material, quarantine/reject/release status, and safety or biohazard warnings where applicable.

8. **Equipment Logs**
   All equipment, especially if used for multiple materials or processing steps, should have a written and signed log of operations performed, and their dates and lot numbers. Cleaning should also be logged.

tasks (eg, analytical methods must be shown to measure accurately). For example, sterile fill operations must be validated by performing fills of sterile medium and demonstrating sterility of the filled containers. Facility validation is generally addressed through generation of a master validation plan that includes construction qualification (CQ), installation qualification (IQ) and operational qualification (OQ). In the biologics arena, process qualification (PQ) is also routinely performed. PQ involves demonstration that the entire process in question can be performed consistently at least three times at full scale, meeting all critical specifications, in full compliance with GMP. Procedures for cleaning and reuse of equipment, or sterilization of equipment, require validation to demonstrate absence of contamination. Regular revalidation of critical systems is also standard practice (eg, twice per year); substantive changes in facilities, utilities or bioburden status require immediate revalidation.

Control and Testing of Source Materials

All materials used for manufacture require acquisition under a controlled purchase or internal manufacturing system. Materials should be inspected on receipt for evidence of shipping problems, then sampled and tested according to industry standard procedures (eg, USP analytical methods) or approved in-house SOPs. Vendor audits for GMP compliance must be conducted for critical purchased materials (eg, culture media). Materials with pending analytical results must be labeled as quarantined and held in a segregated, controlled area until approval of test results and item release are obtained.

Control and Testing of Intermediates and Final Products

Testing of process intermediates and products must reflect an optimal strategy for assurance of product quality. It is helpful for the manufacturing process to have "hold steps" if possible to allow testing of intermediate process materials. In some cases, the product potency or quality is actually harmed by such hold steps (as with some radiopharmaceuticals). For cell products, careful consideration of product testing issues is important in determining whether steps such as cryopreservation to enable sterility testing are advisable.

Stem cell products and expanded or transfected stem cell products face a fairly unique obstacle in that product potency is strictly defined by the ability to deliver an "engrafting dose" of hematopoietic stem cells or a given number of progenitor or precursor cells. The utility of various in-vitro assays in establishing a correlation with long-term in-vivo engraftment remains controversial. Further assay development and strong statistical correlation with in-vivo function will be needed to improve this situation; single cell proliferation assays may provide a means of characterizing the proliferative potential and range of cell populations that contain stem cells as well as other important cell types.[102] It is not clear what type of "composition labeling" is sensible and approvable for expanded stem cell products. Ideally, rapid procedures such as immunophenotyping can be utilized clinically with strong statistical validation to support potency labeling.

Control of Facilities and Procedures

CBER requires maintenance of an appropriate environment for biologics manufacture within the GMP framework. A strong program is required for essentially continuous testing of water-for-injection, clean steam systems and USP-grade purified water. These systems are critical for injected product quality, effective sterilization and cleaning. Air systems and facility bioburden are surveyed by an environmental monitoring program that regularly tests air and surface contamination levels. Trends are to be monitored and contaminating organisms identified to minimize contamination concerns. In general, CBER has expressed a preference for separate facilities for manufacture of different materials (eg, separation of virus manufacture facility from a facility used for viral transduction of transplanted cells). If nearby biohazards are unavoidable (eg, animal facilities, viruses or transfected cells, or patients in a hospital setting), the manufacturer must specifically address these risks and describe a plan for control and segregation when validating the manufacturing facility and operation. Cell processing centers must also address the need for simultaneous culture of multiple patient tissues; strong control through physical segregation procedures and labeling is needed to demonstrate a system to prevent mixups. The FDA is continually reviewing mixed-use manufacturing issues; direct consultation with CBER is advised to review specific issues for a planned processing center.

Operation of Cell Processing Centers

The sections above provide an overview of issues to be considered in establishing an operation seeking licensure of an approved biologics product. The following additional issues arise in the context of handling human tissue for manipulation.

Shipping

The regulatory control issues above will promote centralization of cell processing facilities, with the implication that cell processing may be remote from the donor and/or recipient. The validation plan mentioned above should include a demonstration that procedures for shipping retain high viability and cell function (eg, in-package temperature recording devices are advised), and controls against mixup or mislabeling. Labeling that complies with regulations for shipping biological materials must satisfy regulatory agencies as well as all the parties involved in transportation.

Cryopreservation

Cryopreservation of cells to be used for hematopoietic cell transplantation is routine for some tissues and impossible for others due to loss of function; cryopreservation supports the logistics of expanded cell transplant and allows improved quality control but may be incompatible with the desired schedule for clinical administration. Stem cells themselves can be cryopreserved readily and recovered with full function[132]; however, when mature cells such as granulocytes are present in a cell composition, some degree of cell lysis is expected. Some materials that promote successful recovery through the freeze/thaw process (eg, DMSO) are not yet approved independently by the FDA.

Transfer of Control

While all the steps described above are the clear responsibility of the licensed cell product manufacturer, the critical steps of source tissue acquisition and product administration to the patient fall under the "practice of medicine" with variable degrees and styles of documentation and control. It is critical to develop a strong protocol that clearly outlines the steps that constitute source material testing and acceptance, product release and transfer of responsibility. The parties involved should also address issues of archiving of representative product and clinical tissues; disposal of surplus, expired or unapproved materials; and circumstances under which the procedure should be suspended or canceled. Frequent, detailed communications between the tissue donor site, cell processing site and transplant recipient site are critical to successful coordination of transplants.

Summary

Cell therapies may lead to improved treatments for cancer, AIDS and a variety of genetic diseases. These methods are in an early stage of development; full application of these technologies in a setting of approved biologics products will require the development of facilities and procedures that satisfy regulatory expectations and overcome logistical obstacles.

Acknowledgment

The authors would like to thank Gary C. du Moulin, from Cellcor, Inc, for helpful discussions in the preparation of this manuscript.

References

1. Till JE, McCulloch EA. A direct measurement of the radiation sensitivity of normal mouse bone marrow cells. Radiat Res 1961;14:213-22.
2. Boggs DR, Boggs SS, Saxe DF, et al. Hematopoietic stem cells with high proliferative potential. J Clin Invest 1982;70:242-53.
3. Lord BI, Dexter TM. Purification of haemopoietic stem cells—the end of the road? Immunol Today 1988;9:376-7.
4. Moore MAS. Clinical implications of positive and negative hematopoietic stem cell regulators. Blood 1991;78:1-19.
5. Ploemaker RE, van der Sluijs JP, van Beurden CAJ, et al. Use of limiting dilution type long-term marrow cultures in frequency analysis of marrow-repopulating and spleen colony-forming hematopoietic stem cells in the mouse. Blood 1991;78:2527-33.

6. Weissman IL, Heimfeld S, Spangrude G. Haemopoietic stem cell purification. Immunol Today 1989;10:184.
7. Jones RJ, Celano P, Sharkis SJ, Sensenbrenner LL. Two phases of engraftment established by serial bone marrow transplantation in mice. Blood 1989;73:397-401.
8. Dunlop JM, Firkin F, McNiece IK, Bertoncello I. Accelerated establishment of murine long-term marrow cultures by addition of stem cell factor. Exp Hematol 1993;21:769-73.
9. Spangrude GJ, Heimfeld S, Weissman IL. Purification and characterization of mouse hematopoietic stem cells. Science 1988;241:58-62.
10. Uchida N, Aguila HL, Fleming WH, et al. Rapid and sustained hematopoietic recovery in lethally irradiated mice transplanted with purified Thy-1.1^{lo}, Lin– Sca-1+ hematopoietic stem cells. Blood 1994 (in press).
11. Smith LG, Weisman IL, Heimfeld S. Clonal analysis of hemopoietic stem-cell differentiation in vivo. Proc Natl Acad Sci USA 1991;88:2788-92.
12. Fraser CC, Eaves CJ, Szilvassy J, Humphries RK. Proliferation of totipotent hematopoietic stem cells in vitro with retention of long-term competitive in vivo reconstituting ability. Proc Natl Acad Sci USA 1992;89:1968-72.
13. Harrison DE, Stone M, Astle CM. Effects of transplantation on the primitive immunohematopoietic stem cell. J Exp Med 1990; 172:431-7.
14. Keller DC, Du XX, Srour EF, et al. Interleukin-11 inhibits adipogenesis and stimulates myelopoiesis in human long-term marrow cultures. Blood 1993;82:1428-35.
15. Szilvassy SJ, Fraser CC, Eaves CJ, et al. Retrovirus-mediated gene transfer into purified hemopoietic stem cells with long-term lymphomyelopoietic repopulating ability. Proc Natl Acad Sci USA 1989;86:8798-802.
16. Keller G, Snodgrass R. Life span of multipotential hematopoietic stem cells in vivo. J Exp Med 1990;171:1407-18.
17. Sutherland HJ, Eaves CJ, Eaves AC, et al. Characterization and partial purification of human marrow cells capable of initiating long-term hematopoiesis in vitro. Blood 1989;74:1563-70.
18. Sutherland HJ, Lansdorp PM, Henkelman DH, et al. Functional characterization of individual human hematopoietic marrow stromal layers. Proc Natl Acad Sci USA 1990;87:3584-8.

19. Kyoizumi S, Baum CM, Kaneshima H, et al. Implantation and maintenance of functional human bone marrow in SCID-hu mice. Blood 1992;79:1704-11.
20. Baum CM, Weissman IL, Tsukamoto A, Buckle AM. Isolation of a candidate human hematopoietic stem-cell population. Proc Natl Acad Sci USA 1992;89:2804-8.
21. Rice HE, Flake AW, Emani VR, et al. Ex vivo expansion of hematopoietic stem cells from human fetal liver in an artificial capillary system. Blood 1993:82(Suppl 1):18a.
22. Srour EF, Zanjani ED, Brandt JE, et al. Sustained human hematopoiesis in sheep transplanted in utero during early gestation with fractionated adult human bone marrow cells. Blood 1992;79:1404-12.
23. Baumhueter S, Singer MS, Henzel W, et al. Binding of L-selectin to the vascular sialomucin, CD34. Science 1993;262:436-8.
24. Civin CI. Human monomyeloid cell membrane antigens. Exp Hematol 1990;461-7.
25. Civin CI, Strauss LC, Brovall C, et al. Antigenic analysis of hematopoiesis. III. A hematopoietic progenitor cell surface antigen defined by a monoclonal antibody raised against KG-la cells. J Immunol 1984;133:157-65.
26. Kessler SW, Black AT. Clinical scale CD34+ cell immunomagnetic selection from bone marrow with absolute tumor "reverse purging" capability (abstract). Blood 1992;80(Suppl 1):232a.
27. Civin CI. Identification and positive selection of human progenitor/stem cells for bone marrow transplantation. Prog Clin Biol Res 1992;377:461-72.
28. Berenson RJ, Bensinger WI, Kalamasz DF. Positive selection of viable cell populations using avidin-biotin immunoadsorption. J Immunol Methods 1986;91:11-19.
29. Bradley TR, Metcalf D. The growth of mouse marrow cells in vitro. Aust J Biol Med Sci 1966;44:287.
30. Tushinski RJ, Stanley ER. The regulation of mononuclear phagocyte entry into S phase by the colony stimulating factor CSF-1. J Cell Physiol 1985;122:221-8.
31. Tushinski RJ, Oliver IT, Guilbert LJ, et al. Survival of mononuclear phagocytes is dependent on a lineage specific growth factor (CSF-1) which the differentiated cells selectively destroy. Cell 1982;28:71-81.
32. Bartelmez SH, Bradley TR, Bertoncello I, et al. Interleukin 1 plus interleukin 3 plus colony-stimulating factor 1 are essen-

tial for clonal proliferation of primitive myeloid bone marrow cells. Exp Hematol 1989;17:240-5.
33. Leary AG, Ikebuchi K, Hirai Y, et al. Synergism between IL-6 and IL-3 in supporting proliferation of human hematopoietic stem cells: Comparison with Interleukin-1α Blood 1988;71: 1759.
34. Mochizuki DY, Eisenman JR, Conlon PJ, et al. Interleukin 1 regulates hematopoietic activity, a role previously ascribed to hemopoietin 1. Proc Natl Acad Sci USA 1987;84:5267-71.
35. Moore MAS, Warren DJ. Interleukin-1 and G-CSF synergism: In vivo stimulation of stem cell recovery and hematopoietic regeneration following 5-fluorouracil treatment in mice. Proc Natl Acad Sci USA 1987;84:7134.
36. Brandt J, Briddell RA, Srour EF, et al. Role of c-kit ligand in the expansion of human progenitor cells. Blood 1992;79(3): 634-41.
37. Du XX, Williams DA. Interleukin 11. A multifunctional growth factor derived from the hematopoietic microenvironment. Blood 1994;83:2023-30.
38. Egeland T, Steen R, Quarsten H, et al. Myeloid differentiation of purified CD34+ cells after stimulation with recombinant human granulocyte-monocyte colony-stimulating factor (CSF), granulocyte-CSF, monocyte-CSF, and interleukin-3. Blood 1991;78:3192-9.
39. Haylock DN, To LB, Dowse TL, et al. Ex vivo expansion and maturation of peripheral blood CD34+ cells into the myeloid lineage. Blood 1992;80:1405-12.
40. Iscove NN, Shaw AR, Keller G. Net increase of pluripotent hematopoietic precursors in suspension cultures in response to IL-1 and IL-3. J Immunol 1989;142:2332-7.
41. Kobayashi M, Imamura M, Gotohda Y, et al. Synergistic effects of interleukin-lb and interleukin-3 on the expansion of human hematopoietic stem cells in liquid culture. Blood 1991; 78:1947.
42. Koller MR, Bender JG, Papoutsakis ET, Miller WM. Effects of synergistic cytokine combinations, low oxygen, and irradiated stroma on the expansion of human cord blood progenitors. Blood 1992;80:403-11.
43. McAlister IB, Teepe M, Gillis S, Williams DE. Ex vivo expansion of peripheral blood progenitor cells with recombinant cytokines. Exp Hematol 1992;20:626-8.
44. Ogawa M. Differentiation and proliferation of hematopoietic stem cells. Blood 1993;81:2844-53.

45. Smith SL, Bender JG, Maples PB, et al. Expansion of neutrophil precursors and progenitors in suspension cultures of CD34+ cells enriched from human bone marrow. Exp Hematol 1993; 21:870-7.
46. Ploemaker RE, van Soest PL, Voorwinden H, Boudewijn A. Interleukin-12 synergizes with interleukin-3 and steel factor to enhance recovery of murine hematopoietic cells in liquid culture. Leukemia 1993;7:1381-8.
47. Ploemaker RE, van Soest PL, Boudewijn A, Neben S. Interleukin-12 enhances interleukin-3 dependent multilineage hematopoietic colony formation stimulated by interleukin-11 or steel factor. Leukemia 1993;7:1374-80.
48. Ihle JN, Keller J. Interleukin-3 regulation of hematopoietic stem cell differentiation. Prog Clin Biol Res 1985;184:85-94.
49. Quesniaux VF, Mayer P, Liehl E, et al. Review of a novel hematopoietic cytokine, Interleukin-11. Int Rev Exp Pathol 1993;34(A):205-14.
50. Zsebo KM, Wypych J, McNiece IK, et al. Identification, purification, and biological characterization of hematopoietic stem cell factor from buffalo rat liver-conditioned medium. Cell 1990;63:195.
51. Anderson DM, Lyman SD, Baird A, et al. Molecular cloning of the mast cell growth factor—a hematopoietin that is active in both membrane bound and soluble forms. Cell 1990;63:235-43.
52. Huang E, Nocka K, Beier DR, et al. The hematopoietic growth factor KL is encoded at the Sl locus and is the ligand of the c-kit receptor, the gene product of the W locus. Cell 1990;63: 223-33.
53. Bernstein ID, Andrews RG, Zsebo KM. Recombinant human stem cell factor enhances the formation of colonies by $CD34^+$ and $CD34^+lin^-$ cells cultured with interleukin-3, granulocyte-stimulating factor, or granulocyte-macrophage colony-stimulating factor. Blood 1991;77:2316-21.
54. Brandt JE, Bhalla K, Hoffman R. Effects of interleukin-3 and c-kit ligand on the survival of various classes of human hematopoietic progenitor cells. Blood 1994;83:1507-14.
55. Heimfeld S, Fei R, Tsui J, et al. Ex-vivo expansion of human bone marrow and cord blood CD34+ progenitor cells (abstract). Blood 1993;82(Suppl 1):17a.
56. Lill MC, Lynch M, Fraser JK, et al. Ex vivo production and expansion of functional myeloid cells from CD34 selected hematopoietic cells (abstract). Blood 1993;82(Suppl 1):296a.

57. Mayani H, Dragowska W, Lansdorp PM. Cytokine-induced selective expansion and maturation of erythroid versus myeloid progenitors from purified cord blood precursor cells. Blood 1993;81:3252-8.
58. McNiece IK, Langley KE, Zsebo KM. Recombinant stem cell factor synergises with GM-CSF, G-CSF, IL-3, and EPO to stimulate human progenitor cells of the myeloid and erythroid lineages. Exp Hematol 1991;19:226-31.
59. Miura N, Okada S, Zsebo KM, et al. Rat stem cell factor and IL-6 preferentially support the proliferation of c-kit-positive murine hemopoietic cells rather than their differentiation. Exp Hematol 1993;21:143-9.
60. Sato N, Sawada K, Koizumi K, et al. In vitro expansion of human peripheral blood CD34+ cells. Blood 1993;82:3600-9.
61. Srour EF, Brandt JE, Briddell RA, et al. Long-term generation and expansion of human primitive hematopoietic progenitor cells in vitro. Blood 1993;81:661-9.
62. Tsuji K, Lyman SD, Sudo T, et al. Enhancement of murine hematopoiesis by synergistic interactions between steel factor (ligand for c-kit), interleukin-11, and other early acting factors in culture. Blood 1992;79:2855-60.
63. Brugger W, Mocklin W, Heimfeld S, et al. Ex vivo expansion of enriched peripheral blood CD34+ progenitor cells by stem cell factor, IL-1b, IL-6, IL-3, and interferon-g and erythropoietin. Blood 1993;81:2579-84.
64. Catlett JP, Leftwich JA, Westin EH, et al. C-kit expression by CD34+ bone marrow progenitors and inhibition of response to recombinant human interleukin-3 following exposure to c-kit antisense oligonucleotides. Blood 1991;78:3186-91.
65. Van Zant G, Larson DB, Drubachevsky I, et al. Expansion in bioreactors of human progenitor populations from cord blood and mobilized peripheral blood (abstract). Blood 1993; 82(Suppl 1):296a.
66. Broxmeyer HE, Cooper S, Lu L, et al. Effect of murine mast cell growth factor (c-kit proto-oncogene ligand) on colony formation by human hematopoietic progenitor cells. Blood 1991;77:2142-9.
67. Lyman SD, James L, Vanden Bos T. Molecular cloning of a ligand for the flt3/flk-2 tyrosine kinase receptor: A proliferative factor for primitive hematopoietic cells. Cell 1993;75: 1157-67.

68. Dexter TM, Allen TD, Lajtha LG. Conditions controlling the proliferation of haemopoietic stem cells in vitro. J Cell Physiol 1976;91:335-44.
69. Andrews RG, Singer JW, Bernstein ID. Human hematopoietic precursors in long-term cultures: Single CD34+ cells that lack detectable T cell, B cell, and myeloid cell antigens produce multiple colony-forming cells when cultured with marrow stromal cells. J Exp Med 1990;172:355-8.
70. Brandt JE, Srour EF, Hoffman R. Effects of adherent bone marrow stromal cells on the development and proliferation of highly purified human hematopoietic stem cells. Trans Assoc Am Physicians 1992;105:238-49.
71. Eaves CJ, Cashman JD, Eaves AC. Methodology of long term culture of human hematopoietic cells. J Tissue Culture Meth 1991;13:55-62.
72. Gartner S, Kaplan HS. Long-term culture of human bone marrow cells. Proc Natl Acad Sci USA 1980;77:4756-9.
73. Veraillie C, Blakolmer K, McGlave P. Purified primitive human hematopoietic progenitor cells with long-term in vitro repopulating capacity adhere selectively to irradiated bone marrow stroma. J Exp Med 1990;172:509-20.
74. Brockbank KGM, de Jong JP, Piersma AH, Voerman JSA. Hematopoiesis on purified bone-marrow-derived reticular fibroblasts in vitro. Exp Hematol 1986;14:386-94.
75. Dexter TM. Regulation of hematopoietic cell growth and development: Experimental and clinical studies. Leukemia 1989;3:469-74.
76. Ikebuchi K, Wong GG, Clark SC, et al. Interleukin 6 enhancement of interleukin 3-dependent proliferation of multipotential hemopoietic progenitors. Proc Natl Acad Sci USA 1987;84: 9035-9.
77. Hunt P, Robertson D, Weiss D, et al. A single bone marrow-derived stromal cell type supports the in vitro growth of early lymphoid and myeloid cells. Cell 1987;48:997-1007.
78. Quesenberry PJ, McNiece IK, Robinson BE, et al. Stromal cell regulation of lymphoid and myeloid differentiation. Blood Cells 1987;13:137-46.
79. Whitlock CA, Tidmarsh GF, Muller-Sieburg CE, Weissman IL. Bone marrow stromal cell lines with lymphopoietic activity express high levels of a pre-B neoplasia-associated molecule. Cell 1987;48:1009-21.
80. Spooncer E, Heyworth CM, Dunn A, et al. Self-renewal and differentiation of interleukin-3-dependent multipotent stem

cells are modulated by stromal cells and serum factors. Differentiation 1986;31:111-8.
81. Gordon MY, Riley GP, Watt SM, Greaves MF. Compartmentalization of a haematopoietic growth factor (GM-CSF) by glycosaminoglycans in the bone marrow microenvironment. Nature 1987;326:403-5.
82. Long MW, Briddell R, Walter AW, et al. Human hematopoietic stem cell adherence to cytokines and matrix molecules. J Clin Invest 1992;90:251-5.
83. Zuckerman KS, Wicha MS. Extracellular matrix production by the adherent cells of long-term murine bone marrow cultures. Blood 1983;61:540-7.
84. Coulombel L, Vuillet MH, Leroy C, Tchernia G. Lineage- and stage-specific adhesion of human hematopoietic progenitor cells to extracellular matrices from marrow fibroblasts. Blood 1988;71:329-34.
85. Long MW, Dixit VM. Thrombospondin functions as a cytoadhesion molecule for human hematopoietic progenitor cells. Blood 1990;75:2311-8.
86. Minguell JJ, Tavassoli M. Proteoglycan synthesis by hematopoietic progenitor cells. Blood 1989;73:1821-7.
87. Spooncer E, Gallagher JT, Krizsa F, Dexter TM. Regulation of haemopoiesis in long term bone marrow cultures. IV. Glycosaminoglycan synthesis and the stimulation of haemopoiesis by b-D-xylosides. J Cell Biol 1983;96:510-4.
88. Wight TN, Kinsella MG, Keating A, Singer JW. Proteoglycans in human long-term bone marrow cultures: Biochemical and ultrastructural analysis. Blood 1986;67:1333-43.
89. Roberts R, Gallagher J, Spooncer E, et al. Heparan sulfate bound growth factors: A mechanism for stromal cell mediated haemopoiesis. Nature 1988;332:376-8.
90. Long MW. Blood cell adhesion molecules. Exp Hematol 1992;20:288-301.
91. Issaad C, Croisille L, Katz A, et al. Murine stromal cell line allows the proliferation of very primitive human CD34+/CD38– progenitor cells in long-term cultures and semisolid assays. Blood 1993;81(11):2916-24.
92. Koller MR, Newsom B, Van Zant G, et al. Bioreactor expansion of whole density separated and CD34-enriched human bone marrow (abstract). Blood 1993;82(Suppl 1):649a.
93. Tushinski R, Backer M, O'Toole T, et al. Leukemia inhibitory factor leads to ex vivo expansion of human hematopoietic stem cells (abstract). Blood 1993;82(Suppl 1):19a.

94. Veraillie C. Direct contact between human primitive hematopoietic progenitors and bone marrow stroma is not required for long-term in vitro hematopoiesis. Blood 1992;79:2821-6.
95. Brandt J, Srour EF, van Besien K, et al. Cytokine-dependent long-term culture of highly enriched precursors of hematopoietic progenitor cells from human bone marrow. J Clin Invest 1990;86:932-41.
96. Han M, Kobayashi M, Imamura M, et al. In vitro expansion of murine hematopoietic progenitor cells in liquid cultures for bone marrow transplantation: Effects of stem cell factor. Int J Hematol 1993;57:113-20.
97. Kerst JM, Slaper-Cortenbach ICM, von dem Borne AEGKr, et al. Combined measurement of growth and differentiation in suspension cultures of purified human CD34 positive cells enables a detailed analysis of myelopoiesis. Exp Hematol 1992;20:1188-93.
98. Lansdorp PM, Dragowska W. Maintenance of hematopoiesis in serum-free bone marrow cultures involves sequential recruitment of quiescent progenitors. Exp Hematol 1993:21: 1321-7.
99. Lemoli RM, Tafuri A, Strife A, et al. Proliferation of human hematopoietic progenitors in long-term bone marrow cultures in gas-permeable plastic bags is enhanced by colony-stimulating factors. Exp Hematol 1993;20:569-75.
100. Muench MO, Firpo MT, Moore MAS. Bone marrow transplantation with IL-1 plus kit-ligand ex vivo expanded bone marrow accelerates hematopoietic reconstitution in mice without the loss of HSC lineages and proliferative potential. Blood 1991; 81:3463-73.
101. Muench MO, Moore MA. Accelerated recovery of peripheral blood cell counts in mice transplanted with in vitro cytokine-expanded hematopoietic progenitor cells. Exp Hematol 1992; 20:611-8.
102. Backer MP, Young J, DiGusto D. Expansion kinetics of single fetal hematopoietic progenitor cells: Multipotential differentiation and retention of primitive phenotype (abstract). Blood 1993;82(Suppl 1):17a.
103. Armstrong RD, Koller MR, Paul L, et al. Clinical scale production of stem and hematopoietic cells (abstract). Blood 1993; 82(Suppl 1):269a.
104. Gluck S, Lebkowski J, Porter K, et al Characterization and transfusion of in vitro expanded hematopoietic progenitor cells. Exp Hematol 1992;21:1141.

105. Koller MR, Emerson SG, Palsson BO. Large-scale expansion of human stem and progenitor cells from bone marrow mononuclear cells in continuous perfusion cultures. Blood 1993; 82:378-84.
106. Rummel SA, Emerson SG, Van Zant G. Expansion of human hematopoietic stem/progenitor cells resistant to treatment with 4-hydroperoxycyclophosphamide (abstract). Blood 1993;82(Suppl 1):297a.
107. Silver SM, Adams PT, Hutchinson RJ, et al. Phase 1 evaluation of ex vivo expanded hematopoietic cells produced by perfusion cultures in autologous bone marrow transplant (abstract). Blood 1993;82(Suppl 1):297a.
108. Purdy MH, Shpall EJ, Heimfeld S, et al. Large volume ex vivo expansion of CD34 positive(+) hematopoietic progenitor cells (HPC) for transplantation (abstract). Blood 1993;82(Suppl 1):652a.
109. Berenson RJ, Bensinger WI, Hill RS, et al. Engraftment after infusion of CD34+ marrow cells in patients with breast cancer or neuroblastoma. Blood 1991;77:1717-22.
110. Berenson RJ, Shpall EJ, Franklin W, Bearman SI, et al. Transplantation of CD34 positive marrow and/or peripheral blood progenitor cells (PBPC) into breast cancer patients following high-dose chemotherapy (HDC) (abstract). Blood 1993; 82(Suppl 1):173a.
111. Rurrieri L, Heimfeld S, Broxmeyer HE. Cytokine-dependent ex vivo expansion of early subsets of CD34+ cord blood progenitors is greatly enhanced by cord blood plasma, but expansion of the more mature subsets of progenitors is favored (abstract). Blood 1993;82(Suppl 1):16a.
112. Craig W, Kay R, Cutler RL, Lansdorp PM. Expression of Thy-1 on human hematopoietic progenitor cells. J Exp Med 1993; 177:1331-42.
113. Ayash LJ, Elias A, Wheeler C, et al. Double dose-intensive chemotherapy with autologous marrow and peripheral-blood progenitor-cell support for metastatic breast cancer: A feasibility study. J Clin Oncol 1994;12:37-44.
114. Crown J, Kritz A, Vahdat L, et al. Rapid administration of multiple cycles of high-dose myelosuppressive chemotherapy in patients with metastatic breast cancer. J Clin Oncol 1993; 11:1144-9.
115. Shea TC, Mason JR, Storniolo AM, et al. Sequential cycles of high-dose carboplatin administered with recombinant human granulocyte-macrophage colony-stimulating factor and

repeated infusions of autologous peripheral-blood progenitor cells: A novel and effective method for delivering multiple courses of dose-intensive therapy. J Clin Oncol 1992;10:464-73.

116. Shea TC, Mason JR, Breslin M, et al. Reinfusion and serial measurements of carboplatin-mobilized peripheral-blood progenitor cells in patients receiving multiple cycles of high-dose chemotherapy. J Clin Oncol 1994;12:1012-20.
117. Tepler I, Cannistra SA, Frei III E, et al. Use of peripheral-blood progenitor cells abrogates the myelotoxicity of repetitive outpatient high-dose carboplatin and cyclophosphamide chemotherapy. J Clin Oncol 1993;11:1583-91.
118. Bienzle D, Abrams-Ogg AC, Kruth SA, et al. Gene transfer into hematopoietic stem cells: Long-term maintenance of in vitro activated progenitors without marrow ablation. Proc Natl Acad Sci USA 1994;91:350-4.
119. Food and Drug Administration. Points to consider in human somatic cell therapy and gene therapy. Rockville, MD: Center for Biologics Evaluation and Research, 1991.
120. Food and Drug Administration. Points to consider in the collection, processing, and testing of ex vivo activated mononuclear cells for administration to humans. Rockville, MD: Center for Biologics Evaluation and Research, 1989.
121. Department of Health and Human Services. Application of current statutory authorities to human somatic cell therapy products and gene therapy products. Federal Register 1993; 58:53248-51.
122. Kessler DA, Siegel JP, Noguchi PD, et al. Regulation of somatic-cell therapy and gene therapy by the Food and Drug Administration. N Engl J Med 1993;329:1169-73.
123. Food and Drug Administration. Points to consider in the characterization of cell lines used to produce biologicals. Rockville, MD: Center for Biologics Evaluation and Research, 1993.
124. Food and Drug Administration. Points to consider in the manufacture and testing of monoclonal antibody products for human use. Rockville, MD: Center for Biologics Evaluation and Research, 1987.
125. Prusiner SB. Prion encephalopathies of animals and humans. Dev Biol Stand 1993;80:31-44.
126. Price PJ, Gregory EA. Relationship between in vitro growth and biophysical and biochemical properties of the serum supplement. In Vitro 1982;18:576-84.

127. Hyelone Laboratories. Fetal bovine serum: Variations in components that influence cell growth and function. Art to Science in Tissue Culture. 1986;5: 1-8.
128. Palsson BO, Paek SH, Schwartz RM, et al. Expansion of human bone marrow progenitor cells in a high density perfusion system. Biotechnology 1993;11:368-72.
129. Koller MR, Bender JG, Miller WM, Papoutsakis ET. Expansion of primitive human hematopoietic progenitors in a perfusion bioreactor system with IL-3, IL-6 and stem cell factor. Biotechnology 1993;11:358-63.
130. du Moulin CG, Stack J, Kruger R, Liu V. Quality assurance/quality control compliance program: A cellular therapy developer's perspective. Regul Affairs 1993;5:461-72.
131. du Moulin CG, Liu V, Osband M. Implementation of an effective program for quality assurance and quality control in living cell therapy: A 2-year experience with autolymphocyte therapy. Transplant Proc 1992;24:2803-8.
132. Makino S, Harada K, et al. A simplified method for cryopreservation of peripheral blood stem cells at –80 C without rate-controlled freezing. Bone Marrow Transplant 1991;8: 239-44.

In: Nance ST, ed.
Blood Supply: Risks, Perceptions and Prospects for the Future
Bethesda, MD: American Association of Blood Banks, 1994

7

Reducing the Infectivity of Blood Components—What We Have Learned

Leonard I. Friedman, ScD; Robert R. Stromberg, PhD; and Stephen J. Wagner, PhD

CAREFUL DONOR SELECTION AND increased laboratory testing have greatly improved the safety of the blood supply. Nevertheless, a small risk of virus transmission by transfusion still exists. The most recent estimates for transmission of viruses are: human immunodeficiency virus, type 1 (HIV-1), 1 in 225,000; hepatitis B virus (HBV), 1 in 200,000; hepatitis C virus (HCV), 1 in 3,300; and human T-cell lymphotropic virus (HTLV-I/II), 1 in 50,000.[1] Other blood-borne viruses include cytomegalovirus (CMV), human immunodeficiency virus, type 2 (HIV-2), hepatitis A virus (HAV), non-A,B,C hepatitis and parvovirus B19.[2] If 20 million blood components are transfused annually in the US, and assuming that HIV-1 is 100% fatal, HBV 0.1% fatal,[3] HCV 1.5% fatal[4] and HTLV-I/II (combined) 1% fatal, then the maximum number of related deaths is about 185. Because many of these individuals will die of their primary illness or for unrelated reasons, the number of fatalities as a direct result of virally transmitted disease is much lower. There are also increasing concerns about transmission of bacteria.[5,6] In 1990, the Food and Drug Administration received reports of six fatalities related to bacterial sepsis; five in platelets and one in red cells. Six fatalities due to bacterial sepsis, all in platelet products, were reported during 1991.[7] The incidence of nonfatal sepsis may be as

Leonard I. Friedman, ScD, Head, Product Development Department; Robert R. Stromberg, PhD, Scientist, Product Development Department; and Stephen J. Wagner, PhD, Scientist, Product Development Department; American Red Cross, Rockville, MD
(Reprinted from *Immunological Investigations,* 1994, courtesy of Marcel Dekker, Inc, New York.)

high as 1 per 1700 transfusions of pooled platelet concentrates.[8] Finally, parasitic diseases, such as Chagas' disease, are also being followed with interest.[9]

Infectious diseases are not the only cause of transfusion-related fatalities. In 1990 and 1991, 29 deaths were attributed to "administrative errors," such as the incorrect unit being transfused or testing the wrong crossmatch sample; 58 deaths were attributed to serologic incompatibility and other causes.[7] Although the number of deaths attributable to transfusion is relatively small in comparison to the number of patients transfused, implementation of infectious agent removal and/or inactivation processes should provide an added level of safety. This could possibly limit the need for additional donor screening or testing, and may reduce or eliminate disease transmission due to current or future blood-borne pathogens.

Product Definition

It is useful to think of plasma, red cells and platelets as "impure" blood components. Plasma contains residual platelets, leukocytes and red cells. Red cells contain residual leukocytes, platelets and plasma. Platelets contain residual red cells, leukocytes and plasma. Depending on the infectious agent, it may be "freely" suspended in the plasma; extracellular but "associated" with red cell, leukocyte or platelet membranes; or intracellular. Table 7-1 shows the location of various viruses in these compartments; there are many unknowns. Similarly, bacteria can be found extracellularly and intracellularly, and parasites may also be located in different compartments.

Table 7-1. Location of Viruses in Blood Components

Virus	Plasma	Leukocytes	Red Cells	Platelets
HIV-1	Yes	Yes	?	Yes
HIV-2	?	?	?	?
HBV	Yes	?	?	?
HCV	Yes	?	?	?
HTLV-I	No	Yes	No	?
HTLV-II	?	?	?	?
CMV	No	Yes	No	No
B19	Yes	?	?	?
HAV	Yes	?	?	?

Table 7-2. Estimate of Window Period Virus Load

Virus	Infectious Particles in Plasma (per mL)	Infectious Leukocytes (per mL)
HIV-1	10^2-10^4 [Virus isolates]	10^5-10^3 [DNA hybrid]
HCV	10^2 [Chimpanzee studies]	?
HBV	$<5 \times 10^5$ particles [EIA test]	?
HTLV-I	0	10^4 [DNA hybrid]
CMV	?	?

In order to define an infectious disease removal or inactivation process, the maximum bioburden expected to be present must be estimated. Because it can be assumed that blood components will be derived from fully tested donations, it is likely that a 10^6-fold reduction (99.9999%) in virus titer will need to be achieved in extracellular, intracellular and cell-associated compartments.[10,11] Table 7-2 shows the data used to define the 6 $\log_{10}$ objective. For many of the bacteria associated with blood transfusion, their concentration at the time of blood collection is <10 CFU/mL.[12-14] Since some of these organisms may proliferate during liquid storage, the bioburden at the time of processing must be estimated. It is assumed that red cells and platelets will be prepared from whole blood within 24 hours after collection and undergo any infectious disease removal/inactivation process at that time; plasma will probably be frozen prior to such treatment. Considering the growth rates of some species of bacteria that have been implicated in sepsis, it is possible that their level could be as high as 10^2-10^3 CFU/mL at the time of component preparation.

Overview of Virus Removal and Inactivation Processes

Over the past 10 years a number of virus removal and inactivation processes have been investigated. They are categorized in Table 7-3 for each blood component. Some processes may not be suitable alone, but might be acceptable if combined with another (eg, leukocyte reduction combined with photochemical treatment). It is also important to recognize that "removal" and "inactivation" are equivalent in terms of final product infectivity, as long as the process removes (eg, filtration) or inactivates (eg, chemical) viruses to the same extent.

Table 7-3. Overview of Virus Removal/Inactivation Processes Studied

Process	Plasma	Red Cells	Platelets
Affinity column	X		
Chemical	X	X	
Extended storage		X	
Filtration			
size exclusion	X		
leukocyte reduction		X	X
Heating			
pasteurization	X		
mild heat		X	
high temp/short time	X		
Irradiation			
ultraviolet			X
gamma	X		
Photochemical	X	X	X
Washing		X	

Plasma Processing

Although the indications for fresh frozen plasma for transfusion are limited,[15-17] the clinical demand for this product has not decreased. Approaches for virus removal and inactivation are presented below.

Affinity Column

Affinity adsorption columns have been used successfully for protein purification. In these cases, specific proteins adsorb to selected solid phase matrices; contaminating viruses are washed away. For plasma, however, the approach has to be reversed; viruses and infected cells have to selectively bind to the matrix. When these experiments were attempted, the extent of "free" virus removal was about 1 $\log_{10}$.[18] Another disadvantage of this approach is that the matrices would need to be made selective for each type of virus or infected cell.

Microporous Membrane Filtration

For virus reduction in plasma, size exclusion membrane-based filtration has been studied.[19] In this process, plasma is passed through a microporous membrane in which the mean pore diameter is larger than most proteins, yet smaller than freely suspended viruses and cells containing viruses. Extracellular HIV-1, with a size of about 100 nm, did not pass through a 105 nm pore diameter membrane. However, because of the small size of B19 (18-26 nm), hepatitis delta (28-39 nm), HCV (30-60 nm) and HBV (42 nm),[20] a smaller pore diameter membrane is required. When plasma is filtered through a 40 nm membrane, there is considerable loss of high molecular weight clotting factors.[21]

Gamma Irradiation

High energy gamma irradiation has been used to inactivate viruses in fresh frozen plasma. At 40 kGy, $10^{6.5}$ infectious dose (ID)/mL of HIV-1 was inactivated in plasma at –40 C.[22] However, there was concurrent clotting factor activity loss of 14.6, 38.8 and 23.3% for Factors VIII:C, VIII:vWF and IX, respectively. In an unrelated study, using similar irradiation conditions, more significant protein damage occurred and the process was found to be unacceptable for further development.[23]

Iodine

Two iodine-based methods for virus inactivation have been investigated. Iodine, when bound to cross-linked polyvinylpyrrolidone (PVP), was able to inactivate >5 $\log_{10}$ of vesicular stomatitis virus (VSV) in cryoprecipitate-poor plasma while decreasing Factor IX activity by <10%.[24] However, since cross-linked PVP was not able to bind iodine as tightly as was desired, another carrier was considered. Iodine bound to cross-linked starch inactivated >9 $\log_{10}$ of VSV and >7 $\log_{10}$ encephalomyocarditis virus (a model virus for HAV and B19).[25] Under these conditions there was retention of 70% Factor VIII and >75% Factor IX activity. The disadvantages to such a process are the need to remove the starch-iodine following incubation, the potential release of iodine from the matrix and a reduction in coagulation factor activity with increasing starch-iodine concentration or incubation time.

Pasteurization

Pasteurization (10 hours at 60 C) of thawed, pooled and stabilized plasma has been implemented in France.[26,27] Studies indicate preservation of 75-95% clotting factor activity and no protein denaturation or coagulation factor activation. In-vitro studies demonstrated that >5 $\log_{10}$ HIV-1 and >5.7 $\log_{10}$ Sindbis (a model virus for HCV) were inactivated. However, no chimpanzee studies, using HIV-1-, HBV- and HCV-spiked and processed plasma, have been reported. These data are needed in order to evaluate the overall effectiveness of this specific pasteurization process.[28]

Preliminary virus inactivation studies in plasma were also conducted using a high-temperature short-time heating method.[29] The problem is to determine the temperature and time conditions where the rate of virus inactivation exceeds the rate of protein damage. For example, with a process duration of 0.25 seconds and a hold time of 0.006 seconds at 77 C, ≥4.4 $\log_{10}$ of HIV-1 was inactivated with a 15-20% loss of Factors VIII and IX activity; there was a greater loss of Factor V activity. Three $\log_{10}$ of HIV-1 (74 C), ≥5.8 $\log_{10}$ EMC (≥72 C) and ≥4.4 $\log_{10}$ VSV (75 C) could also be inactivated.

Solvent/Detergent

Virus inactivation in plasma, using a solvent/detergent process, has been implemented. In it, the thawed and blood-group-specific pooled plasma is incubated with 1% tri(n-butyl)phosphate and 1% Triton X-100 (a nonionic detergent) at 30 C for 4 hours.[30] Subsequently, the chemical additives are removed by chromatography and the resulting plasma is sterile filtered and refrozen. The final product contains approximately 200 mL and has a shelf life of >2 years when stored at –30 C. Protein recovery is good and coagulation factors are not activated. In-vitro inactivation studies demonstrated HIV-1, Sindbis and VSV kills of ≥7.2, ≥6.9 and ≥7.5 $\log_{10}$, respectively. Chimpanzee studies resulted in virus inactivation of 10^6 CID_{50} for HBV and ≥10^5 CID_{50} for HCV.[31] Extensive clinical studies have been under way for over 3 years and show comparability between untreated fresh frozen plasma (FFP) and solvent/detergent-treated plasma.

Solvent/detergent processes have been used for virus inactivation of plasma derivatives for many years. One drawback is their inability to inactivate nonlipid enveloped viruses, such as HAV and B19. HAV transmission has recently been reported in Europe following treatment of plasma derivatives.[32-34] Another potential issue may relate to residual solvent and/or detergent in transfusions to neonates. Also, as with pasteurization or any process based on the treatment of pooled components, a breach in manufacturing or a process inadequacy will have an effect on many patients.

Methylene Blue

A photodynamic method, using methylene blue (MB), has been introduced in parts of Germany and Switzerland for virus inactivation of plasma for transfusion.[35] In this process, MB is metered into individual thawed units of previously frozen plasma by sterile connection, to make a 1 μM concentration. The units are then incubated in the dark with agitation at 4 C for 1 hour before irradiation by visible light (50,000 lux) for 1 hour. Refreezing is the final step in this process. Most plasma proteins are not influenced by the process[36]; there is usually less than a 20% impact on those that are. For example, under slightly different irradiation conditions there is a loss of approximately 13% of Factor VIII and 17% of Factor IX activity.[37] These studies indicated that ≥2.5, ≥5.7, ≥3.0, ≥5.5 $\log_{10}$ extracellular HIV-1, VSV, HSV and influenza, respectively, were inactivated. However, nonlipid enveloped viruses were not greatly affected; poliovirus was not inactivated and only 1 $\log_{10}$ adenovirus was inactivated. Of additional concern is the fact that treatment with MB does not inactivate intracellular virus. The initial freeze-thaw step is intended to lyse residual leukocytes or make the intracellular virus more accessible to the MB treatment. However, the freeze-thaw treatment is not 100% effective.[38] It is reasonable to expect that leukocyte reduction or microporous membrane filtration would be more effective in removing intracellular viruses.

In terms of toxicity, MB has been used clinically for many years and at significantly higher doses. There have been only occasional reports of adverse effects. More than 100,000 units of MB-treated FFP have been transfused in Germany. In comparison with transfusions of untreated FFP, there has been no increase in adverse outcomes. A more controlled clinical study of MB-treated FFP is now being conducted in Germany and a review comparing MB and solvent/detergent methods for virus inactivation in FFP has recently been published.[39]

Miscellaneous Approaches

A number of other virus inactivation processes for plasma have been studied. For example, beta-propiolactone in combination with ultraviolet irradiation has been used in Germany for cold-sterilization of pooled serum and several types of plasma derivatives for many years.[40] Psoralen compounds and ultraviolet A (UVA) light have also been studied, but usually as part of investigations involving platelets and/or red cells. In one study, aminomethyltrimethylpsoralen (AMT) was found to inactivate $\geq 6 \log_{10} ID_{50}$ of VSV; Factor VIII recovery averaged 57%.[41] Use of glutathione as a quenching agent increased the recovery to 87% without affecting the virus kill. A second study used a newly developed brominated psoralen derivative; $\geq 6 \log_{10}$ inactivation of two nonenveloped bacteriophages was obtained while retaining 90% Factor VIII activity.[42] Ozone, administered through a microporous membrane system, was demonstrated to inactivate HIV-1 in plasma and Factor VIII concentrate.[43] Medium-chain saturated and long-chain unsaturated fatty acids and monoglycerides have also been shown to inactivate significant levels of HIV-1, HIV-2 and herpes simplex virus in plasma and serum.[44]

Summary of Plasma Processes

Three processes have been implemented outside the US for inactivating viruses in plasma: chemical (solvent/detergent); heat (pasteurization); and photochemical (methylene blue). Table 7-4 shows

Table 7-4. Virus Inactivation of Plasma

Consideration	Solvent/ Detergent Treatment	Pasteurization	Methylene Blue Treatment
Extracellular virus	Yes	Yes	Yes
Intracellular virus	Yes	Yes	?
Virus limitations	Lipid	?	Lipid
Chimpanzee studies	Yes	?	?
Protein loss	Yes	Yes	Yes
Potential toxicity	Low	No	Low
Controlled trials	Yes	?	?
Central manufacturing	Yes	Yes	Possible
Pooled plasma	Yes	Yes	No
Uniform product	Yes	Yes	No
Product quality control	Yes	Yes	No
Process quality control	Yes	Yes	Yes
Suitable for all patients	?	Yes	?
Hospital practice change	No	No	Minor

some of the process considerations and indicates data that have not yet been reported. Whether as stand-alone processes or in combination with one or more additional steps, it is likely that they are able to reduce the virus transmission risk of plasma for transfusion. The solvent/detergent and pasteurization processes should also be able to inactivate contaminating bacteria and parasites; it is not known whether the MB process is effective. This may, however, be a moot point, since most plasma products are frozen during storage and proliferation of pathogens or generation of significant endotoxin is unlikely.

Red Cell Processing

Many research groups have studied virus depletion and inactivation processes in red cells using various approaches. In addition, since several species of bacteria can grow in red cell suspensions during storage and some parasites are associated with red cells, the "ideal" process would be one in which pathogens would be removed or inactivated in all compartments. The section below reviews some of the work that has been reported.

Leukocyte Reduction

Leukocyte reduction has been investigated as a means of removing leukocyte-associated viruses. Early clinical studies in which approximately 1-2 $\log_{10}$ of leukocytes were removed by washing or filtration resulted in significant reduction or elimination of CMV transmission.[45-50] As leukocyte reduction filters became more efficient, the data indicating CMV elimination became more compelling. Finally, in a recent multicenter controlled clinical study involving bone marrow transplant patients, the use of filtered red cells was compared to the use of CMV-seronegative red cells for prevention of CMV infection. There was no significant difference in the incidence of CMV between the tested and filtered red cells.[51] Thus, the use of filtered red cells should be comparable to the use of seronegative red cells for prevention of CMV disease. Leukocyte reduction may have an effect on other pathogens. In the case of HTLV-I, at least a 3 $\log_{10}$ reduction in infectivity was reported after leukocyte removal by filtration of blood spiked with cultured HTLV-I-transformed cells.[52] With HTLV-I-infected individuals, the number of infected cells was reduced by 1-3 $\log_{10}$. Although filtration does reduce infectivity, there are no data to demonstrate that filtration will prevent its transmission. With HIV-1, both "free" and cell-associated viruses are present. Therefore, it is not feasible for transmission to be prevented by filtration alone. However, using polymerase chain reaction (PCR) and/or coculture methods, it has been demonstrated that filtration reduced the number of infected leukocytes in HIV-1-spiked red cells[53-55] and in blood obtained from seropositive donors.[54,55] Thus, leukocyte removal may reduce the infectious disease bioburden. Additional studies have indicated that *Yersinia* and other bacteria in red cells can be reduced by plasma proteins and filtration.[56-60]

Platelet Reduction

Platelets are a major "contaminant" in red cells. A number of human viruses such as influenza,[61] vaccinia[62] and herpes[63] have been associated with platelets. More recently, a strong association between platelets and free HIV-1 has been reported.[64,65] Leukocyte-reduced and washed platelets obtained from HIV-1 seropositive donors were found to be positive for HIV-1 PCR-RNA and negative for PCR-DNA, showing that the detected virus was not incorporated in leukocytes. Extensive washing did not remove significant quantities of virus, indicating binding between the platelets and HIV-1. The presence of HIV within platelets has also been shown by electron microscopy.[66] Thus, although the infectivity of HIV-1 associated with platelets has not been demonstrated, residual platelets in red cells may need to be considered as a vector for virus transmission.

Washing

In the late 1970's it was believed that red cell freezing, deglycerolization and washing would eliminate HBV. Initial reports based on retrospective analyses suggesting a substantial reduction in hepatitis infectivity[67] were not confirmed. In a prospective study, no clinical hepatitis was contracted with frozen, deglycerolized and washed red cells compared to several cases in the control arm. However, the number of experiments were not sufficient to be statistically significant.[68] On the other hand, frozen, deglycerolized and washed cells have been reported to have no effect on reducing the incidence of posttransfusion hepatitis.[69] Further evidence that such treatment does not prevent transmission of hepatitis was shown by transfusing four chimpanzees with human red cells that had been frozen, deglycerolized and washed after being spiked with hepatitis virus that were negative by counter electrophoresis but positive by radioimmunoassay.[70] All chimpanzees demonstrated unequivocal evidence of infection.

More recently, a series of leukocyte reduction and washing experiments were conducted.[71,72] Prior to processing, the red cells were spiked with VSV, Sindbis, pseudorabies or the bacteriophage $\phi 6$. Experimental filters were used to remove 6 $\log_{10}$ of leukocytes[73-75]; about 2+ $\log_{10}$ of platelets were concurrently removed. Based on dye experiments, it was estimated that commercially available cell washers would remove about 5+ $\log_{10}$ of plasma. Under conditions that should have resulted in approximately 6 $\log_{10}$ virus washout, the maximum reduction observed was typically 4-5 $\log_{10}$ from the supernatant fluid, but <2 $\log_{10}$ from the red cells.[71] Extensive test tube experiments were also conducted in which the wash solution to red cell volume ratio was considerably increased from that in the cell washers. Although virus reduction was improved, residual model virus was always present in the red cell portion. These results suggested virus association with red cells or with contaminating platelets.

Virus reduction was not improved by modifying the wash conditions. This was done by slightly elevating the temperature or changing the ionic strength or protein level of the wash solution. A series of experiments was conducted in which different detergents were added to VSV-spiked red cells to determine whether they could augment the release of virus from the red cell membrane and thus improve washout efficiency. The detergents included nonionic and anionic, short- and long-chain aliphatic and aromatic compounds. No improved virus depletion was observed unless accompanied by significant red cell damage.[72]

Mild Temperature Elevation

Although a slight temperature elevation will not inactivate most blood-borne pathogens, HIV inactivation in culture media was reported to occur at a rate of about 1 $\log_{10}$/hour at 45 C.[76] Thus, if inactivation occurred linearly, a simple 6-hour incubation would be able to reduce or eliminate HIV from red cells. Unfortunately, when the studies were conducted using red cell suspensions, only about 0.25 $\log_{10}$/hour was inactivated at 45 C.[77] In addition, the red cells were irreversibly damaged. These data indicate that heat treatment will not be effective for HIV inactivation.

Extended Storage

In a retrospective study of individuals who were later found to have been HIV-1 positive at the time of donation, the infectivity of transfused red cells was significantly reduced during storage. There was an 89% transmission rate for products stored from 8-14 days, compared to a 50% transmission rate after 22+ days of storage.[78] In an unrelated study using coculture assays, the infectivity of red cells spiked with HIV-1-infected T cells declined exponentially during storage, although the rate appeared to be dependent on the suspension medium.[79] Thus, while this is a simple approach, most infectivity of intracellular virus is retained during storage.

Chemical Approaches

Chemical approaches have also been explored for virus inactivation in red cells. The literature indicates that ozone is capable of inactivating HIV-1[80,81] and other pathogens.[82-84] In a series of test tube experiments using VSV and φ6, it was demonstrated that a 5-6 $\log_{10}$ virus kill was only achieved at low [approximately 0.05 (5%)] hematocrit and that extensive hemolysis (approximately 30%) occurred.[85] It was unexpected that this level of hemolysis could not be visually observed in the supernatant fluid because of ozone-induced destruction (bleaching) of extracellular hemoglobin. The use of sodium chlorite and lactic acid to generate chlorous acid and chlorine dioxide for HIV inactivation has been suggested.[86,87] Recent studies were unable to achieve effective virus kill without significant damage to red cells, using ClO_2 generated from sodium chlorite by addition of lactic acid and chloride ions.[88] One report in the literature also indicated that decreasing the pH in cell-free media inactivated HIV-1.[89] The authors have been unable to achieve HIV-1 inactivation at pH levels as low as 4.9 in the absence of red cells. Medium-chain saturated and long-chain unsaturated fatty acids have been reported to inactivate enveloped viruses. Monoglycerides of the acids were also found to have antiviral activity, frequently at considerably lower concentrations.[90] However, the authors have found that monoglyceride ethers caused unacceptably high hemolysis.

Photochemical Approaches

Most studies on the inactivation of viruses in red cells have utilized photochemicals such as merocyanine 540 and its derivatives,[91,92] benzophorphyrin derivative,[93-95] aluminum phthalocyanine and related compounds[96,97] and MB.[98,99] Evidence suggests that the hydrophobic dyes merocyanine 540 and benzophorphyrin derivative target virus envelopes for damage. Thus, these photochemicals are dependent on subtle differences between virus and red cell membranes to inactivate viruses without significantly altering the structure or function of red cells. Although they inactivate lipid-enveloped extracellular (and in some cases, intracellular) viruses, it has been difficult to maintain red cell properties, especially during subsequent storage.

Less information is available about the likely mechanism for virus inactivation using aluminum phthalocyanine and its derivatives. However, phototreatment of red cells with aluminum phthalocyanine tetrasulfonate under virucidal conditions resulted in some alteration of red cell surface properties and reduction of circulatory half-life.[100] More recent studies using new phthalocyanine derivatives show model virus and HIV-1 inactivation with maintenance of selected in-vitro red cell properties.[101]

Methylene blue, a phenothiazine dye that can intercalate between nucleic acid bases,[102] has also been studied as a virucidal photochemical. Upon exposure to visible light of wavelengths that hemoglobin does not appreciably absorb, a variety of nucleic acid lesions have been observed. More than 5 $\log_{10}$ of some model viruses can be inactivated in 0.30 (30%) hematocrit suspension with modest alterations of in-vitro red cell properties, and stability over 42 days of storage.[98] Although MB can inactivate extracellular HIV-1 under conditions that do not compromise in-vitro red cell properties, other results have been discouraging. Different viruses have very different sensitivities to MB photoinactivation.[103] The conditions required to inactivate MB-resistant viruses, such as VSV, result in large changes in red cell ion permeability and the binding of plasma proteins to the red cell surface[98]; nonlipid-enveloped viruses are not usually inactivated.[99] Furthermore, MB treatment does not inactivate HIV-1-infected H9 cells or Sindbis-infected Vero cells under conditions that readily inactivate extracellular virus.[99]

Other photoactive chemicals are currently under investigation. Hypericin, a drug being evaluated in clinical trials in AIDS patients, has recently been reported to inactivate $\geq 10^4$ TCID of HIV-1 in whole blood.[104] No red cell damage was observed during 21 days of post-treatment storage. There have been limited studies using a novel brominated psoralen derivative.[42] In this case, 6.6 $\log_{10}$ of $\phi 6$ was reported to be inactivated in a 0.60 (60%) hematocrit suspension with no significant alterations to selected in-vitro red cell properties. For UVA activated photochemicals, however, light absorption by hemoglobin strongly inhibits virucidal activity.[105]

Summary of Red Cell Processes

In spite of the large number of studies of both physical and chemical processes, there are no near-term approaches that appear to be suitable for "generic" inactivation of viruses and/or bacteria in red cells. High efficiency leukocyte reduction is expected to eliminate the transmission of CMV disease. With other approaches, significant virus inactivation is usually accompanied by red cell damage. Thus, a combination of processes may be needed. For example, leukocyte reduction by filtration could remove most white-cell-associated viruses, and to a lesser extent, those which may be associated with residual platelets. In addition, this step may potentially reduce bacterial bioburden. A subsequent photochemical step would inactivate "free" and membrane-associated viruses. The photochemical should be one that is activated at a wavelength largely unaffected by the presence of hemoglobin and plasma proteins.

Platelet Processing

For platelet products, a process to inactivate bacteria as well as viruses might permit extension of the shelf life of platelets, thus reducing a portion of the outdating that now occurs.

Miscellaneous Approaches

While leukocyte reduction may be an important step in platelet virus depletion and inactivation methods, filtration alone has not been shown to be satisfactory. For bacteria associated with platelet products, it is unlikely that leukocyte reduction will have much of a positive effect.[106] Washing is not an acceptable method due to platelet activation, high losses and the strong association with HIV-1.[64,65] When UVB alone was used to inactivate extracellular virus, platelet damage resulted.[107,108]

Photochemical Approaches

Several photochemical-based approaches have been studied. Those that used merocyanine 540 or aluminum phthalocyanine sulfonate in combination with visible light resulted in significant inactivation of viruses, but with platelet damage.[97,108-110] Considerable effort has been directed at studying the use of psoralens in conjunction with UVA light. With psoralens, such as 8-methoxypsoralen (8-MOP) or aminomethyltrimethyl (AMT), which form psoralen-nucleic acid adducts, inactivation of 5-6 $\log_{10}$ of several model viruses and 4-6 $\log_{10}$ inactivation of extracellular HIV-1[111,112] has been demonstrated, sometimes under conditions that do not affect in-vitro platelet properties.[105,109,113,114] Intracellular HIV-1 is also inactivated by both 8-MOP and AMT.[112,115] In addition, 8-MOP has been shown to inactivate duck hepatitis B, a model for HBV.[116-118] Free radical quenchers were able to reduce platelet damage resulting from use of AMT under conditions that inactivated $\geq 6 \log_{10}$ cell-free virus and $\geq 5 \log_{10}$ cell-associated virus in 100% plasma.[119,120] These studies used high UVA doses to compensate for reduced virus inactivation due to AMT binding to serum albumin.[121] At such doses in the presence or absence of AMT, irreversible platelet damage can occur.

Preservation of hemostatic effectiveness of AMT-UVA-treated human platelets, using virucidal conditions, has been demonstrated in a rabbit model.[103] However, the light exposure to achieve this must be carefully controlled. In addition, AMT (in the dark) produces frame-shift mutations in bacteria; the frequency of these mutations is greatly enhanced by an S9 metabolic activation system used to simulate drug metabolism in the liver.[121] Thus, the residual photochemical and its breakdown products may require removal.

Efforts to synthesize less mutagenic psoralens that retain virucidal activity without harming the in-vitro properties of platelets have recently been reported. Limited data regarding use of a brominated psoralen derivative indicate $\geq 6 \log_{10}$ inactivation of a bacteriophage with no reported genotoxicity.[42,122] Data have also been presented on a series of novel primary aminopsoralens.[123] In platelet concentrates, 5-6 $\log_{10}$/mL of cell-free HIV-1 was inactivated by several of them. Little or no frame-shift or base substitution mutagenicity was observed with these compounds or their photoproducts. After 5 days of storage, normal aggregation was exhibited, although platelet concentrate pH was lower than controls. One of them, S-59, inactivated $>10^6$/mL duck hepatitis B and $>10^5$/mL HCV based on a PCR assay.[124] It also inactivated $>10^5$/mL cell-associated HIV-1. Genotoxicity was examined in both bacterial and mammalian systems and found to be acceptable. S-59 was weakly mutagenic in one Ames test strain (TA1537) without metabolic activation; this result disappeared after light activation.

As pointed out previously, bacterial sepsis is also associated with platelet products. Studies have been conducted that demonstrated that 8-MOP can inactivate many bacterial species spiked into platelet concentrates while preserving platelet function during 5 days of storage.[125-128] Greater than 10^5 CFU/mL of five gram-positive, and two of seven gram-negative, organisms were inactivated. Four of the more resistant bacteria were inactivated >10^5 CFU/mL when the plasma protein level was reduced to 15% (through use of a new synthetic storage medium) and the 8-MOP concentration increased. *Pseudomonas aeruginosa*, the most resistant organism, was inactivated by $10^{4.6}$ CFU/mL. In conjunction with these studies, the pharmacokinetics of intravenous 8-MOP were studied.[129] Five or 10 mg were infused over 60 minutes to normal subjects; peak plasma levels were less than those used for psoralen-UVA therapy. No drug was measurable after 2 hours and no side effects or adverse reactions were observed.

Summary of Platelet Processes

Although many approaches have been investigated, no process is yet available for the inactivation of viruses and/or bacteria in platelets. As with red cells, a photochemical process, possibly coupled with leukocyte reduction filtration, is likely to be successful. There is a reasonable chance that a novel photochemical will be developed that will permit concurrent virus and bacterial inactivation. Table 7-5 reviews some of the process considerations for known photochemicals and indicates data still needed.

Table 7-5. Virus Inactivation of Platelets

	Photochemical Type	
Consideration	**Visible Light MC540, AlPc**	**UVA Light 8-MOP, AMT, PSR-Br, S-59**
Extracellular virus	Yes	Yes
Intracellular virus	No	Probably
Virus limitation	Lipid only	?
Bacteria	No	Possibly
Chimpanzee studies	No	8-MOP
Platelet damage	Depends on photochemical	
Plasma interferes	Depends on photochemical	
Genotoxicity	Depends on photochemical	

Issues To Consider

Over the years we have learned that the use of model viruses for evaluating proposed depletion and/or inactivation approaches may not be suitable. Model virus interactions with red cells, leukocytes, platelets and plasma may differ significantly from those of the viruses of concern. These differences may affect how efficiently a specific approach will work. As a result, many investigators have focused on HIV-1 as their primary target virus. However, there may also be differences among laboratory strains of HIV-1, HIV-1 from newly seroconverted individuals and HIV-1 from antigen-positive, antibody-negative blood donors. The latter case, which represents donors in the "window period," is most relevant to the blood banking community. Studies of removal and inactivation processes should include a broad range of transfusion-transmitted pathogens, in addition to HIV-1.

Another issue is how to demonstrate the safety and efficacy of a removal or inactivation process. Because disease transmission as a result of known blood-borne pathogens is infrequent, controlled clinical trials to demonstrate process effectiveness would be virtually impossible to carry out in the US. Instead, we will most likely need to rely on in-vitro virus and bacteria studies as well as in-vivo chimpanzee studies. A series of in-vitro and in-vivo platelet and red cell studies of treated components should be acceptable to demonstrate safety. In-vitro genotoxicity studies and pharmacokinetic studies will also be required, but it may be hard to demonstrate with a high degree of certainty that the risk of a process is significantly lower than its benefit.

Provided that sufficient data are available, the medical and scientific community may be able to decide on the relative safety and efficacy of virus and bacteria removal or inactivation processes. In addition, in the current atmosphere of concern for health-care costs, the issue of cost-effectiveness of any process should be discussed.

An analysis has been conducted to estimate the cost of blood-borne infectious diseases per unit of red cells transfused.[130] The medical costs and lost earnings potential due to morbidity and mortality associated with HIV-1, HBV, HCV, CMV, syphilis, Epstein-Barr virus, *Yersinia*, malaria, *Babesia* and Chagas' disease were considered. Other inputs included the incidence of infection, the occurrence of subsequent clinical disease and the age and sex of the patients. All costs were presented in 1990 dollars. Using a 5% discount rate to calculate net present value, the results indicated

Table 7-6. Process Acceptability Factors

Consideration	Highly Acceptable	Less Acceptable
Virus type	Generic	Selected
Inactivation/reduction	$\geq 6\ \log_{10}$	$<6\ \log_{10}$
Bacteria type	Generic	Selected
Inactivation/reduction	$\geq 6\ \log_{10}$	$<6\ \log_{10}$
Component yield	Unaffected	Reduced
Component survival	Unaffected	Reduced
Shelf life	Unchanged	Reduced
Process type	One (for all components)	Several
Single vs pooled	Single unit	Pooled
Complexity	Easy	Complex
Throughput	High	Moderate
Disposables	Current	New or additional
Toxicity	None	Toxicity less than disease risk
Cost	Low	High
Process location	Blood center	Specialized facility
Suitability	All patients	Screening required
Hospital	No change	Change required

that the medical, morbidity and mortality cost to society was $18.78 per unit: $0.63 for HIV/AIDS; $0.05 for HBV; $17.34 for HCV; and $0.76 for all other infections combined. These figures are currently being recalculated and the cost may be even lower, depending on HCV test improvements and on the mortality associated with HCV. Additional studies of this type need to be undertaken.

It is unlikely that any one process will be perfect. Therefore, the ultimate acceptability of a virus and/or bacteria depletion or inactivation process will likely depend on many interrelated factors and trade-offs will need to be made. Some examples of these are shown in Table 7-6. Undoubtedly, different people will have diverging views of the relative importance of these factors.

What Have We Learned?

Extensive virus removal and inactivation studies have been conducted in plasma, red cells and platelets by many groups. Much has been learned about what will and will not be suitable for use with blood components. For plasma, although some issues remain, three methods have been implemented outside the US: pasteurization, solvent/detergent and methylene blue. For red cells and possibly platelets, leukocyte reduction should be safe and effective for the elimination of CMV disease and may prove to be beneficial for the reduction of some bacteria, at least in red cells. Several novel photochemicals are being developed for virus inactivation in platelets. They may also have the potential to inactivate bacteria. However, since these photochemicals are new drugs, licensing studies will take several years. Although several photochemicals may have limited value in inactivating some viruses in red cells, no generic methods have been identified that inactivate all species of viruses without damaging red cells. However, despite the difficulty in identifying processes that inactivate a broad range of extracellular and intracellular pathogens without harming the cells being preserved or the patients who receive the blood components, significant knowledge has been accumulated. It is realistic to anticipate that virus and bacteria removal and inactivation processes will continue to be developed for future implementation.

References

1. Dodd RY. The risk of transfusion-transmitted infection. N Engl J Med 1992;327:419-20.
2. Dodd RY. Will blood products be free of infectious agents? In: Nance SJ, ed. Transfusion medicine in the 1990's. Arlington, VA: American Association of Blood Banks, 1990:223-51.
3. Esteban JI, Camps J, Genesca J, Alter HJ. Hepatitis C and B: New developments. In: Nance SJ, ed. Blood safety: Current challenges. Bethesda, MD: American Association of Blood Banks, 1992:45-96.
4. Alter HJ. You'll wonder where the yellow went: A 15-year retrospective of posttransfusion hepatitis. In: Moore SB, ed. Transfusion-transmitted viral diseases. Arlington, VA: American Association of Blood Banks, 1987:53-86.
5. Blajchman MA, Ali AM. Bacteria in the blood supply: An overlooked issue in transfusion medicine. In: Nance SJ, ed. Blood safety: Current challenges. Bethesda, MD: American Association of Blood Banks, 1992:213-28.
6. Wagner SJ, Friedman LI, Dodd RY. Transfusion associated bacterial sepsis. Clin Microbiol Rev 1994;7:290-302.
7. Regulatory Affairs column. Fatality statistics. AABB News Briefs 1992;14(8):14.

8. Morrow JF, Braine HG, Kickler TS, et al. Septic reactions to platelet transfusions. A persistent problem. JAMA 1991;266: 555-8.
9. Appleman MD, Shulman IA, Saxena S, Kirchhoff LV. Use of a questionnaire to identify potential blood donors at risk for infection with *Trypanosoma cruzi*. Transfusion 1993;33:61-4.
10. Fratantoni JC, Prodouz KN, Horowitz MS. Viral inactivation of blood products. Transfusion 1990;30:480-1.
11. Wagner SJ, Friedman LI, Dodd RY. Approaches to the reduction of viral infectivity in cellular blood components and single donor plasma. Transfus Med Rev 1991;5:18-32.
12. Arnow PM, Weiss LM, Weil D, Rosen NR. *Escherichia coli* sepsis from contaminated platelet transfusion. Arch Intern Med 1986;146:321-4.
13. Buchholz DH, Young VM, Friedman NR, et al. Detection and quantitation of bacteria in platelet products stored at ambient temperature. Transfusion 1973;13:268-75.
14. Buchholz DH, Young VM, Friedman NR, et al. Bacterial proliferation in platelet products stored at room temperature. Transfusion-induced Enterobacter sepsis. N Engl J Med 1971; 285:429-33.
15. Chapman RG. The use of fresh-frozen plasma (letter). JAMA 1986;255:905.
16. Oberman HA. Inappropriate use of fresh-frozen plasma (editorial). JAMA 1985;253:556-7.
17. NIH consensus conference. Fresh-frozen plasma. Indications and risks. JAMA 1985;253:551-3.
18. Tsao IF, Shipman C, Wang H. The removal of adventitious viruses and virus-infected cells using cellular adsorbent: A feasibility study. Biotechnol Appl Biochem 1989;6:1330-3.
19. Hamamoto Y, Harada S, Kobayashi S, et al. A novel method for removal of human immunodeficiency virus: Filtration with porous polymeric membranes. Vox Sang 1989;56:230-6.
20. Suomela H. Inactivation of viruses in blood and plasma products. Transfus Med Rev 1993;7:42-57.
21. Smith KJ, Friedman KD, Sekiguchi S, et al. Recovery of coagulation factors after 40 nm microporous membrane filtration of plasma or cryoprecipitate (abstract). Blood 1991; 78(10)(Suppl 1):352a.
22. Kitchen AD, Mann GF, Harrison JF. Effect of gamma irradiation on the human immunodeficiency virus and human coagulation proteins. Vox Sang 1989;56:223-9.

23. Hiemstra H, Tersmette M, Vos AHV, et al. Inactivation of human immunodeficiency virus by gamma radiation and its effect on plasma and coagulation factors. Transfusion 1991; 31:32-9.
24. Highsmith FA, Caple M, Walthall B, et al. Viral inactivation of vesicular stomatitis virus in normal human serum by cross-linked polyvinylpyrrolidone. J Infect Dis 1993;167:1027-33.
25. Highsmith FA, Xue H, Caple M, et al. Inactivation of lipid- and non-lipid-enveloped model viruses in normal human plasma by crosslinked starch-iodine. Transfusion 1994;34:322-7. [See also correction 1994;34:557.]
26. Burnouf-Radosevich M, Burnouf T, Huart JJ. A pasteurized therapeutic plasma. Infusionsther Transfusionsmed 1992;19: 91-4.
27. Burnouf-Radosevich M, Burnouf T, Huart JJ. Pasteurisation industrielle du plasma et critères de qualité. Rev Fr Transfus Hemobiol 1993;36:93-102.
28. Brackman HH, Egli H. Acute hepatitis B infection after treatment with heat inactivated factor VIII concentrate. Lancet 1988;2:967.
29. Charm SE, Landau S, Williams B, et al. High-temperature short-time heat inactivation of HIV and other viruses in human blood plasma. Vox Sang 1992;62:12-20.
30. Horowitz B, Bonomo R, Prince AM, Chin SN, et al. Solvent/detergent-treated plasma: A virus-inactivated substitute for fresh frozen plasma. Blood 1992;79:826-31.
31. Kaplan JS, Reid ME, Read EJ. Current status of solvent/detergent-treated plasma. AABB News Briefs 1993:12-13.
32. Mannucci PM. Outbreak of hepatitis A among Italian patients with hemophilia. Lancet 1992;339:819.
33. Azzi A, Ciappi S, Zakvrewska K, et al. Human parvovirus B19 infection in hemophiliacs first infused with two high-purity, virally attenuated factor VIII concentrates. Am J Hematol 1992;39:228-30.
34. Mannucci PM, Gdovin S, Gringeri A, et al. Transmission of hepatitis A to patients with hemophilia by factor VIII concentrates treated with organic solvent and detergent to inactivate viruses. The Italian collaborative group. Ann Intern Med 1994;120:1-7.
35. Mohr H, Pohl U, Lambrecht B, Wieding JU, et al. Durch methylenblau/licht-behandlung virusinaktiviertes humanplasma: Herstellung und bisherige klinische erfahrungen. Infusionsther Transfusionsmed 1993;20(Suppl 2):19-24.

36. Tissot J-D, Hochstrasser DF, Schneider B. No evidence for protein modifications in fresh frozen plasma after photochemical treatment: An analysis by high-resolution two-dimensional electrophoresis. Br J Haematol 1994;86:143-6.
37. Lambrecht B, Mohr H, Knuver-Hopf J, Schmitt H. Photoinactivation of viruses in human fresh plasma by phenothiazine dyes in combination with visible light. Vox Sang 1991;60:207-13.
38. Wieding JU, Vehmeyer K, Dittman J. Contamination of fresh-frozen plasma with viable white cells and proliferative stem cells. Transfusion 1994;34:185-6.
39. Wieding JU, Hellstern P, Köhler M. Inactivation of viruses in fresh-frozen plasma. Ann Hematol 1993;67:259-66.
40. Stephan W. Inactivation of hepatitis and HIV in plasma and plasma derivatives by treatment with beta-propiolactone/UV irradiation. Curr Stud Hematol Blood Transfus 1989;56:122-7.
41. Margolis-Nunno H, Chin SN, Geacintov N, et al. Virus sterilization of plasma and platelet concentrates: Enhancement of the specificity of psoralen photoinactivation (abstract). Blood 1991;78(10)(Suppl 1):352a.
42. Yerram N, Platz MS, Forster P, et al. Selective viral inactivation in RBC, platelets and plasma using a novel psoralen derivative plus ultraviolet A (UVA) light (abstract). Transfusion 1993;33(Suppl):50S.
43. Wells KH, Latino J, Gavalchin J, Poiesz BJ. Inactivation of human immunodeficiency virus type 1 by ozone in vitro. Blood 1991;78:1882-90.
44. Isaacs CE, Schneidman K, Chen J, Kim KS. Inactivation of enveloped viruses including human immunodeficiency viruses (HIV-1, HIV-2) and herpes viruses in human blood and blood derivatives by lipids and the effect of serum chemistry measurements (abstract). In: Program and Abstracts of the Fifth National Forum on AIDS, Hepatitis, and other Blood-Borne Diseases. Princeton, NJ: Symedco, 1992:75.
45. Eisenfeld L, Silver H, McLaughlin J, et al. Prevention of transfusion-associated cytomegalovirus infection in neonatal patients by the removal of white cells from blood. Transfusion 1992;32:205-9.
46. Sayers MH, Anderson KC, Goodnough LT, et al. Reducing the risk for transfusion-transmitted cytomegalovirus infection. Ann Intern Med 1992;116:55-62.

47. Boland GJ, deGast GC, Hene RJ, et al. Early detection of active cytomegalovirus (CMV) infection after heart and kidney transplantation by testing for immediate early antigenemia and influence of cellular immunity on the occurrence of CMV infection. J Clin Microbiol 1990;28:2069-75.
48. de Graan-Hentzen YCE, Gratama JW, Mudde GC, et al. Prevention of primary cytomegalovirus infection in patients with hematologic malignancies by intensive white cell depletion of blood products. Transfusion 1989;29:757-60.
49. Gilbert GL, Hayes K, Hudson IL, James J. Prevention of transfusion-acquired cytomegalovirus infection in infants by blood filtration to remove leucocytes. Lancet 1989;1:1228-31.
50. DeWitte T, Schattenberg A, Van Der Meer JWW, et al. Prevention of primary cytomegalovirus infection after allogeneic bone marrow transplantation by using leukocyte-poor random blood products from cytomegalovirus-unscreened blood-bank donors. Transplantation 1990;50:964-8.
51. Skolnick AA. Blood banking not what it used to be, experts say. JAMA 1994;271:809-11.
52. Al EJM, Visser SCE, Broersen SM, et al. Reduction of HTLV-I-infected cells in blood by leukocyte filtration. Ann Hematol 1993;67:295-300.
53. Rawal B, Yen TSB, Vyas GN, Busch MP. Leukocyte filtration removes infectious particulate debris but not free virus derived from experimentally lysed HIV-infected cells. Vox Sang 1991;60:214-18.
54. Bruisten SM, Tersmette M, Wester MR, et al. Efficiency of white cell filtration and a freeze-thaw procedure for removal of HIV-infected cells from blood. Transfusion 1990;30:833-7.
55. Rawal BD, Busch MP, Endow R, et al. Reduction of human immunodeficiency virus-infected cells from donor blood by leukocyte filtration. Transfusion 1989;29:460-2.
56. Nusbacher J. *Yersinia enterocolitica* and white cell filtration. Transfusion 1992;32:597-600.
57. Kim DM, Brecher ME, Bland LA, et al. Prestorage removal of *Yersinia enterocolitica* from red cells with white-cell-reduction filters. Transfusion 1992;32:658-62.
58. Wenz B, Burns ER, Freundlich LF. Prevention of growth of *Yersinia enterocolitica* in blood by polyester fiber filtration. Transfusion 1992;32:663-6.
59. Buchholz DH, AuBuchon JP, Snyder EL, et al. Removal of *Yersinia enterocolitica* from AS-1 red cells. Transfusion 1992; 32:667-72.

60. AuBuchon JP, Pickard C. White cell reduction and bacterial proliferation. Transfusion 1993;33:533-4.
61. Terada H, Baldini M, Ebbe S, Madoff MA. Interaction of influenza virus with blood platelets. Blood 1966;28:213-28.
62. Bik T, Sarov I, Livne A. Interaction between vaccinia virus and human blood platelets. Blood 1982;59:482-7.
63. Forghani B, Schmidt NJ. Association of herpes simplex virus with platelets of experimentally infected mice. Arch Virol 1983;76:269-74.
64. Lee T-H, Stromberg RR, Henrard D, Busch MP. Effect of platelet-associated virus on assays of HIV-1 in plasma. Science 1993;262:1585.
65. Lee T-H, Stromberg RR, Henrard DR, Busch MP. Detection of high levels of platelet-associated HIV-1: Implication for quantitation of plasma viremia (abstract). Transfusion 1993;33 (Suppl):37S.
66. Zucker-Franklin D, Seremetis S, Zheng ZY. Internalization of human immunodeficiency virus type I and other retroviruses by megakaryocytes and platelets. Blood 1990;75:1920-3.
67. Meryman HT. Red cell freezing: A major factor in the future of blood banking. In: Dawson RB, Barnes A Jr, eds. Clinical and practical aspects of the use of frozen blood. Washington, DC: American Association of Blood Banks, 1977:1-21.
68. Tullis JL, Hinman J, Sproul MT, Nickerson RJ. Incidence of posttransfusion hepatitis in previously frozen blood. JAMA 1970;214:719-23.
69. Haugen RK. Hepatitis after the transfusion of frozen red cells and washed red cells. N Engl J Med 1979;301:393-5.
70. Alter HJ, Tabor E, Meryman HT, et al. Transmission of hepatitis B virus infection by transfusion of frozen-deglycerolized red blood cells. N Engl J Med 1978;298:637-42.
71. Stromberg RR, Cole ML, Sadoff BJ, et al. Viral depletion in red cells by cell washing (abstract). In: Book of Abstracts from the ISBT/AABB Joint Congress. Arlington, VA: American Association of Blood Banks, 1990:196.
72. Stromberg RR, Hanson CV, Sawyer L, et al. Viral association with red cells (abstract). Blood 1992;80(10)(Suppl 1):220a.
73. Sadoff BJ, Stromberg RR, Miller K, et al. Experimental 6 log white-cell-reduction filters for red cells. Transfusion 1992;32: 129-33.
74. Sadoff BJ, Dooley DC, Kapoor V, et al. Methods for measuring a 6 log white cell depletion in red cells. Transfusion 1991;31: 150-5.

75. Friedman LI, Sadoff BJ, Stromberg RR. White cell counting in red cells and platelets: How few can we count? (editorial). Transfusion 1990;30:387-9.
76. McDougal JS, Martin LS, Cort SP, et al. Thermal inactivation of the acquired immunodeficiency syndrome virus, human T lymphotropic virus-III/lymphadenopathy-associated virus, with special reference to antihemophilic factor. J Clin Invest 1985;76:875-7.
77. Stromberg RR, Kuypers FA, Sawyer L, et al. Loss of red blood cell viability associated with limited thermal inactivation of extracellular HIV-1. Vox Sang 1994 (in press).
78. Donegan E, Lenes BA, Tomasulo PA, Mosely JW. Transmission of HIV-1 by component type and duration of shelf storage before transmission. Transfusion 1990;30:851-2.
79. Geyer SJ, Blay R, Epstein JS. Rate of HIV-1 inactivation in packed red cells stored at 1-6 C in CPDA and ADSOL (abstract). Transfusion 1991;31(Suppl):47S.
80. Wagner KF, Mayers DL, Linette GP. Effect of ozone on HIV in experimentally infected human blood (abstract). CDC AIDS Weekly 1989;Jan 30:17.
81. Freeberg JK, Carpendale MT. Ozone inactivates extracellular human immunodeficiency virus at non-cytotoxic concentrations. OzoNachrichten 1988;7:14-24.
82. Burleson GR, Murray TM, Pollard M. Inactivation of viruses and bacteria by ozone, with and without sonication. Appl Environ Microbiol 1974;29:340-4.
83. Sproul OJ, Pfister RM, Kim CK. The mechanism of ozone inactivation of water-borne viruses. Water Sci Tech 1982;14: 303-14.
84. Vaughn JM, Chen YS, Lindburg K, Morales D. Inactivation of human and simian rotaviruses by ozone. Appl Environ Microbiol 1987;53:2218-21.
85. Wagner SJ, Wagner KF, Friedman LI, Benade LE. Virucidal levels of ozone-induced hemolysis and hemoglobin degradation. Transfusion 1991;31:748-51.
86. Rubinstein AI, Rubinstein DB. Sodium chlorite and lactic acid RBC sterilizing solution also significantly inactivates intracellular HIV-1 (abstract). In: Book of Abstracts from the ISBT/AABB Joint Congress. Arlington, VA: American Association of Blood Banks, 1990:93.
87. Rubinstein AI, Rubinstein DB. Sodium chlorite and lactic acid treated units of RBCs to inactivate HIV-1 to produce sterile units of red cells (abstract). In: Book of Abstracts from the

ISBT/AABB Joint Congress. Arlington, VA: American Association of Blood Banks, 1990:170.

88. Chapman JR, Sun C-S, Stromberg RR, Kross RD, et al. Red cell damage under conditions of HIV inactivation by chlorine dioxide/chlorite (abstract). Blood 1992;80(10)(Suppl 1):482a.
89. Martin L, McDougal JS, Louderback AL. Disinfection and inactivation of the human T lymphotropic virus type III/ lymphadenopathy-associated virus. J Infect Dis 1985;152: 400-3.
90. Thormar H, Isaacs CE, Brown HR, et al. Inactivation of enveloped viruses and killing of cells by fatty acids and monoglycerides. Antimicrob Agents Chemother 1987;31:27-31.
91. Sieber F, O'Brien JM, Krueger GJ, et al. Antiviral activity of merocyanine 540. Photochem Photobiol 1987;46:707-11.
92. O'Brien JM, Montgomery RR, Burns WH, et al. Evaluation of merocyanine 540-sensitized photoirradiation as a means to inactivate enveloped viruses in blood products. J Lab Clin Med 1990;116:439-47.
93. Neyndorff HC, Bartel DL, Tufaro F, Levy JG. Development of a model to demonstrate photosensitizer-mediated viral inactivation in blood. Transfusion 1990;30:485-90.
94. North J, Neyndorff HC, King D, Levy JG. Viral inactivation in blood and red cell concentrates with benzoporphyrin derivative. Blood Cells 1992;18:129-40.
95. Stromberg RR, Cole M, Friedman LI, et al. Viral inactivation of red cells with a benzoporphyrin derivative (abstract). Blood 1991;78(10)(Suppl 1):353a.
96. Horowitz B, Williams B, Rywkin S, et al. Inactivation of viruses in blood with aluminum phthalocyanine derivatives. Transfusion 1991;31:102-8.
97. Horowitz B, Rywkin S, Margolis-Nunno H, et al. Inactivation of viruses in red cell and platelet concentrates with aluminum phthalocyanine (AIPc) sulfonates. Blood Cells 1992;18:141-50.
98. Wagner SJ, Storry JR, Mallory DA, et al. Red cell membrane alterations associated with virucidal methylene blue phototreatment. Transfusion 1993;33:30-6.
99. Wagner SJ, Robinette D, Storry J, et al. Differential sensitivities of viruses in red cell suspensions to methylene blue photosensitization. Transfusion 1994;34:521-6.
100. Rywkin S, Geacintov N, Lenny L, et al. Virus inactivation and red cell cytotoxicity: The role of oxygen-derived reactants

photogenerated with phthalocyanine derivatives (abstract). Photochem Photobiol 1992;55:115S-16S.
101. Rywkin S, Ben-Hur E, Pascual D, et al. New photosensitizers to inactivate viruses in red blood cells (abstract). Blood 1993; 82(10)(Suppl 1):205a.
102. Hagmar P, Pierrou S, Nielsen P, et al. Ionic strength dependence of the binding of methylene blue to chromatin and calf thymus DNA. J Biomol Struct Dyn 1992;9:667-79.
103. Wagner SJ, Bardossy L, Moroff G, et al. Assessment of the hemostatic effectiveness of human platelets treated with aminomethyltrimethyl psoralen and UVA light using a rabbit ear bleeding time technique. Blood 1993;82:3489-92.
104. Meruelo D, Prince AM, Pascual D, et al. The potential use of hypericin as an inactivator of retroviruses and other viruses in blood products (abstract). Blood 1993;82(10)(Suppl 1): 205a.
105. Moroff G, Wagner S, Benade LE, Dodd RY. Factors influencing virus inactivation and retention of platelet properties following treatment with aminomethyltrimethylpsoralen and ultraviolet A light. Blood Cells 1992;18:43-56.
106. Wenz B, Ciavarella D, Freundlich L. Effect of prestorage white cell reduction on bacterial growth in platelet concentrates. Transfusion 1993;33:520-3.
107. Prodouz KN, Fratantoni JC, Boone EJ, Bonner RF. Use of laser-UV for inactivation of virus in blood products. Blood 1987;70:589-92.
108. Prodouz KN, Lytle CD, Bonner RF, Fratantoni JC. Effects of two viral inactivation methods on platelets: Laser-UV radiation and merocyanine 540-mediated photoinactivation. Blood Cells 1992;18:101-16.
109. Dodd RY, Moroff G, Wagner S, et al. Inactivation of viruses in platelet suspensions that retain their in vitro characteristics: Comparison of psoralen-ultraviolet A and merocyanine 540-visible light methods. Transfusion 1991;31:483-90.
110. Prodouz KN, Lytle CD, Keville AP, et al. Inhibition by albumin of merocyanine 540-mediated photosensitization of platelets and viruses. Transfusion 1991;31:415-22.
111. Watson AJ, Klaniecki J, Hanson CV. Psoralen/UV inactivation of HIV-1-infected cells for use in cytologic and immunologic procedures. AIDS Res Hum Retroviruses 1990;6:503-11.
112. Benade LE, Shumaker J, Xu Y, Dodd RY. Inactivation of free and cell-associated HIV in platelet suspensions by amino-

methyltrimethylpsoralen (AMT) and ultraviolet light (abstract). Transfusion 1992;32(Suppl):33S.

113. Lin L, Wiesehahn GP, Morel PA, Corash L. Use of 8-methoxypsoralen and long-wavelength ultraviolet radiation for decontamination of platelet concentrates. Blood 1989;74:517-25.
114. Corash L, Lin L, Wiesehahn G. Use of 8-methoxypsoralen and long wavelength ultraviolet radiation for decontamination of platelet concentrates. Blood 1992;18:57-74.
115. Lin L, Londe H, Hanson CV, et al. Photochemical inactivation of cell-associated human immunodeficiency virus in platelet concentrates. Blood 1993;82:292-7.
116. Eble BE, Chan A, Corash L. A duck hepatitis B virus (DHBV) model to correlate in vitro and in vivo inactivation of virus in humans (abstract). Blood 1992;80(10)(Suppl 1):261a.
117. Eble BE, Villena F, Chen C, Corash L. Photochemical inactivation of duck hepatitis B virus (DHBV) in human platelet concentrates: Correlation of in vitro and in vivo effects (abstract). Blood 1993;82(10)(Suppl 1):205a.
118. Lin L, Cook D, Londe H, et al. Use of variable length amplicons to determine the efficiency of viral inactivation by psoralen mediated photochemistry (abstract). Blood 1993;82(10)(Suppl 1):401a.
119. Margolis-Nunno H, Bartley A, Ben-Hur E, et al. Quencher mediated protection of platelet integrity during psoralen photoinactivation of viruses in platelet concentrates (abstract). Blood 1993;82(10)(Suppl 1):401a.
120. Margolis-Nunno H, Williams B, Rywkin S, et al. Virus sterilization in platelet concentrates with psoralen and ultraviolet A light in the presence of quenchers. Transfusion 1992;32:541-7.
121. Wagner SJ, White R, Wolf L, et al. Determination of residual 4′-aminomethyl-4,5′,8-trimethylpsoralen and mutagenicity testing following psoralen plus UVA treatment of platelet suspensions. Photochem Photobiol 1993;57:819-24.
122. Yerram N, Forster P, Goodrich T, et al. Comparison of virucidal properties of brominated psoralen with 8-methoxypsoralen (8-MOP) and aminomethyl trimethyl psoralen (AMT) in platelet concentrates (abstract). Blood 1993;82(10) (Suppl 1):402a.
123. Wollowitz S, Fang Y, Jiatao P, et al. Novel psoralens with enhanced UVA dependent inactivation of human immunodeficiency virus and reduced mutagenicity in the absence of UVA light (abstract). Blood 1993;82(10)(Suppl 1):402a.

124. Wollowitz S, Cook D, Londe H. Inactivation of pathogenic viruses in human platelet concentrates with a novel psoralen (abstract). In: Book of Abstracts from the 23rd Congress of the International Society of Blood Transfusion. Paris: ISBT, 1994:162.
125. Lin L, Londe H, Janda M, et al. Photochemical inactivation of pathogenic bacteria in platelet concentrates (abstract). Blood 1993;82(10)(Suppl 1):205a.
126. Lin L, Londe H, Janda M. Photochemical inactivation of pathogenic bacteria in human platelet concentrates. Blood 1994 (in press).
127. Lin L, Rheinschmidt M, Metchette K. Storage of platelets in synthetic media. Preservation of in vitro platelet function following photochemical decontamination (abstract). In: Book of Abstracts from the 23rd Congress of the International Society of Blood Transfusion. Paris: ISBT, 1994:161.
128. Londe H, Alfonso R, Janda M. Photochemical inactivation of bacteria in platelet concentrates (abstract). In: Book of Abstracts from the 23rd Congress of the International Society of Blood Transfusion. Paris: ISBT, 1994:21.
129. Billard V, Gambus PL, Barr J, et al. Pharmacokinetics of 8-methoxypsoralen (8-MOP) administered intravenously (IV) to humans (abstract). Blood 1993;82(10)(Suppl 1):402a.
130. Mendelson D, Mossburg P, Pinkert D, et al. The societal cost of transfusion-transmitted infections from allogeneic red cell (rbc) transfusions. Paper presented at 46th Annual Meeting of the American Association of Blood Banks 1993.

In: Nance ST, ed.
Blood Supply: Risks, Perceptions and Prospects for the Future
Bethesda, MD: American Association of Blood Banks, 1994

8

Impact of Legal and Regulatory Changes During the Past Decade

Kathleen Sazama, MD, JD

TRANSFUSION MEDICINE AND BLOOD collection are practiced differently in 1994 from the way they were practiced in 1984. Changes have arisen from legal decisions, new regulatory requirements and actions, legislative initiatives and actions undertaken voluntarily by blood banking and transfusion medicine professionals when opportunities to improve were identified. Legal decisions have refocused attention on patient rights, donor expectations, establishing and following standard procedures with appropriate documentation, performance and decision-making. United States governmental agencies with renewed or new interest in blood banking/transfusion medicine issues include the Food and Drug Administration (FDA), the Occupational Safety and Health Administration (OSHA), the Health Care Financing Administration (HCFA), the Environmental Protection Agency (EPA), the Department of Transportation (DOT), the Department of Justice (DOJ), the Department of Health and Human Services (DHHS) [including the Office of the Inspector General (OIG)], the Federal Trade Commission (FTC) and the Centers for Disease Control and Prevention (CDC). Each of these agencies has published new regulations and/or guidelines and has focused inspectional activities to address concerns about safety in blood transfusion practices. Some individual states have taken similar action. Other nongovernmental entities such as the Postal Service, the Airline Pilots Association and private

Kathleen Sazama, MD, JD, Professor of Pathology and Laboratory Medicine and Director of Laboratory Medicine and Transfusion Services, Medical College of Pennsylvania, Philadelphia, Pennsylvania accrediting bodies have also voiced new concerns about activities derived from or integral to blood banking.

The blood banking community has responded by introducing new concepts of quality management and improvement and is engaged in reengineering and emphasizing compliance with good manufacturing practice. All of these actions can be tied, in one way or another, to the completely unanticipated advent of a new infection in the blood supply, the human immunodeficiency virus (HIV) causing acquired immunodeficiency syndrome (AIDS).

Historical Beginnings

Transfusion-transmitted diseases have provided impetus for change in legislation and increased regulation, beginning with hepatitis transmission in the 1960's and 1970's. At that time, the public response, evidenced by activity in individual state legislatures, was to provide protection to blood collection and transfusion facilities in the form of so-called "blood shield" statutes. In 1985, when the HIV test for blood screening was first available, all 50 states except three (New Jersey, Rhode Island and Vermont) provided such protection (Appendix 8-1) recognizing that blood for transfusion differs in significant ways from other goods offered for sale in commerce. These blood shield statutes were enacted when medical paternalism was prevalent and physicians were esteemed professionals in society whose recommendations were unquestioned. The foundation for the statutes was a seminal 1954 decision in *Perlmutter v. Beth David Hospital*,[1] which distinguished the provision of blood for transfusion from sale of commercial goods by finding that furnishing blood was a service provided as part of medical therapy for the patient's benefit. However, the federal government was concerned even earlier than 1954 that tighter oversight of blood banking was necessary (Table 8-1).

Beginning with the deaths from contaminated diphtheria antitoxin, which resulted in the origins of the Public Health Service (PHS) in 1902, continuing through the 1970's, the US government has taken numerous steps to control and improve the safety of biologic products, including blood and blood components and derivatives. When these measures were insufficient to prevent relabeling and distribution of blood for transfusion after its intended shelf life, blood was also specifically defined to be a "drug" within the meaning of the Food and Drug Law, which brought blood banking

Table 8-1. Selected Chronology of FDA Oversight of Blood Banking

Year	Act	Effect
1902	Virus-Toxin Act = Public Health Service Act	Licensed establishments and biologicals in interstate commerce if shipped for sale, barter or exchange Biologicals = virus, therapeutic serum, toxin, antitoxin or analogous product applicable to the prevention, treatment and cure of diseases and injury to man; required to be "safe, pure and potent" Biological Control Service of PHS (forerunner of FDA) established
1906	Food and Drug Act	Drugs regulated
1938	Food, Drug and Cosmetics Act	Drugs must be "safe," cosmetics added
1962	FD and C amended (Kefauver)	Drugs must also be "efficacious"
1970	PHS amended	Biologics also included: vaccines, blood, blood components or derivatives and allergenic products; added "responsible head," biennial inspections, label control, registration requirements
1972	HBsAg testing approved	Division of Biologics Standards (NIH) transferred to FDA Bureau of Biologics; blood defined as a drug
1976	FD and C amended to include devices	Blood banking reagents, equipment and instruments affected
1980	Regulatory relief requested by President Reagan	Significant regulatory revisions prepared/proposed

(continued)

Table 8-1. Selected Chronology of FDA Oversight of Blood Banking (continued)

Year	Act	Effect
1982		Drugs and Biologics combined into FDA National Center, renaming "BoB" Guidelines, memoranda, points to consider began to replace regulations for many changes
1985	Anti-HTLV-III testing approved	Recommendations for use distributed as FDA memoranda
1986		Drugs and Biologics split: CDER/ CBER
1987	Anti-HTLV-I testing approved	Recommendations for use distributed as 1988 FDA memoranda
1988	Clinical Laboratory Improvement Amendments	Testing done in blood centers brought under federal regulation
1988	Regulations requiring anti-HIV testing finalized	
1988	Annual inspections instituted	
1990	Anti-hepatitis C testing approved	Recommendations for use distributed as FDA memoranda
1991	Anti-hepatitis B core testing approved	Recommendations for use distributed as FDA memoranda
1993	Quality assurance guideline (draft)	Drug regulations used to create new requirements
1993	Computer validation guideline (draft)	Drug regulations used to create new requirements

under the more rigorous drug regulations, an event that has attained additional meaning for blood banking in recent years.

Legal Changes Following AIDS Transmission by Transfusion

Soon after the recognition of the new disease, AIDS, the first lawsuit alleging transfusion-transmission of AIDS was filed, naming all possible wrongdoers: the treating physician, the hospital, the blood bank and collection center. One can imagine how awful it was to be the patient who, expecting a blood transfusion to be healing therapy, instead found shortened life expectancy and significant morbidity when infected with HIV-1 through that transfusion. The patient's family and other loved ones would demand justice: someone should have to pay for their tragic loss.

While scientists and transfusion experts struggled to acquire, assimilate and analyze rapidly emerging information, the lay press found in the AIDS epidemic all the necessary elements for continued public interest: sex, sensationalism and death.[2] The number of publications and media features about AIDS soared in both the scientific and lay press, the latter not always distinguishing between HIV transmission via blood transfusion from its transmission via injections for illicit drug use or promiscuous sexual conduct. Once the public interest was stimulated, the inevitable and predictable response occurred. At least 500 lawsuits arising from transfusion-transmitted AIDS have been filed during the past 10 years. The issues raised in those lawsuits have covered all possible legal bases, focusing primarily on issues of negligence (Table 8-2).

It has been said that there are "three opportunities for a blood bank to be liable to a patient...when the blood bank selects the donor..., when the blood bank processes the blood, including the necessary testing..., [and] if...the blood bank comes into possession of information which the patient or the patient's physician...ought

Table 8-2. Elements of Negligence

1. A duty was owed to the injured person.
2. The responsible entity failed to fulfill the duty owed.
3. There was a breach of duty.
4. As a result of the breach of duty, the person was injured.
5. Compensation (damages) can be ascertained.

to have and this information is not appropriately provided."[3] Blood banks and transfusion services have been sued for all three reasons and more. Negligence has been alleged for failure to obtain informed consent, for improperly transfusing, for failing to provide surrogate testing, for lack of confrontational donor questioning, for not following proper procedures, for implementing testing too slowly, for failing to test and quarantine inventory, for improper testing, for failing to inform a recipient of receipt of a blood component that subsequently tested positive, for failure to provide directed donors, for misrepresenting the center's policy for directed donations, for improper procedures necessitating transfusion and many other bases. Many lawsuits have absolved blood banking, while others have given huge financial awards to the suing party. Of greatest concern is that, although many issues have been decided similarly in a number of states, some courts have ruled in complete opposition with each other on others, with continuing controversy over some fundamental questions (Table 8-3).

Scientists and physicians renewed their efforts to improve existing tests and evaluate and propose new ones, to assess appropriateness of use of blood components by participating in developing consensus practice guidelines[4] and to become better informed about all of the legal issues likely to surface.[5] With AIDS, proposals to change therapeutic interventions included recommendations for

Table 8-3. Litigation About Transfusion-Transmitted AIDS

Issues	Decisions
Blood shield statute protection	Generally upheld; AIDS seen to be same as hepatitis; some states amended their laws
Informed consent	Implied consent usually found; some states passed explicit legislation protecting individual right
Standard of care	States divided—professional vs reasonable person standard
Donor anonymity	Split decisions
Confrontational questioning	Upheld as not required
Surrogate testing	Generally held to be not required
Negligent performance	Where documents are flawed, courts find negligence

limiting donor exposure of each recipient, to prevent disease transmission as well as to avert alloimmunization. However, strong public concerns forced blood banking professionals to provide additional customized services, such as patient-directed and autologous blood (Table 8-4). These latter services have mushroomed due to the consumer's fear of lack of safety of the allogeneic volunteer blood supply.

An underappreciated negative effect of the increasing use of customized blood components is that errors also multiply[6,7] when there are unpredictable variations from a single standard operating procedure.[8] Improvement in systems to recognize and prevent such errors is the impetus for new voluntary and regulatory actions. In an effort to meet customer (patient) expectations, organizations are instituting changes that in themselves may result in less safe conditions. Any of these variations can provide the basis for future lawsuits for negligence.

Regulatory Requirements

The FDA's Response

Coincident with the lawsuits brought by individuals and their families, federal agencies were also taking a closer look at practices within the blood banking community, making frequent suggestions

Table 8-4. Impacts of Consumer Awareness

Request for New/Improved Service	Response	
	Legislative	**Regulatory**
Autologous blood components	State initiatives protecting individual rights	Specific federal guidelines
Patient-directed components	State initiatives protecting individual rights	Selected federal guidelines
Safer factor concentrates	—	Federal intervention with manufacturers
Fewer/no transfusions (informed consent)	State initiatives protecting individual rights	—

for change. Between 1984 and 1993, no fewer than 50 letters (to blood establishments) have been sent from the Director of the FDA's Center for Biologics Evaluation and Research (CBER) or its equivalent announcing new requirements for blood banking. Very few of these issuances have been undertaken consistent with the requirements of the Administrative Procedures Act,[9] which mandates public notice and an opportunity to respond before new requirements can be enforced. During the decade of the mid-1970's through mid-1980's, requirements were generally announced as a proposed regulatory change, with appropriate comment opportunities. Since 1984, nearly all FDA requirements have, of necessity, been distributed to blood centers and transfusion services via memoranda and guidelines. One notable exception is that of the 1988 regulatory requirement that all blood for transfusion be found negative by a test for anti-HIV.[10]

The scope of regulatory changes includes specific handling of autologous and directed donations, use of various testing methods, reentry of donors, donor screening, irradiation practices, detailed instructions for quality assurance and, most recently, clarification of requirements for computerization. Although the bases for most of these actions exist in regulations, the instructions for application have become increasingly detailed. Meanwhile, other federal agencies have joined the FDA in scrutinizing blood banking practices.

"Other" Federal Agencies

Although the principal federal regulatory agency that oversees blood banking and transfusion medicine is the FDA, others have an interest in and responsibilities for some aspects of this profession. These agencies include HCFA, which has responsibility for regulating laboratory testing under the Clinical Laboratory Improvement Act of 1988 (CLIA '88) regulations and for Medicare reimbursement; OSHA, with responsibility for worker safety; EPA, whose environmental concerns have included the blood banking arena since reports of empty blood bags and used syringes washing up on the New Jersey shoreline suggested unsafe practices in disposal of these materials; DOT, for safe packaging and limitations on volumes of infectious materials that can be transported; and DOJ and FTC for possible antitrust issues (Appendix 8-2). Intersecting responsibilities have the potential to create conflict between agencies to the detriment of the blood banking profession, particularly when numerous inspections by each of these agencies occur.

Table 8-5. Summary of CLIA '88 Requirements—Regulatory Scheme Based on Test Complexity Model

1. Certification
2. Personnel requirements
3. Proficiency testing
4. Standard operating procedures
5. Quality control/assurance
6. Inspections

HCFA

CLIA '88. Blood banking organizations that do not provide transfusion or other clinical laboratory services have considered themselves exempt from the requirements of CLIA '67. However, the 1988 amendments eliminate any such exemption, as documented by a rejection of a petition by the AABB, American Red Cross and Council of Community Blood Centers and others to clarify and continue that exemption.[11] The CLIA '88 requirements impose specific new detailed obligations on blood centers (Table 8-5). For reimbursement under Medicare, CLIA certification is required.

Medicare. The DHHS OIG is charged with eliminating fraud and abuse in reimbursements to various providers for Medicare patients. Enforcement under the CLIA '67 and '88 regulations has already resulted in a $111 million penalty against one clinical laboratory, the National Health Laboratory (NHL), which was held legally accountable for unnecessary tests ordered by physicians because NHL "induced" the excess orders.[12] Whether similar reasoning may be applied to orders for crossmatching when only screening is ordinarily required is open to question. Certainly, the availability of practice guidelines will assist in defending against charges of fraud and abuse.[13] However, ownership and patient referral patterns of blood centers may fall outside the "safe harbor" protection if analogies to clinical laboratories are applied or no specific exemption is granted.

OSHA

The OSHA, using its own[14] and PHS guidelines published by the CDC,[15] is sending more of its inspectional force into health-care settings to assess unnecessary and avoidable employee risks. Federal law[16] specifies that each employer is under a "general duty" to furnish a place of employment that is free from recognized hazards causing or likely to cause death or serious physical harm. While it is axiomatic that health-care workers are exposed to infectious agents as occupational hazards, with the AIDS epidemic the OSHA has been taking another look into health-care settings. Traditionally, health-care workers were assessed infrequently by the OSHA inspectors; instead, OSHA relied on educational information distributed for individual reading and application. However, several cases from the pre-AIDS era affirmed the duty of a hospital to use "reasonable care to protect against dangers of employment which might reasonably be expected to produce disease."[17] Today, failure to provide hepatitis B vaccine to persons in health care, including employees in blood centers and transfusion services, is actionable[18-20] because vaccination to prevent occupationally acquired hepatitis represents the standard of care. Cases have generally limited the employee's recovery to that allowed by workers' compensation; however, employers who know of and fail to correct hazardous conditions may be additionally liable for negligence.[21] For example, a recent Pennsylvania case involved HIV transmission to an employee during a 1986 plateletpheresis procedure in which donor blood spurted over the employee's ungloved hands and arms. The case raised important issues such as whether the employer's failure to require the wearing of gloves during every apheresis procedure was a hazardous condition that the employer failed to correct or whether negligence could be found.[22] Because of the employee's own failure to promptly and thoroughly wash off the blood, the jury did not penalize the employer, but did find unspecified negligence.

Some blood centers and even transfusing facilities that have received unfavorable OSHA inspection reports have provided valuable notice to the rest regarding the necessity for establishing and maintaining safe working conditions. Unsafe working conditions that can result in significant financial consequences when brought to the attention of OSHA are often identified by a disgruntled employee who may or may not have voiced objections about those conditions to the employer. The fines accompanying adverse findings are $10,000 per offense per day of noncorrection.

OSHA created specific new requirements, giving very short notice for implementation, to ensure that health-care workplaces, including blood centers, established policies and practices for safe employment. Safety concerns include not only those from blood-borne pathogens, but also chemical, radiation, fire and other preventable hazards. The 6th District US Court of Appeals recently strengthened

OSHA's interpretation of its Hazard Communication Standard by ruling that American Cyanamid Co. must include specific target-organ effects in the labeling of chemicals it manufactures.[23] Safety instruction in the use of those chemicals in the blood center and transfusion service should incorporate similar specific information.

EPA

New requirements for waste management are in place for numerous health-care providers, including blood centers and transfusion services. Generally, states also have specific requirements that must be met.

DOT

The DOT has imposed new restrictions on both packaging and labeling of blood-containing materials when shipped by commercial carriers such as trucks, trains, buses, planes, etc. In addition, the Airlines Pilots Association has voiced concerns over the safety of its members, passengers and crews when blood is being transported.

FTC and DOJ

These agencies are only now beginning to look closely at blood banking in the realm of health-care providers. Other health-care providers have been subjected to increased antitrust scrutiny during the past 12 years, focused primarily on cooperative agreements between physicians,[24] dentists[25] and optometrists.[26] These intra-professional agreements have generally been found to be violative of antitrust principles, while exclusion of either physicians or hospitals from preferred provider organization or health maintenance organization networks are not violative because the exclusion was not viewed as having any significant competitive effect.[27-29]

The climate of health-care reform encouraging the establishment of alliances and health-care networks may not be as favorable to blood banking as to other affected entities. Antitrust issues of sufficient gravity exist[30] such that the DOJ and the FTC issued statements on September 15, 1993, delineating federal enforcement policies with specified "safety zones" that provide some guidance for progress.[31] These policy statements do not provide express immunity from application of the antitrust laws, but they signal a willingness by these agencies to provide future guidelines. A seminal question is whether blood centers are considered to be separate health-care providers or if they will be viewed as analogous to independent clinical laboratories, drug manufacturers or other free-standing services. Thus, for blood centers in particular, careful attention should be paid to any joint venture with other health-care providers such as hospitals, health maintenance organizations, ambulatory care sites, etc, that may in fact be mergers or would be treated legally as mergers. Any new relationship that ends or seriously compromises competition in a relevant market would raise significant antitrust questions.[32] If these new ventures restrict price or output, restrict competition between the venture participants or between the venture and the participants or restrict membership in the venture, antitrust scrutiny will surely occur. A March 1994 statement announced that "both agencies (Department of Justice and Federal Trade Commission) reiterated their strong distaste for granting health providers any special protections."[33]

Blood Banking Responses

Transfusion-transmitted AIDS (TT-AIDS) has led to more changes in blood banking in its 12-year existence than any prior impetus, including the ability to "bank" blood to support life-threatening illnesses for which blood transfusions are the only therapy, wars, or other transfusion-transmitted illnesses. These changes have not necessarily resulted from litigation or even regulation; they were frequently initiated by the professionals themselves in anticipation of harm but often reinforced by a lawsuit in which the issues were decided (Table 8-6). Nevertheless, decision-making in blood banking in the 1990's is clearly attuned and responsive to the ever-changing legal and regulatory environment.

Donors

Protection From Disclosure

TT-AIDS litigation has stripped away donor anonymity in several states, sometimes by compelling answers to questions, other times by forcing the donor to appear in court. Previously, donors were shielded from such identification in the interest of preserving the

Table 8-6. Changes Implemented by the Blood Banking Profession

1. Additional/improved testing
2. Additional questions/confrontational administration
3. Uniform (standardized) donor history
4. Attention to donor privacy, comprehension
5. Quality assurance/improvement actions
6. Computer system validation
7. Reengineering/reorganization of services
8. Creation of compliance officers/departments
9. Informed consent
10. Donor deferral registries
11. Look-back procedures
12. Reentry of deferred donors

quantity of blood collected. Courts in several states no longer accept the premise that the amount of blood available would be threatened if donors are compelled to testify regarding their actions that resulted in TT-AIDS. However, other states are still persuaded that compelling donors to testify has a chilling effect on the availability of blood and should not be undertaken. With different opinions between states, blood collecting organizations are understandably wary of how to respond to these decisions, not only whether to advise donors that they may be subject to subpoena to explain their actions if they do not disqualify themselves appropriately but also how to explain this eventuality in terms that will not adversely affect many other donors whose suitability is unquestioned. No specific action has been proposed in those states where donor protection has been removed.

Comprehension

The earliest and possibly most effective preventive measure against TT-AIDS was the institution of donor questions and information about transmission of AIDS. Early in 1983, donors began receiving AIDS information and were strongly encouraged to avoid donating blood if they had been or might have been exposed to this disease. Despite the fact that in several instances in which donors have been compelled to testify in TT-AIDS cases, they have testified that they did not understand the information provided to them during the donation process that would have prevented or was intended to prevent their inappropriate donation; in fact, many unsuitable donors were deterred by this effort. The information about AIDS is not only scientifically complex, it was also changing frequently. Concerns about donors whose primary language is not English have resulted in translations or translators being available. One large study has provided some scientific data for future implementation.[34] In addition, a uniform donor history questionnaire has been approved by the AABB to standardize the content of questions asked of donors. Physical adjustments to donor questioning areas have resulted in greater privacy during the medical history evaluation, with more confrontational questioning to elicit histories of possible activities for which deferral would occur. Some centers have even investigated use of computerized questioning.[35]

Informed Consent

Donors are being instructed about the testing and consequences of positive results, including having their name placed on a registry of deferred donors. Consent for donation should include assurances that the donor is aware of these consequences and agrees to donate. Whether donors should be warned about possible testimony regarding their donations is unresolved.

Organizational Changes

Creation of Compliance Departments

Quality improvement movements have entered the American business world, including the health-care arena, during the past decade. While confusion over terminology continues, the essence of this philosophy is to apply a set of principles that will ideally prevent errors and produce goods correctly the first time every time. In blood banking, a new administrative department whose focus is compliance with laws, regulations and principles of quality management has been created. Inherent in these activities is attention to legal decisions and regulatory mandates, which, if not present already, must be changed to prevent significant adverse consequences, including loss of licensure, fines and monetary judgments. Establishments have devoted up to 10% of their operating budgets to these new compliance activities and to educating personnel about quality improvement philosophies and methods. Emphasis on areas that have resulted in settlements or loss of lawsuits is the focus of renewed efforts. Documentation, training and competency of personnel, following established standard procedures and evidence of regular review with appropriate corrective actions, are fundamental targets for improvement.

Reorganization/Reengineering of Services

Various models of blood banking exist throughout the US. Some organizations simply collect and distribute blood components, while others perform both collection and transfusion functions. In some, all of the activities related to blood collection, processing, testing, labeling, storage and distribution are performed within a single structure, while in others these functions occur in separate facilities or by contract with another organization. The health-care arena and regulatory agencies have put pressure on some organizations to completely redesign their services, including adding automation and computerization to minimize errors. Other facilities are receiving additional guidance to avoid such draconian consequences.

The growing tendency for courts to conclude that blood banks are not health-care providers will have far-reaching consequences because negligence will be measured only by a "reasonable person" standard rather than by the "medical malpractice" requirement for expert testimony to establish standard of care. The complexity of blood collection and transfusion services does not fall within the usual body of knowledge of a lay person, so loss of the benefit of expert testimony may provide blood centers little protection for unavoidable occurrences such as TT-AIDS. This is an area where legislative protection should be sought for future, as yet unknown, transfusion-transmitted diseases.

Implementation of New Tests

In 1984, when the FDA required only two tests for possible disease transmission by blood (the serologic test for syphilis [STS] and the hepatitis B surface antigen (HBsAg) test], numerous studies of possible additional testing were undertaken for such things as numbers of T lymphocytes of various subtypes, beta$_2$-microglobulin levels, hepatitis B core antibodies (anti-HBc) and others for their possible association with AIDS. These studies have been misinterpreted in subsequent lawsuits as implying that all such testing could and should have been undertaken by all blood establishments. Most courts have seen through these allegations, recognizing that scientific inquiry is necessary to establish a sound basis for creating a standard. When appropriate information was provided by such studies, indeed, appropriate testing was implemented. Between March 1985, when anti-HIV testing was first approved, and May 1990, four new tests (anti-HIV, anti-HBc, anti-human T-cell lymphotropic virus and anti-hepatitis C virus) were instituted, including additional more specific testing methodologies. Several other tests (HIV antigen, alanine aminotransferase) were evaluated but are not required by the FDA.

To support these new tests, entire systems of testing have been replaced, with automation for large centers lagging behind the necessity for institution of additional tests. The addition of these four new tests and improvements to them in such a short time interval has wreaked havoc with systems designed for only two tests. Efforts to upgrade automated systems and add computerization have occasionally resulted in inspectional deficiencies and even license suspension.

Computerization

While addition or replacement of computers with state-of-the-art capabilities is desirable, the FDA is interested in appropriate validation of systems to preclude inadvertent errors. Although no lawsuit to date has specifically implicated computerization failure, many have hinged on issues of adequate and complete documentation for which computerization is thought to be the solution.

Donor Deferral Registries

Individual centers have always maintained a roster of names of donors who have been deferred, either temporarily or indefinitely, for positive test results or a questionable history of exposure to diseases transmissible by transfusion. Efforts to nationalize this process raise important questions of individual rights of privacy and adequacy of security measures to protect against inadvertent disclosure. Even in the largest collecting facilities, eg, the armed forces blood program or the American Red Cross, the ability to correctly identify and prevent donation from a previously deferred donor is not fully operational. Having such information available to prevent donation from ever occurring is an ideal that may not be possible to achieve.

Donor Reentry Procedures

The first approved kits for anti-HIV testing were ultrasensitive, creating a sizable number of donors deferred for what were very likely false-positive results. As test methods improved and additional testing (eg, Western blot and immunofluorescence assay procedures) became available, it was clear that most of these donors were not infected by HIV and could safely resume donating. Strategies to ensure noninfectivity depended on an understanding of the duration of infection with undetectable antibody response and reliance on testing by several manufacturers' methods. While these procedures were being developed, donors were frequently deferred without notification, returning regularly to donate units that were simply discarded. These practices ensured a safe blood supply but were less satisfactory for donors.

Look-Back

When a positive test result was obtained from a repeat donor, blood collecting facilities were faced with the dilemma of how to deal with the prior donations from this donor that had often already been transfused. For components still available (eg, fresh frozen plasma) quarantine and disposal were performed. For red blood cells and platelets, the only alternative available was notification of recipients via their physicians. Because the transfused unit had tested negative (or was untested) at the time of transfusion, its infectivity was uncertain. The period for look-back notification depends on the infecting agent.

Directed Donor Programs

Still controversial, patient-directed donors have been mandated in some states and are not available in others. Safety issues are hotly debated.

Recipient

Informed Consent

Patients have the right to be informed[36] of medical procedures, including blood transfusions, so that they can make an "informed and intelligent choice."[37] The nature of the information can be either what a reasonable physician[38] or what a "prudent person in the patient's position"[39] would require to make a decision. The AABB has stated its support for specific informed consent for transfusion since 1988,[40,41] relying on the *Circular of Information* to form the basis for the communication of risks and benefits to the patient, and providing a videotape and suggested forms for use by physicians in their offices. It is prudent for blood center physicians to continue to provide educational updates for their hospital colleagues in transfusion medicine and other medical specialties. It is probably not reasonable to assume that other practitioners will be as fully informed as the blood center physician about the current risks and benefits of transfusion.

Look-Back Notification

The federal government has proposed regulations specifying the details of such notification to recipients. This is still the responsibility of the treating physician, although, as with informed consent, the blood bank physician may be more knowledgeable and can provide assistance.

Future Shock

The "New" FDA

The enforcement mandate of the FDA in this decade has changed, perhaps forever, the previous scientific and collegial relationships between the agency and its regulated "industry." No new regulations were specifically enacted; rather, a "by the book" attitude was adopted that meant reinterpretation of existing ones. Liaison contacts should maintain communication with CBER scientists, but field investigators are likely to continue closing blood centers when they believe serious deficiencies exist.[42] Manufacturers have lost their FDA licenses for: 1) failure to follow adequate written standard operating procedures for determining donor suitability; 2) failure to follow adequate written standards of procedures for the collection, processing, storage and distribution of blood and blood components for further manufacturing; 3) failure to maintain complete, accurate and concurrent records that clearly traced the steps of each significant procedure in the collection, processing and storage of blood products; and 4) failure to observe, standardize and calibrate equipment. New bases for deficiencies may include invalid test runs, age of recipient sample and other issues. Transfusion services that do not collect blood are generally less well equipped than blood centers to respond to this new agenda.

Unresolved TT-AIDS Issues

Despite the seemingly constant change that is occurring in blood banking, many of the issues surrounding TT-AIDS have created additional questions for which there are few answers or for which data are lacking. These include: issues of donor motivation, veracity, comprehension and accuracy; how to prevent unsuitable donors from continuing to donate; whether directed donors are less safe than volunteer ones; how to improve the sensitivity and specificity of testing for viral diseases; appropriate strategies for implementing new tests including whether and when inventory testing should be undertaken, when is look-back appropriate, how to educate the public when a previously unknown threat to the blood supply occurs—before and after testing becomes available; improving recipient safety by proper identification and transfusion of safer blood components; how to establish systems of storing and issuing blood components so that autologous, directed and then allogeneic components are given in proper sequence; and many more.

Actions by Other Regulatory Agencies

Lurking in the background of the litigation that has transpired is the constant threat of additional requirements from a variety of federal and state agencies. With the erosion of the protection afforded by defining blood banking by a professional medical practice standard, these statutes and regulations may be the basis for determining standard of care. The newest threat is that posed by possible antitrust violations that have yet to be articulated for blood banking.

"Individual" Actions

Whenever federal statutes are violated, it is possible for a private person, even someone involved in the wrongful act, to sue in the name of the US. This type of lawsuit, a *qui tam* action, has been very lucrative for several persons involved in clinical laboratories found to have violated Medicare requirements. If the US decides there is merit to the private claim, the *qui tam* suer can recover as much as one-third of what the federal government obtains from a successful outcome. Now that it has been determined that the CLIA '88 requirements apply to blood centers, similar opportunities for actions against blood centers and transfusion services exist.

Safety issues in blood centers can be identified and lawsuits initiated by individual employees. The organization can be liable for huge fines to the federal government as well as compensation and perhaps larger damages for negligence to the individual employee, donor or volunteer.

Conclusions

The challenges of blood banking and transfusion medicine for the rest of this decade and into the next century will continue to derive from actual or threatened litigation and from heightened interest by regulatory bodies with legal authority to act. These agencies may derive their authority from public health issues or from reimbursement and business interests. TT-AIDS litigation should begin to wane as the time since implementation of testing lengthens. However, issues of negligence for other transfusion-transmitted harm (bacterial contamination, graft-vs-host disease, failure to use autologous units, etc) will likely continue because consumers are aware and interested in blood transfusions. The impact of unsafe working conditions or improper reimbursement and business arrangements that might be violative of federal laws has yet to be measured. The essential question remains whether and to what extent litigation and regulatory actions affect the safety of the blood supply.

NOTE: This chapter is not intended to substitute for legal advice required in particular situations; rather, it is intended to provide the reader with some general principles and definitions so that ethically and legally sound practices continue within transfusion medicine.

References

1. Perlmutter v. Beth David Hospital, 308 N.Y. 100, 123 N.E.2d 792 (1954).
2. Shilts R. And the band played on. New York: St. Martin's Press, 1987.

3. Willett DE. Transfusion-transmitted diseases: Legal aspects. In: Clark GM, ed. Legal issues in transfusion medicine. Arlington, VA: American Association of Blood Banks, 1986:58.
4. NIH consensus conference. Perioperative red blood cell transfusion. JAMA 1988;260:2700-3.
5. Clark GM, ed. Legal issues in transfusion medicine. Arlington, VA: American Association of Blood Banks, 1986.
6. Murphy WG, McClelland DBL. Deceptively low morbidity from failure to practice safe blood transfusions: An analysis of serious blood transfusion errors. Vox Sang 1989;57:59-62.
7. Linden JV, Paul B, Dressler KP. A report of 104 transfusion errors in New York State. Transfusion 1992:32:601-6.
8. Taswell HF, Smith AM, Sweatt MA, Pfaff KJ. Quality control in the blood bank: A new approach. Am J Clin Pathol 1974;62:491-5.
9. Administrative Procedure Act, 60 Statutes 237-244, 5 USC §§551-559.
10. Department of Health and Human Services. General biological products standards, additional standards for human blood and blood products; test for antibody to human immunodeficiency virus (HIV). 21 CFR Parts 606, 610 and 640. Fed Regist 1988;53: 111-17.
11. HCFA affirms that donor testing falls under CLIA regulation. AABB Blood Bank Week, 1994;March 4:2.
12. Mazer R. Take precautions before scandal hits. CLMA Management Briefs 1993;15:1.
13. Goodnough LT, Johnston MF, Ramsey G, et al. Guidelines for transfusion support in patients undergoing coronary artery bypass grafting. Ann Thorac Surg 1990;50:675-83.
14. Clark RA. Enforcement policy and procedures for exposure to tuberculosis (memorandum for regional administrators). Washington, DC: Occupational Safety and Health Administration Oct. 8, 1993.
15. Centers for Disease Control and Prevention/National Institutes of Health. Biosafety in microbiological and biomedical laboratories. Washington, DC: US Government Printing Office; 1993.
16. 21 U.S.C. 654 (a)(1).
17. Thigpen v. Executive Committee of Baptist Convention of State of Georgia, 114 Ga. 839, 152 SE2nd 920 (1966).
18. Kapuschinsky v. United States, 248 F. Supp. 732 (D.S.C. 1966).
19. Booker v. Duke Medical Center, 297 NC 458, 256 SE2nd 189 (1979).

20. Sacred Heart Medical Center v. Department of Labor and Industries, 29 Wash 2d 631, 600 P2d 1015 (1979).
21. Blankenship v. Cincinnati Milacron Chemicals, 433 NE2d 572 (Ohio 1982), cert. denied, 103 S.Ct. 127 (1982).
22. James v. Nolan, 614 A.2d 709 (Pa. Superior Ct., 1992).
23. In the News. MT TODAY, February 7, 1994:15.
24. Arizona v. Maricopa County Medical Society, 457 U.S. 332 (1982).
25. FTC v. Indiana Federation of Dentists, 476 U.S. 447 (1986).
26. Massachusetts Board of Registration in Optometry, 110 F.T.C. 549 (1988).
27. Capital Imaging Medical Assocs. v. Mohawk Valley Medical Assocs., 791 F. Supp. 956 (N.D.N.Y. 1992) aff'd 996 F.2d 537 (2d Cir. 1993).
28. Ball Memorial Hosp., Inc., v. Mutual Hosp. Ins., Inc., 784 F.2d 1325 (7th Cir. 1986).
29. Northwest Medical Lab., Inc., v. Blue Cross & Blue Shield of Or., Inc., 794 P.2d 428 (Or. 1990).
30. Grady KE. The role of antitrust in a reformed health care system. Antitrust 1993;8:2-7.
31. US Department of Justice and Federal Trade Commission. Statements of Antitrust Enforcement Policy in the Health Care Arena (Sept. 15, 1993). Riverwoods, IL: Commerce Clearinghouse, Inc, 1993.
32. Kattan J, Balto DA. Analyzing joint ventures' ancillary restraints. Antitrust 1993;8:13-8.
33. McCormick B. Reform without relief? Antitrust enforcers oppose exemptions for physicians. Am Med News, March 7, 1994:1.
34. Mayo DJ, Rose AM, Matchett SE, et al. Screening potential blood donors at risk for human immunodeficiency virus. Transfusion 1991;31:466-74.
35. Locke SE, Kowaloff HB, Hoff RG, et al. Computer-based interview for screening blood donors for risk of HIV transmission. JAMA 1992;268:1301-5.
36. Salao v. Leland Stanford Jr. University Board of Trustees, 317 P.2d 170 (Cal. Dist Ct. App 1957).
37. Sard v. Hardy, 281 Md. 432, 379 A.2d 1014 (1977).
38. Natanson v. Kline, 350 P.2d 1093 (Kan 1960).
39. Canterbury v. Spence, 464 F.2d 772 (DC 1972).
40. Widmann FK, ed. Informed consent for blood transfusion. Arlington, VA: American Association of Blood Banks, 1989.
41. Informed consent for transfusion: A physician's resource kit. Arlington, VA: American Association of Blood Banks, 1989.
42. HHS/FDA-product licenses. The Federal Health Monitor, January 17, 1994:1.

Appendix 8-1. State Laws That Preclude Strict Liability for the Provision of Blood (So-Called "Blood Shield Statutes")

Alabama Code, title 7, §2-314(4)
Alaska Stat §45.02.316
Ariz. Rev. Stat. §32-1481 and §36-1151
Ark. Stat. Ann. §82-1608 and §85-2.316(3)(d)
Cal. Health and Safety Code §1606
Colo. Rev. Stat. §41-2-11
Conn. Gen. Stat. Title 19, §139-1
Del. Code §6-2-316(5)
Fla. Stat. §672-316(5)
Ga. Code Ann. §51-1-28 and §11-2-316
Haw. Rev. Stat. §327.15
Idaho Code §6-1402(3) and §39-3702
Ill. Rev. Stat, Ch 111 1/2 §5102
Ind. Code §16-8-7.2
Iowa Code §142A.8
Kan. Stat. §65-37d
Ky. Rev. Stat. §139.125
La. Civil Code, Article 1764 (Act No. 301, 1968)
Me. Rev. Stat. Ann. Tit. 11, §2-108
Md. Health-General Code Ann. §18-402
Mass. Gen Laws §2-316(5)
Mich. Comp. Laws, 1970, §691.1511
Minn. Stat. §525.928
Miss. Code §41-41-11
Mo. Rev. Stat. §431.069
Mont. Rev. Codes Ann. §50-33-102
Neb. Rev. Stat. §71-4001
Nev. Rev. Stat. §460.010
N. H. Rev. Stat. Ann. Ch.507.8-b
N.M. Stat. Ann. §24-10-5
N.Y. Public Health Law §580.4
N.C. Gen. Stat. §90-220.10
N.D. Stat. §41.02-33(3)(d)
Ohio Rev. Code §2108.11
Okla. Stat. §34-2151
Or. Rev. Stat. §97.300
Pa. Stat. Ann. Tit. 35, §10021
S.C. Code §44-43-10

continued on page 192

Appendix 8-1. Continued

S.D. Cod. Laws. §57A-2-315.1
Tenn. Code Ann. §47-2-316(5)
Tex. Bus. Com. Code Ann. §2.316(e)
Utah Code Ann. §26-31-1
Va. Code §32.1-297
Wash. Rev. Code §70.54.120
W.V. Code §16-23-1
Wis. Stat. §146.31
Wyo. Stat. §34-21-233 and §35-221-10

Appendix 8-2. United States Governmental Agencies Whose Authority Embraces Blood Banking Activities

1. FDA—Food and Drug Administration
2. CDC—Centers for Disease Control and Prevention
3. HCFA—Health Care Financing Administration
4. OSHA—Occupational Safety and Health Administration
5. EPA—Environmental Protection Agency
6. DOT—Department of Transportation
7. DOJ—Department of Justice
8. FTC—Federal Trade Commission

Index

Italicized page numbers indicate tables or figures